Prophet of Rage

Prophet of Rage

A Life of Louis Farrakhan and His Nation

ARTHUR J. MAGIDA

BasicBooks
A Division of HarperCollins*Publishers*

FIRST EDITION

Designed by Elliott Beard

Library of Congress Cataloging-in-Publication Data
Magida, Arthur J.
    Prophet of rage : a life of Louis Farrakhan and his nation /
Arthur J. Magida. — 1st ed.
        p.   cm.
    Includes index.
    ISBN 0-465-06436-1
    1. Farrakhan, Louis.   2. Black Muslims—Biography.
3. Afro-Americans—Biography.   I. Title.
BP223.Z8.F3846   1996
297'.87—dc20.
    [B]   96-2767

96 97 98 99 00 ❖/RRD 10 9 8 7 6 5 4 3 2 1

For a nation that, in its heart, can still . . .

hold fast,
All together . . .
For ye were enemies
And He joined your hearts
In love, so that by His Grace,
Ye became brethren.

—Koran 3:103

Contents

Foreword

Julian Bond

Louis Farrakhan. These two words immediately summon fear and loathing in many minds; in others, devotion, admiration, and respect.

Who is this highly charged "Prophet of Rage"? Why should anyone care? What does he mean to us all?

Is he a fearless spokesman for black America, unafraid to speak harsh truths to the powerful?

Or a shameless panderer to ancient prejudices, a promoter of bigotry and anti-Semitism?

Is he the leader of a peculiar sect born from the forced marriage of orthodox Islam and the made-up religion of a charlatan and mystic?

Or the inspirational leader of the reclamation of lost souls, a rebuilder of fallen men and women?

For the first time between the covers of a book, Arthur J.

Magida has traced the route of the former Louis Eugene Walcott from his birth in New York's Bronx to Boston's Roxbury and—through a life more complex than either Farrakhan's critics or defenders may believe—to the nation's front pages.

In these pages are the clues to the growth and development of young Louis Eugene Walcott into Louis X and then into Louis Farrakhan, the story of one man and the movement he helped to build.

Here, too, is a history of that man's assessment of the American dream, of opportunity promised and denied, and that man's response.

Farrakhan is important for who he is. But he is also important for what he and his prominence say about us, Americans black and white, our present and our past.

In 1905, the scholar and activist W. E. B. Du Bois predicted that the problem of the twentieth century would be the problem of the color line. He became the towering figure in racial uplift of his time.

Du Bois and others founded the National Association for the Advancement of Colored People (NAACP) in 1909, and black Americans and their white allies have generally followed Du Bois's early prescription for action—pursuing civil rights and political strength, seeking coalitions, fighting for entry into the American mainstream.

But absolute consistency was never Du Bois's strong point. He never blindly followed the path he had prescribed without some deviation. America's black population has been filled with departures from the common view and alternative visions from long before Du Bois's day until today.

One ancient, strong, and persistent strain of black thought has been black nationalism, expressed variously as rigid separatism—complete rejection of all things white—and as a prag matic strategy designed to strengthen black communities as an antecedent to black negotiation with white power.

Louis Farrakhan represents an alternative to Du Bois's integrationist vision. He is Du Bois's opposite. The degree of acceptance he has received says much about the failure of the American dream.

Nearly a century after Du Bois's dire prediction, the chasm between black and white Americans seems as great as ever. One could safely predict that the twenty-first century will be as preoccupied with race as the century we will soon leave behind.

Du Bois spoke in a world where there was absolute separation of the races. White power was absolute. Federal courts had declared that blacks had no rights that white men were bound to respect.

While undeniable progress has been made since 1900 in removing state-sanctioned racial barriers, the sad differences between black and white life chances—in health status, housing, education, life expectancy, and income—persist.

The conservative ascendancy of the last half-decade of the twentieth century sent frightful signals to black Americans that progress won at great cost and sacrifice would be rolled back and further gains stymied.

Republican candidates for the presidency in 1996 competed to see who could loose tougher assaults on affirmative action, whose policy toward immigrants was harsher, which of them could extract the largest savings from squeezing the poor and transfer the most income to the wealthy.

Scientific racism and social Darwinism enjoyed a renaissance.

The federal courts began to dismantle the 1965 Voting Rights Act and weakened the 1954 Supreme Court decision integrating public schools.

Fresh accounts of each day's racially motivated attacks competed with yesterday's grim reports.

The failure of the American dream for more than 10 percent of the nation's population and the resistance of many in the American majority to any palliative measures, however weak, could not help but feed the flames of rejectionist thought and separatist sentiment.

The wonder is not that so many are attracted to Louis Farrakhan; it is that the numbers of black Americans revealed in public opinion polls as favoring his brand of racial politics aren't greater than they are.

Centuries of failed attempts at amelioration of what was called in Du Bois's day "the Negro problem" should have created a stronger reaction. Farrakhan correctly understands—and has never doubted—that it was a "white problem" all along.

On that, most black Americans would agree.

But Farrakhan does more than blame whites. He also calls on blacks to account for themselves, for criminality and licentiousness and other bad behavior, for the group's failure to adhere to higher standards of behavior.

That message attracts and repels. It attracts many who have abandoned any hope that white resistance to black progress and development will ever yield, while it repels those who believe it echoes the age-old description of blacks as "unworthy" of admission into the larger body politic.

Louis Farrakhan is a unique individual whose life is worth examination. His present prominence ought to make the nation question itself. An understanding of who he is and where he comes from and from what sources his thinking arises and his views were formed is important to our understanding of ourselves.

His life and works can be our mirror, and if many reject the message he proclaims and the accusatory finger he aims, we ought to wonder about the impulses that cause the blaming and the pointing and question whether or not the target isn't all of us.

How does one respond, in turn, to Louis Farrakhan? Is he a fringe character, operating on the edge of American civic life? Don't the crowds he can command—more than 800,000 at the Million Man March, 15,000 to 20,000 nightly in municipal auditoriums across the country—suggest that he must be granted a seat in the front ranks of black leadership? Do the crowds endorse the entire package? Can one select from Farrakhan's expansive menu of complaints, suggestions, accusations, and demands?

This is a fascinating story. Arthur Magida has done a great service to assemble this history at a moment when Americans grapple, once again, with race.

Whatever role Louis Farrakhan has played in the past, and whatever role others may wish to assign to him, he must be understood if we are to move beyond the current impasse.

That understanding can begin here.

Prologue

At his Million Man March on October 16, 1995, Louis Farrakhan did not wear the yarmulke I had given him during dinner at his nineteen-room mansion in Chicago the previous summer. During that meal, Farrakhan had mentioned the march. One million men would converge on Washington to atone for their trespasses, while black women around the country prayed in their local churches for unity and strength. Also attending these churches would be politicians who, instead of wearing yarmulkes as they do when they go to synagogues to meet their Jewish constituents, would wear kufis—small, round African hats.

As he spoke of his hopes for what the march would accomplish, I withdrew from my pocket a gleaming white yarmulke: "Minister Farrakhan, I would like *you* to wear this at the march."

Visibly moved, Farrakhan held the yarmulke briefly between

his palms: "I know what this means, Mr. Magida. I thank you."[1]

Farrakhan did not promise to wear the yarmulke at the march—or at any other time. But for a brief moment, a millisecond, the gesture of reconciliation—his and mine—short-circuited the verbal mayhem that has been waging between Jews and Farrakhan since 1984.

Dinner with Farrakhan was, in effect, a private audience with Farrakhan. He held court for more than two hours, directing each diner to his chair, introducing each guest to the others, dominating any chatter at the table, keeping it from devolving into mere dinner party chitchat. At the roughly eighteen-foot-long table, all conversation revolved around him. He was the verbal centerpiece, the catalyst, the conversational alchemist.

Since this was my third encounter with Farrakhan, I knew the drill. After a guard's polite but efficient frisking, I was ushered into a small room just inside the front door. There, I was asked to take off my shoes and was given a pair of fresh white socks to slip on. Next, I was shown to a rather formal room where the assembled guests sat on small, white circular couches awaiting their host. When Farrakhan appeared about ten minutes later, he was wearing a pair of casual slacks and a light cotton shirt open at the collar. As usual, he was friendly, articulate, and eager to remedy his image as white America's worst bogeyman.

Farrakhan can be immensely charming. His voice is finely calibrated, with all the nuances and controls of a born orator and entertainer. He worked the dinner table like a born politician, telling jokes about himself and tales from the distant past of the Nation of Islam; quoting liberally, when necessary, from the Koran and the Jewish and Christian Bibles; orating with the tireless cadence of the black preacher, the hip lingo of the street, and the propulsive conviction of the newly converted (even though he joined the Nation of Islam in 1955). He has an immense sense of self and of his own presence and often refers to himself in the third person. Explaining this phenomenon, he once told me, "I represent so many persons who . . . have helped make me who I am. It's an outgrowth of humility."[2]

Farrakhan has rarely, in public or private, retreated from the turf he has staked out for himself as the one black leader unafraid to scold white America about its sins and atrocities against blacks. He so magnificently mirrors—and so well satisfies—blacks' fury because he has the audacity to refract back to whites the very pain blacks say they have suffered at the hands of whites. It is the voice of retribution and reparation. It is, say some, the voice of God.

In his eyes, Farrakhan is perhaps the *only* legitimate voice in this country. His passions, his sense of chosenness, his commitment to his people cannot be denied, although his ploys and tactics may be questionable. As a youth, he cried when told that the back-to-Africa messiah Marcus Garvey had died. As a teen, he soaked up the adulation and the praise of the crowds that heard him play classical music on his violin at recitals or sing calypso at nightclubs. As a young adult, he cursed the heavens when he heard that God had chosen another man—Elijah Muhammad—to ease his people's suffering. Farrakhan has *always* had outsized assumptions about himself, and now, with Garvey and Muhammad long gone and the African-American community in disarray and distress, *he* speaks truths, *he* is allied with the power of God, *he* can redeem his people and lead them to the Promised Land through his Nation of Islam, the conduit for respect and esteem. In 1982, Farrakhan may have said, with a half-smile, alluding to the Nation of Islam's trademark fashion statement, "We are not a bow-tie cult," but the NOI's bow tie confers status, power, authority, and *civility* on a community hungry for all four.[3]

Despite the fury of his theology and his preaching, there is a certain chasm between the public Farrakhan and the private

Farrakhan. At dinner, for instance, as the only white and the only Jew among the seventeen guests (several top Nation of Islam officials, an old friend of Farrakhan's from New York, a business associate or two, a young black singer and his fiancée, two of Farrakhan's nine children, and Farrakhan's wife, Khadijah), I felt comfortable and at ease, as Farrakhan seemed to be with me. It was as if he can shelve the pitch of his public rhetoric and embrace the humanity of individuals when they are flesh-and-blood individuals before him, not stirred into the anonymous stew of their specific tribe.

After dinner: No coffee. No wine. No tea. Not even dessert. Farrakhan remained seated as, one by one, the guests filed by him to say farewell and went out into the summer night, where two or three Fruit of Islam guards stood around the mansion gates. This may have been Chicago's Hyde Park, but it was also the Nation of Islam's National House, possibly the safest spot in the city.

I first approached Farrakhan in June 1993, shortly after he had played a Mendelssohn concerto on his violin in North Carolina, ostensibly as an overture of reconciliation toward Jews. He was reportedly casting about for ways to mend his very ragged fences with the Jewish community. I was then senior editor of a Jewish newspaper. Assuming he wanted to reach as broad an audience as possible in the Jewish community, I faxed Farrakhan a request for an interview, advising that if he really wanted to alter his relations with Jews, sitting down with me would let him reach tens of thousands of Jews in one fell swoop.

As a Jew, I had been appalled, sickened, frightened by some of Farrakhan's rhetoric, which had labeled Judaism "a gutter religion" in 1984. But as a liberal and as a believer in what Judaism calls *teshuvah*—defining moments of "turning" toward grace, forgiveness, and exemplary acts of redemption—I was equally appalled, sickened, frightened by the downward trajectory of black-Jewish relations, some of which stemmed from the feuding between Jews and Farrakhan. I believed that if Farrakhan's motives were pure and his words of conciliation were genuine, there might be hope yet for black-Jewish relations.

In that context, interviewing Farrakhan might serve a higher purpose than achieving a mere journalistic "scoop."

Sitting down with Farrakhan almost guaranteed an extraordinary story. But it would only be a *proper* story if it was balanced by the right research augmented by the proper inner resources. I had been warned that Farrakhan and the aura surrounding the Nation of Islam—the secrecy, the guards, Farrakhan's fortress-like home—were all designed to intimidate. I concluded that the only way to withstand such pressures and exit the interview with my integrity intact was to know Farrakhan better than he assumed I did. So I intensively studied his theology and his history and previewed through videotapes his intriguing, compelling personality.

As a journalist from a Jewish publication, it was preordained that I would be criticized for even being in the same room as Farrakhan. To most Jews, Farrakhan is an extremist, and almost by definition, extremists are to be shunned. But Farrakhan's growing influence upon the political center made him a legitimate, proper subject for inquiring, critical reportage. Pretending otherwise would be to indulge in a pretense that Farrakhan's influence extended no further than the meager membership of the Nation of Islam.

During the almost four-hour interview, Farrakhan was tireless and determined to be understood. He quickly apologized after the one and only time he exploded at me. I had asked whether he would accede to Jews' requests to apologize for what were widely perceived as anti-Semitic remarks.

"Why is it that Jews feel they have to extract from black people this apology?" he shouted, his voice growing in volume and ire. "What is it in your makeup? I'm sorry. Get down on your knees, Farrakhan! And if I did, you know what your people would tell me? Too little. Too late. . . . Who the hell do you think you are that I should bow down before you and beg for forgiveness when your people helped to bring my people into slavery and I have never heard a Jew apologize to me or my people for what you brought my people to. . . . You're too arrogant. You're too proud of your power. You want everybody to bow down to you, and I ain't bowing down to nothing or nobody but God."[4]

Farrakhan was also adept at quickly turning the tables and shifting the argument. When I asked how he could persuade others that he is not "the devil incarnate," he countered, "To blacks, . . . there's more evidence . . . [that Jews and whites are] the devil than there is that I am for telling about their devilishment. . . . I can't be judged except by my actions. I have done nothing wrong to white people. I have no criminal record. In high school, the Jews who came to hear my music and who taught me never found me to be disrespectful. Any Jew that's come into my home, I've treated with respect and honor."[5]

I can vouch for that, as can those Jews who went to high school with Farrakhan. But Farrakhan's damage to our commonweal does not stem from how he treated whites or Jews long ago or how he treats them now in the comfort of his home. Instead, his impact stems from what he says at press conferences and in vast public arenas where his audiences number in the tens of thousands.

Farrakhan's eventual obituary will cite two career milestones: his reputation as the preeminent anti-Semite of the 1990s, and the lingering questions about his role in Malcolm X's assassination in 1965. He will always be haunted by the words he wrote in late 1964 in the Nation of Islam's newspaper, *Muhammad Speaks*: "The die is set, and Malcolm shall not escape.... Such a man as Malcolm is worthy of death." By 1994, Farrakhan's formulation about Malcolm's killing was studiously bland: "I can't say that I approved, and I really didn't disapprove. I was numb. But today, looking back, Malcolm would be so much more valuable to us alive."[6]

Instead, Malcolm has become a fashion. In any black ghetto, men, women, teens—even infants—wear black caps or sweatshirts emblazoned with a large white "X." In early 1994, when passing by 72 Dale Street, the dilapidated frame house with boarded-up windows where Malcolm lived with his half-sister in the early 1940s in Roxbury, Boston's black ghetto, an African-American woman saw black teens sitting on what remained of the steps. Each wore a cap with an "X."

"Do you know who walked on those steps?" she asked. "Do you know who slept in that house?" The answer, not unexpectedly, was negative. The teens knew style; they didn't know history. They knew fashion; they didn't know heritage.[7]

In some ways, Farrakhan is also a fashion, a collective emblem of frustration and bitterness. But unlike the present-day Farrakhan, Malcolm had been edging in his last months toward some form of accommodation with whites. First, of course, he had to overcome his fourteen years in the Nation of Islam, where he had heard and preached day and night that whites were no more than "blue-eyed devils." At the same time, the civil rights movement was embracing an entirely different vision, one that rejected the concrete experience of bondage, lynchings, and rape for an ideal whose prerequisite was hope, faith, compassion, and goodness.

As James Baldwin wrote in 1960, the civil rights movement

depends, at bottom, on an ability to see beneath the cruelty and hysteria and apathy of white people, their bafflement and pain

and essential decency. This is superbly difficult. It demands a
perpetually cultivated spiritual resilience, for the bulk of the evidence contradicts the vision. But the Muslim movement has all
the evidence on its side. . . . It is quite impossible to argue with
a Muslim concerning the actual state of Negroes in this country—the truth, after all, is the truth.

This, to Baldwin, was

the great power a Muslim speaker has over his audience. His
audience has not heard this truth—the truth about their daily
lives—honored by anyone else. Almost anyone else, black or
white, prefers to soften this truth, and point to a new day which
is coming in America. But this day has been coming for nearly
one hundred years. Viewed solely in the light of this country's
moral professions, this lapse is inexcusable.[8]

Farrakhan's public message is almost identical to what Baldwin heard from the Muslims more than three decades ago. But
put Farrakhan before a tableful of dinner guests, and he quickly
re-earns the stage name he adopted when performing calypso in
the 1950s: "The Charmer."

The challenge today is not to reconcile these two halves of
Farrakhan's psyche, for his persona itself is symptomatic of our
persistent, corrosive national difficulty and uncertainty about
race and class. Nor is the challenge to reconcile the polarized
sectors of the Nation of Islam: the sometimes likable veneer that
can emanate from its top leader, and the wrath stirring underneath that can erupt suddenly. On an airplane flight in 1994, for
instance, Farrakhan responded graciously, if noncommittally,
when a Jewish man asked him to "tone down your rhetoric
about Jews." The man was then followed by one of Farrakhan's
guards out of the plane when it landed, staying three paces
behind him through the airport, muttering over and over again,

"You fucking Jew bastard. We're gonna get you. Motherfucker. Motherfucker. Fucking, fucking Jew bastard."[9]

Nor is the challenge to bridge the chasm between the Nation of Islam's radical theology and its severe discipline—and its reliance on the Christian lore, text, and imagery that resonates with the masses of blacks whom the Nation of Islam wishes to reach, even as one of Farrakhan's most fiery ministers had the apparent leeway—and the implicit permission—to be covertly baptized at a sunrise service on the Chicago shores of Lake Michigan in the mid-1980s.[10]

The real challenge is to reconcile the dualities swirling around race and class and faith in our *national* psyche; to rehabilitate the lives and the image of blacks that has currency not only among whites but also among blacks. This is an era when black males, who comprise 7 percent of the nation's population, constitute about 48 percent of the prison population. So it was not necessarily incongruous when one of my middle daughter's black friends said, upon hearing that I was going to the Million Man March, "I hope they don't beat him up."

Not incongruous, but certainly tragic. Tragic that young blacks should carry this burden of their males being so prone to violence. And tragic that the notion of some sort of black-white amity at an adult level was deemed improbable by the young.

That, not Farrakhan, is the nub of the issue. Solve that, and Farrakhan is neutralized. Let it fester, and Farrakhan's influence expands and dilates. Reconciling these national dualities is a far more difficult task than somehow aligning them "correctly" in the mind and the heart of this one man, this "bogeyman," this barometer of our vexing past, our unsettling present, and, perhaps, our troubling future.

I

"Up, You Mighty Race"

Boston, the national cradle of liberty, nurtured Farrakhan as it had nurtured Malcolm X. When Malcolm first came to Boston in 1941, he was sixteen-year-old Malcolm Little; Farrakhan was then eight-year-old Louis Eugene Walcott. Both would be raised without a father, both by overburdened mothers who had immigrated from the Caribbean, Malcolm's from Grenada, Farrakhan's from St. Kitts. But Malcolm's mother was sent to a state mental hospital in Kalamazoo when he was fourteen, and the boy was effectively orphaned; Farrakhan's mother, on the other hand, kept a tight, caring rein on their small, Depression-era household, stressing the gentility and fine manners of the islands left behind and urging her sons to cultivate, as vehicles for advancement in her new country, education, culture, honesty, diligence, industry, perseverance—the same qualities cultivated by her many West Indian neighbors. These earned the West Indians an assortment of nicknames, including "black Jews," and contributed in no small way to the open derision from other Roxbury blacks for their "island" affectations, such as wearing silk shirts, straw hats, and white flannel pants.[1]

Roxbury's West Indian community was singularly cohesive, despite—or maybe because of—the hardships of being relatively recent black immigrants in a mainly white culture at the height of the Depression. They had a strong sense of community, of place, of identity. The community also had a very robust proletarian version of castes and classes, much of which depended on one's ancestors' country of origin. According to Boston University professor Hillel Levine and journalist Lawrence Harmon:

[L]ower Roxbury had long served as a way station for various ethnic groups. The Irish ruled in the 1870s and 1880s, staying long enough to save for homes in more desirable sections of the city. Canadians, mostly Nova Scotians in the building trades, followed. By the early 1930s, however, the Jews had already established a three-decade presence in much of Roxbury and Dorchester. . . . Since they [had] arrived en masse at the turn of the century, Boston's Jews had served as a convenient buffer between black neighborhoods in lower Roxbury and the Irish neighborhoods in the eastern section of nearby Dorchester. It was, for most concerned, a cozy . . . arrangement. . . . It was expected that the Jews, as latecomers to the city, would live next to the ramshackle houses in lower Roxbury, where many of the city's small black population (only 2 percent of the city's 560,000 residents at the turn of the century) resided. The occasional "black Brahmin" who fancied a house in upper Roxbury could expect no resistance from the Jews, newcomers themselves. Similar incursions, however, were unthinkable in Irish strongholds.[2]

Each group more or less kept to itself, although they eventually had to rub up against each other. That was the life of the streets and, surely, of the schools, which had been legally desegregated in 1855. Beneath a fragile patina of amicability lurked tensions, resentments, suspicions, and, sometimes, violence, which was usually initiated by the Irish and was sometimes implicitly spurred on by the hate-preaching radio priest Father Charles E. Coughlin of the Shrine of the Little Flower in Royal Oak, Michigan. He may have been popular in Chicago, Cincinnati, Baltimore, and St. Louis, where passionate, adoring crowds filled large auditoriums, but Boston, proclaimed its Irish-gened mayor Michael Curley, was "the strongest Coughlin city in America."[3]

The West Indians' considerable sense of community often buffered them from the turf wars waged in the neighborhood. As George Guscott, who lived next door to Farrakhan, later remembered, "Most people knew one another. If they didn't, at least they'd heard the last name. People were totally different in those days: it was a tight-knit situation. Everybody was poor, and we knew we were poor. As a consequence, there was much unity and we helped one another."[4]

Helping could take many forms. "We knew if we did something wrong, our parents would know about it," said John Bynoe, whose family lived at 714 William Street, one block away from Gene Walcott. "It was one big extended family. We used to sit on the steps and name all the families for five blocks around. So how much bad could you do if you even *tried* to do something wrong? We all had good, strong West Indian mothers. When your mother told you to do something, you listened. If you didn't, they smacked you alongside your head."[5]

Guscott concurred: "If you did something wrong on your way home from school, and somebody saw you do it, an adult would grab you right there and give you a whipping, and then you were afraid they would tell your parents about what you did. If they did, your parents would give you another whipping."[6]

The family solidarity, communal cohesiveness, and sense of oneness that would later be among Louis Farrakhan's most dominant themes as a Nation of Islam leader were forged in the streets and homes of lower Roxbury. "We used to look out for ourselves and for each other," observed Guscott. "That's the way we grew up, and that's what Farrakhan is still talking about today."[7]

Louis Eugene Walcott, as Farrakhan was baptized (he was sometimes called "Louis" and most often called "Gene"), had firm, motherly steering almost from birth. Two decades later, his path would intersect with Malcolm's. In the meantime, the two were on vastly different trajectories. Gene was a true straight arrow: violin in one hand, books in the other, he was no mama's boy, but he was his mama's pride.

Malcolm, on the other hand, with *his* mother in a mental institution back in Michigan, became a hustler, a scam artist, a player of games, and a master of psyches. Street-smart and white-wary, he looked for the angle—*any* angle. His father, who beat his wife and sometimes their seven children, had been killed in a streetcar accident when Malcolm was six. Wherever he went, Malcolm learned early on that the world around him was white-dominated and white-favored: he believed that, to the whites who ran the schools, where he consistently did poorly, and to the social agencies that thought they knew best how children should be raised, blacks were faceless, soul-less nonentities; empty, rudderless ciphers. Until he joined the Nation of Islam in 1949, Malcolm had been adrift with few moorings. His only anchor seemed to be his obsession with out-smarting whites and outwitting the law. One way or another, he had always been on the lam: moving from city to city when his father was alive; being shifted from school to school, often because of his surliness; running from cops and from fellow hustlers whom he had crossed.

Malcolm came to Boston from the Ingham County juvenile home about ten miles south of Lansing, Michigan, to live with his older half-sister, Ella Little. Ella would try to be the scolding matriarch Malcolm had never had, constantly trying to keep him to some version of the straight and narrow, which he, with his usual rambunctiousness and curiosity, would invariably spurn for quick (and sometimes cheap) thrills.

Ella lived on Harrishof Street in Roxbury, where most of the city's eleven thousand blacks lived. Also in Roxbury were a hefty contingent of Irish and most of the city's one hundred thousand Jews. To be exact, Ella lived in *upper* Roxbury, also known as "The Hill." Though she hardly qualified as one of them, many on The Hill comprised "The Four Hundred," the city's black elite. But there was a certain sham to the label: although Yankee-born and Yankee-educated, most of The Four Hundred couldn't hold a candle to the financial stature and hereditary sinecure of the city's white Brahmins, many of whose ancestors antedated the nation itself. To compensate, many in The Four Hundred put on airs and assumed the manners of the white elite. They were patrician in style, but style then, as now, went only so far and was surely less than skin-deep. Some of these black Brahmins took their cues from upper-class whites: they summered on Cape Cod or Martha's Vineyard and attended the Boston Symphony on Friday afternoons the rest of the year. A few managed to escape the confines of Roxbury and live on Beacon Hill or in the South End in apartments or homes "filled with books, potted palms . . . and antique furniture." Some even had servants who were white, not black, believing that "more gentility and culture would come from exposure to whites."[8]

Malcolm was contemptuous of the

Hill Negroes [who] were breaking their backs trying to imitate white people . . . under the pitiful misapprehension that it would make them "better." . . . Eight out of ten of the Hill Negroes . . . despite the impressive-sounding job titles they affected, actually worked as menials and servants. . . . "I'm with an old family" was a euphemism used to dignify the professions of white folks' cooks and maids who talked so affectedly among their own kind in Roxbury that you couldn't even understand them. I don't know how many forty- and fifty-year-old errand boys went down the Hill dressed like ambassadors in black suits and white collars, to downtown jobs "in government," "in finance," or "in law." It has never ceased to amaze me how so many Negroes, then and now, could stand the indignity of that kind of self-delusion.[9]

On foot and by subway, Malcolm explored the Boston area: the Common and the Public Garden; Cambridge and its universities; the history that was everywhere. To Ella's dismay, Malcolm found that he preferred *lower* Roxbury to The Hill. This maze of a neighborhood, whose meandering streets, in an old Boston tradition, followed former cow paths, was Boston's black ghetto, full of "grocery stores, walk-up flats, cheap restaurants, poolrooms, bars, storefront churches, and pawnshops. . . . Not only," he later recalled, "was this part of Roxbury much more exciting, but I felt more relaxed among Negroes who were being their natural selves and not putting on airs."[10]

What Malcolm didn't know was that one of the Negroes who did not reside on The Hill was young Gene Walcott, who lived about one mile to the northeast of upper Roxbury in a three-family brick house at 687 Shawmut Avenue with his mother and his brother, Alvan Walcott, twenty months his senior. Gene, remembered an old family friend, had more talent—academically, musically, athletically—than Alvan, who was "more quiet" and with whom "you didn't feel you could take the same chances and liberties as you could with Gene."[11]

Gene stood out not just in his family but in the rest of lower Roxbury. He was a beacon for some, such as John Rice, who lived about four blocks away from the Walcotts and who had a scarcity of bearing and direction—until he found out about Gene Walcott, who was two years older than he was. Rice had moved to Boston in 1935, with his mother and an older brother, from Gamaria, South Carolina, a town "you could ride through in a minute. There were a few stores, a cotton gin. A judge would hold court in a barn where he set up a few bales of cotton. You were guilty as soon as you walked in there. They took from my grandfather two pigs, a cow, two mules. They never told him what his crime was. I later found out he had one half of a half a pint of corn whiskey in his back pocket covered up. All they wanted was his livestock. They used the whiskey as an excuse to get it."

In Boston, Rice, tall, gangly, a bit awkward, had no male role models in his family. His father was still in South Carolina; his brother "wasn't worth much." But he "had to have a big brother or a father figure somewhere. So I picked Eugene Walcott. I'd heard about . . . how smart he was in school. I watched how he walked. How proud he was of himself. I thought, 'I want to be just like him.'"[12]

The underlying values, the warmth, the unity and security that pervaded Roxbury were urban counterparts to the small-town America that Norman Rockwell would later depict. But Gene Walcott's Shawmut Avenue, of course, encapsulated little of Rockwell's airbrushed white picket fences and packed town meetings and freckle-faced kids sipping milk shakes at the corner soda fountain. Not with a small playground on the southeastern side of the street that was barely big enough for baseball and, on the northwestern side, houses with apartments for two or three families, most of which had been built for workers in the late nineteenth century. Not with the Robert Gould Shaw Settlement House at Windsor and Shawmut, two blocks to the south, named after the white Bostonian who commanded the all-black Fifty-fourth Massachusetts regiment during the Civil War. Not with the smell of such Caribbean food as curry and coconut bread permeating the streets while being cooked for Saturday or Sunday night dinners. And surely not with St. Cyprian's Episcopal Church, whose congregants were mostly from the Caribbean and which was built in 1925 in response to an incident at the all-white Church of the Ascension on Washington Street, where for several years most of Roxbury's black Episcopalians had worshiped, whites in the morning, blacks in the late afternoon. This arrangement lasted until John Leo Bynoe, a native of Barbados, returned to the church one Sunday to retrieve a straw hat he had left there. When he found the sanctuary being fumigated, he "was insulted for life." Neither he—nor his fellow West Indians—went back. Instead, they built St. Cyprian's, a one-floor, Spanish-style brick structure with a sanctuary for four hundred congregants and stained-glass windows depicting such African Americans as Marcus Garvey; Richard Allen, the founder of the African Methodist Episcopal Church; and Absalom Jones, the first black Episcopal minister. At St. Cyprian's, the West Indians could have their pride and their dignity. On Sundays there was a literary society, a tea, musical performances by youngsters, and three separate worship services.[13]

Each service was full, said the Reverend Nathan Wright, minister at St. Cyprian's from 1950 to 1964, because, "if you wanted to get out of your tenement, this is where you went. Or maybe you went to the candy store or the pool hall. But this was free, and this was uplifting, and this was where most of your friends were."[14]

It was also where Gene Walcott worshiped. As an acolyte, he carried the cross into the sanctuary for Sunday services, sang in the choir, and played his violin at Sunday concerts.

"The women of the church loved [Gene]," said Elma Lewis, whose mother was Farrakhan's godmother. "They adored him. He behaved. He was obedient. He was mannerly. He was faithful and kind. He was everything you would want a child to be."[15]

Louis Eugene Walcott, the boy, was everything that the world at large would later say Louis Farrakhan, the preacher, was not. But late at night, known only to himself and his God, he would cry himself to sleep as he lay in bed, eavesdropping on his mother and her friends as they talked in the dining room about the "condition of black people, about the suffering of our people. I would wonder why, if God had sent a deliverer to an oppressed people in the past, why that same God wouldn't send *us* a deliverer? I never heard my pastor speak on the question of the liberation of my people. I couldn't understand why we would have to be buried in a separate cemetery if we were all going to the same heaven. I couldn't understand why it was an honor to go downtown to sing with a white choir in a white church. As a youngster, I loved Jesus and I loved scripture, but I just wanted answers."[16]

Sarah Mae Manning, Gene's mother, had come to the United States in the mid-1920s. "A fiery, strong-willed, abundantly attractive" woman, she had arrived, as had most West Indians, "with crazy expectations and hopes." And like most, she "worked hard as hell and met a nightmare."[17]

She settled first in New York's Bronx, working primarily as a domestic for whites and marrying a cab driver named Percival Clarke, a Jamaican immigrant who Mae soon discovered "was a 'lover man,' and she didn't want that. He got out of her life." During one of Clarke's extended absences, Mae fell in love with a cab driver named Louis Walcott, with whom, in October 1931, she had her first son, Alvan. But in the fall of 1932, Clarke briefly surfaced—and Mae became pregnant again, this time by her own husband. A panicked Mae tried three times to abort the pregnancy with a coat hanger, then finally gave birth to a boy whom she named after her lover, not her husband. In fact, Farrakhan's birth certificate would list Louis Walcott as his father, not Percival Clarke.[18]

The pregnancy thoroughly complicated Mae's life—and the circumstances certainly throw Farrakhan's racial pedigree into question. Even Farrakhan knew that the pregnancy had initially been a disaster for his mother. As he told an audience in Newark in April 1995, "She's with a man, but I'm not his child. She don't want to tell the man, 'I've been unfaithful,' so she's hoping, since my brother was here from this man, . . . that I'll be what *he* wanted: a girl. And she was hoping that I wouldn't be light . . . 'cause both my mother and the man she was living with were dark."[19]

At this point, the Newark audience hearing this story burst into laughter, as if privy to some secret joke. And also as if Farrakhan was hinting that his father was not just "light," but even "white." He compounded the punch line by adding, "Any resemblance to any persons living or dead is not a coincidence at all. *This* is our life story"—the story of white abuse of blacks, of white appropriation of black virtue, honor, integrity.[20]

"Well, my mother's scared to death," continued Farrakhan, "so she's praying all the time, . . . begging the Higher Power to make her secure. Her prayers go into me. She's making a servant for God. She don't know that. An unfortunate circumstance is producing something of value."[21]

Whether Farrakhan's father was all-white or was just light-skinned—whether, indeed, Farrakhan has even a single drop of white blood in him—neither makes him an anomaly nor dilutes his authority as a black leader. Rather, if true, it may lend him an even greater authority, since it centers him in the norm of black life in the United States, a nation that long defined "blackness" as having *any* known African ancestry, no matter how slight. This definition is a residue of the frequent miscegenation that occurred during slavery and the hate and suspicions that animated more than a century of Jim Crow segregation.

The principle that determined whether one was defined—and treated—as black was known in the South as the "one-drop rule": a single "drop" of "black blood" made one black. It was also known as the "one black ancestor rule," and some courts called it the "traceable amount rule." Somewhere between 75 to 90 percent of all those defined as black in the United States have some white ancestry. Those blacks with no white lineage can usually be found in the more isolated, rural areas of the Deep South, especially in South Carolina.[22]

The one-drop rule was uniformly observed in the Deep South, except in New Orleans, where, even late into the 1900s, white and black could sit next to each other on public transportation, not because local whites exercised any great tolerance (although the city's jazz and relatively loose sexual mores hint at something there that was uncommon in the rest of America), but simply through sheer expediency: the local streetcar company balked at implementing Jim Crow laws in a city that was so aware of the gradations of skin color that it honored them with such names as "mulatto," "quadroon," "octoroon," "white Creole," and "Creole of color."[23]

The differences in skin color within Gene Walcott's family were obvious to all, just as they were obvious to those who knew Malcolm Little's family. Gene's mother "was black as ink," said Elma Lewis. "His brother was black as ink. But *he* is light as hell." In Malcolm's family, the color lines were reversed. His father was pitch-black, while his mother, who proclaimed herself the

daughter of "a white 'prince' and plantation owner," was quite
light. She took great pride in Malcolm's whiteness, sometimes
even vigorously scrubbing his face and neck because she
believed she could make him "look almost white if I bathe him
enough."[24]

The notorious one-drop rule gave Malcolm and Gene Walcott little choice. Though their blackness, like that of most
African Americans, was diluted with whiteness, they were, for all
intents and purposes, biologically, legally, socially, and psychologically black. But each still had a choice in how to adjudicate
his blackness, and each may have harbored a vast resentment
that his Caucasian ancestors had not somehow "rescued" their
progeny from the misfortunes of being black in white America.
Unlike W. E. B. Du Bois, the formidable black intellectual whose
family tree included white French and white Dutch, Malcolm
and the adult Louis Walcott would harness a vision of whites as
corrupt, insincere, unredeemable. By embracing blackness as
morally and historically pristine, Malcolm and Gene elevated
color until it became the final arbiter of justice and redemption,
of obligation and reward and destiny. To them, their white genes
notwithstanding, whiteness was deviltry itself, brutal and profane; blackness was hallowed, sacred, divine. And the world at
large was a troubled, bifurcated place: goodness on one side, evil
on the other, and the apocalypse dead-ahead. The stakes for
which they would play were among the highest in town: freedom, dignity, divine retribution, and ultimate deliverance. And
the odds, they were certain, were all on their side because God,
virtue, and justice were also on their side.

Boston has been called "arguably the country's most insular
city," one where "nothing was more important than finding
one's niche." In Boston, Mae and her family quickly located their
niche. In 1937, she and Louis Walcott and their two boys first

lived at 23 Melrose Street in the city's South End. But the next year, the Boston directory lists only a Mrs. Mae Walcott residing at 51 Westminster Street in Roxbury. Louis Walcott's absence from the directory strongly suggests that he and Mae had separated, or as an old family friend described what happened to Farrakhan's mother's lover, "he joined the missing."[25]

Mae, Louis, and Alvan remained on Westminster Street for two years. In 1940, they moved to Shawmut Avenue, smack in the middle of the West Indian community where everyone seemed to know their place—and to keep to it. But ethnic and racial tensions were never far away. At the Dudley Street station, blacks often had to jump off the trolley and run for safety "because the Irish people were always picking on them," just as they enjoyed picking on Jews. In Nat Hentoff's bittersweet remembrance of growing up in Roxbury, *Boston Boy*, he recalls walking one evening with three friends through Franklin Park,

> on the way to a dance at Hebrew school. Coming toward us are four bigger boys. When they are close enough, it is clear they are not Jewish. And since they are not Italian, they are Irish. Their leader swaggers up to me and asks—what else?—"Are you Jewish?" . . . I nod.
>
> "You got a light?" he asks.
>
> As I go to my pocket, I look down, and a stone, a huge stone, smashes into my face. Or so it feels. The shock and pain are such that it takes a few moments for me to taste the blood and feel the space where a second ago, there had been a tooth.
>
> Their leader, rubbing his fist with satisfaction, waits for a revengeful lunge and is not surprised when it doesn't come. So few of these kikes fight back. He and his sturdy companions move on, guffawing.[26]

In Roxbury, Gene Walcott had a few Jewish friends, some of whom he defended from the marauding Irish, probably because, as Hentoff said, "so few of these kikes fight back." When Gene was thirteen, he had a further lapse of the civility that had been inculcated in him by his mother and the other West Indians of lower Roxbury: "I punched a white boy in front of my friends. I was trying to show off. He didn't do anything to me. It bothered my conscience. That boy did nothing to me, although, of course, he was a member of a group that did much to me and my people. I felt bad for so doing. That's the only incident where I struck somebody."[27]

The incident seems somewhat out of character, if we are to believe this testimony from Malik Abdul Khallaq, who knew Farrakhan while he was growing up: "Louis Farrakhan is not a fighter. No fisticuffs for him. He cannot fight his way out of a paper bag. But he'll talk *you* into fighting *your* way out."[28]

As she had in New York, Mae earned a fitful living. She was often on welfare and would supplement her meager income with ironing and sewing or working as a domestic, sometimes for physicians at Massachusetts General Hospital, and often for Jews. One Jew in whose house she lived for about eighteen months in the late 1950s as a caretaker for his children was impressed that she "knew the laws of *kashrut* [the Jewish dietary code]. It was obvious that she had worked for other Jews. She just stepped in and immediately knew what to do. My wife had recently died, and I had three small children. She was great with them, but she was very strict about manners, such as keeping their hands off the table at mealtime."[29]

For kindergarten through fourth grade, Gene attended the Asa Gray Elementary School (about four blocks away from his home); for fifth through eighth grades, he attended the Sherwin School (about two blocks away). And in the typical fashion for the neighborhood, Mae saved her pennies and nickels for the twenty-five to fifty cents it cost per lesson for Alvan to learn piano and for Gene to learn violin, which he began at the age of six. Gene first studied with Preston Williams, the local teacher from whom most neighborhood kids learned; as Gene's skills improved and his talent surfaced, he studied with a Jewish woman who had immigrated from Russia. The instrument became an all-consuming passion. Demonstrating a mature self-discipline, he "would play three, four, five hours a day" by the time he got to high school. "I liked to play in the bathroom. The violin seemed to resonate better there, and I could watch myself better in the mirror. Nobody could get into the bathroom while I was playing."[30]

But there was much more to life in Roxbury than music and education. Many Caribbean immigrants there were attracted to Marcus Garvey, who had come to the United States from Jamaica in 1916 and whose Universal Negro Improvement Association (UNIA) became the largest black social movement in American history. The UNIA had nearly two thousand branches around the world and up to six million dues-paying members in the United States. It was probably the most influential of any black militant organization in the first half of this century, and it helped shape almost every militant group that came after it. Its ideology spoke to black impotence and frustration, to black religiosity and spirituality, and to black frustrations in the marketplace, the church, the voting booth. Garvey's genius was that he fused longings for power, God, and community into constructive, self-enhancing venues without diluting their strength or energy.

From the 1920s to the mid-1930s, the seat of the Garvey movement in Boston was Toussaint L'Overture Hall at 1065 Tremont Street, right next door to St. Cyprian's. At meetings, usually held on Sunday evenings, Garvey organizers exhorted about the need for education, pride, land, and economic self-sufficiency. Youngsters read poems from the NAACP's publication *The Crisis*, and thirteen-to-sixteen-year-olds marched around in their khaki Garvey "cadet" uniforms when they weren't studying flag signals, military training, black history, and the *Universal Negro Ritual*, which was roughly modeled after the Episcopalian *Book of Common Prayer*. And everyone's spirit was raised by the call from Garvey himself: "Up, you mighty race, you can accomplish what you will."[31]

Gene's mother was almost certainly a Garvey sympathizer, if not a UNIA member, and at least one member of his family was a committed, passionate Garveyite. Once, when visiting an uncle in New York, eleven-year-old Gene was surprised that he had a picture of a black man on his mantel, since immigrants from the British West Indies usually reserved this spot of honor for such luminaries as King George. Gene's uncle said the black man "was the greatest leader our people had ever had." Gene, who was short for his age, stood on a chair for a few minutes, looking into the face of the black man, studying his features.

"Where is this man, that I might meet him and help him?" he asked his uncle.

"He's dead," came the reply.

Gene "was so hurt that after hoping, all my young years, to meet the right man for our people, that when I found him, he was already dead. Tears rolled down my cheeks, and I cried and cried because Marcus Garvey was dead."[32]

As would the Nation of Islam, the Garvey movement turned skin into the arbiter of virtue and greatness; economic self-sufficiency into the vehicle for liberation from white domination; and land into the means for ultimate emancipation. Garvey wanted land in Africa, the Nation of Islam would want it carved out of the contiguous United States. As with the Nation, the language, the fervor, the symbolism that animated Garvey's quest for sovereignty was, at its core, deeply religious. But unlike the Nation, which would adopt the Koran (but would never ignore the Old and New Testaments), Garvey was preoccupied solely with the Jewish and Christian texts, and he rarely used religion as a pretext for divisiveness. Garvey let his followers stay in their own faith, as long as it was led by blacks. But beyond that, his religious principles, fired in the crucible of racial imperatives, were close to what would eventually be espoused by the Nation of Islam: since Jesus was black, continuing to believe that God was white was to engage in a gross, race-defeating error: "God has no color, yet it is human to see everything through one's own spectacles, and since the white people have seen their God through white spectacles, we have only now started out . . . to see our God through our own spectacles. . . . When you bow down to a graven image, you dishonor the God that is in you. . . . Therefore, the UNIA desires every Negro to destroy the image of the white God that you have been taught to bow to."[33]

The "structure" Garvey assigned to God was traditionally Christian: an omniscient, omnipotent trinity, "not a person," but "a spirit." But to the future Nation of Islam, God was a physical force that could be touched, viewed, argued with, but never suppressed: *every* black man was God. Gene Walcott—a.k.a. Louis Farrakhan—would later champion this elevation of race to the rarefied category of divinity. But in the meantime, surrounded by determined Garveyites and proud West Indians, he was absorbing—by osmosis, if not directly—a less vitriolic but no less potent brand of theological black pride, one that he would echo, if not outright mimic in his own fashion, decades later.

II

Telegram for "The Charmer"

While Gene Walcott had never assumed the uppity, patrician airs of The Four Hundred of upper Roxbury, he didn't turn down the chance in 1947 to join the small handful of blacks who attended the most patrician of the city's secondary pubic schools, the Boston Latin School. Entry depended on grades, and Gene's were good enough for him to rank with the city's academic elite.

Psychologically, Boston Latin was light-years away from the safe, nurturing cocoon of Roxbury. Founded in 1635, it was the oldest public school in America. Alumni included Samuel Adams, Benjamin Franklin, Ralph Waldo Emerson, George Santayana, the art historian Bernard Berenson, and the conductor-composer Leonard Bernstein. This unrelentingly serious school on the somewhat presumptuously named Avenue Louis Pasteur didn't accept slouches, it didn't produce slouches, and it surely didn't coddle a single one of its students. As an alumnus wrote on the school's 350th anniversary in 1985, "Even today when old graduates reminisce, you will barely hear them say of any teacher, 'He really understood me.' They are more apt to say, 'He certainly taught me trigonometry and the ablative absolute.'"[1]

The legacy of another alumnus, the fearsome, stern Puritan preacher Cotton Mather, seemed to have a vestigial stranglehold on Boston Latin. Sobriety of intention and single-minded devotion to academics underlay Boston Latin's unwritten maxim. Given such a stricture, it is not difficult to imagine Gene Walcott squirming in his seat, waiting for the school bell to ring at 3:00 P.M. so he could return to the somewhat looser—and certainly more African American—ambience of Roxbury.

After one year at Boston Latin, Walcott transferred to English High, which, after Latin, was the second-best academic high school in the city. Years later, Farrakhan said he had left Latin because he felt out of place and conspicuous in such an overwhelmingly white school. At English High, he had the company of more blacks (the school was about 15 percent African American) and was consistently on the honor roll (as he had been at Latin). But he became conspicuous in a way he hadn't been at Latin: he joined the track team, specializing in the one-hundred-yard dash. Although according to the mythology that later enveloped Farrakhan declaring him to be a star who set records, documents at English High suggest that he was an average member of the team, someone who neither excelled nor broke records but instead was reliable, steadfast, and determined.[2]

In the 1930s and 1940s, high school track was the rage in Boston. If one was on a winning team (as Gene Walcott was), he became a mini-celebrity, surrounded by the penumbra that adheres to any teen who stands out from the crowd: a juvenile "otherworldliness" is attributed to them that falls somewhere between being a minor god and just another kid who hangs out on street corners with his peers, who view him with puerile respect, adulation, and envy.

"In those days, being a track star was like being a president," recalled a former Roxbury resident who has always admired Farrakhan. "Louis was 'the president' of Roxbury. But he wouldn't flaunt it. People would try to hang out around him; they would rub up against him. It wasn't important to him. He would go home and do his homework and wouldn't bathe in the glory just because he had won a fifty-yard dash."[3]

On Walcott's track team was a Roxbury Jew who became "very close" to the black athlete. In relay races, Walcott passed the baton to him; on weekends or after school, they visited each other at their homes. Looking back at the friendship years later, and weighing all that Farrakhan had said in the intervening years about Jews, this ex-teammate said, "I wish I could say otherwise, but Gene was a *mensch* [Yiddish for an "upright, honorable, trustworthy person"]. He could charm the rubber off a rubber duck. He had a quick, facile mind and was just a nice, enormously decent young man. I liked him tremendously."[4]

Walcott's running abilities got him a job as a counselor during the summers in the late 1940s at Camp Breezy Meadows, a summer camp for disadvantaged black youths from New England in Holliston, Massachusetts, about twenty-five miles west of Boston. Boys attended in July, girls in August. As with any camp, there were histories and traditions and ways to ensure that your name passed down in the oral legends from one generation of campers and counselors to the next. At Breezy Meadows, one way was to carve your name in the wooden walls of the bunks or high up in the rafters. Several years after he stopped working there, campers could still see "Walcott" carved on the walls of the boys' dormitory, and they would look at it with a certain reverence. *The* track star had been here. *The* honor roll student had been here. Maybe some of his glory would brush off on *them.*

At camp, Walcott sometimes held a running "clinic" in which he advised youngsters how to run faster and more efficiently. One day he spied the awkward thirteen-year-old John Rice, who was "stumbling around and being beat by everyone."

"Come here," he called to Rice, who would be a freshman at English High that fall.

"At that time," remembered Rice, "we didn't have starting blocks. Instead, we dug small holes in the ground with our feet. He said, 'Dig a hole here and another hole here.' That way I got leverage, and he taught me how to use my leverage to go forward. He taught me only once. After that, the kids who were beating me couldn't even touch me. And no one could ever beat me."[5]

Rice would soon presume that his victories at track and his straight A's in high school would catapult him into the same league of neighborhood leadership and fame as Walcott. But while track and academics were indeed Walcott's forte, Rice possessed neither Walcott's will to constantly pursue an audience nor Walcott's certainty that he had been chosen for a noble and invaluable task. Without those qualities, Rice would always look up to Walcott as the hero he could have been; with those qualities, Walcott had his ticket out of Roxbury.

Young Walcott wanted to be a star in more than just track. About 1947 or 1948, John Bynoe, who was a few years older than Walcott, organized a fundraising concert at Ruggles Hall in Roxbury so that a local football team, the Panthers, could buy jackets. The draw was an act from New York: Joe Clark and His Calypsonians. This was perhaps the first time that a calypso group had played in Roxbury, although the neighborhood's

West Indian complexion certainly made it receptive to the Caribbean beat. With the West Indian in him intuitively responding to the music and the trained musician in him assuming that mastering calypso was a cinch (and surely easier than playing classical music on the violin), Gene turned to Bynoe and said, "I can do that."[6]

Soon, the sixteen-year-old Louis Eugene Walcott, never one to be upstaged by a new fad, was playing in Boston's black night-clubs under the name of "The Charmer," a child in a Gomorrah of marijuana, loose sex, and double entendres. On the sidelines was a very displeased Mae Clarke, confused about what had happened to her polite, proper Louis and dismayed at the sen-suality emanating from the stage: "She came a few times when I was in the nightclub and, of course, singing the music of the Caribbean . . . and some of them were songs with double mean-ings. On the surface, it was one thing, but underneath it was kind of filthy. She would hear me sing these kinds of songs. She would register some of her disapproval of my gyrations in my dance and some of the songs that I sung."[7]

The Charmer, who was still, really, just a kid, made the rounds of black clubs, especially Eddie's Lounge and the Hi-Hat, both on Massachusetts Avenue, where he was fresh bait for both men and women. "I could have been on Broadway if I wanted to entertain homosexuality as a young seventeen-year-old boy," he recalled years later.

> I said, "The hell with you. If my talent ain't good enough for you, then the hell with you. I don't need Broadway. I need God's way." . . . Women came to me. . . . I was . . . playing in the night-clubs, and I wouldn't go to bed with them. They wanted to give me money. And I said, "Oh no, you've worked so hard for your money." I was making eighty-five dollars a week, but I wouldn't take a dime from nobody to make them think they had bought

my life. . . . I told them, "You're out of your damn mind." They said, "I think you're a faggot." And I said, "I *know* what I am. You'll never find out."[8]

Fending off women, sipping alcohol, smoking some marijuana, Gene Walcott may have been living the fantasy life of the average teenager.

At the same time that he was singing in nightclubs, Walcott even appeared on national television on *The Ted Mack Original Amateur Hour,* but not as a calypso singer. Instead, he played classical music on his beloved violin, possibly because a Negro who played such music on such an instrument was more of a novelty act than one who sang calypso. For the TV audience, with his suit jacket buttoned up and a dark tie knotted close to his neck, Walcott looked like anything but a nightclub crooner of Caribbean melodies. And his peppy banter with Ted Mack suggested only that he was a fine, upstanding youth:

MACK: It says here you're a track runner in English High School, that you've equaled every record in school. Right?

WALCOTT: Yes, but I hope to break a few when I put on a little more weight.

MACK: How about your violin? Can you play that as fast as you can run?

WALCOTT: Not quite, but I hope to break some records with this someday.

MACK: You're just a champion at heart, aren't you?[9]

With high school ending and a very ambitious mother behind him, the "champion" began thinking about college. He considered attending the Juilliard School of Music in New York but ended up in September 1950 at Winston-Salem Teachers' College, an all-black school in Winston-Salem, North Carolina, with about seven hundred women and one hundred men. According to Farrakhan, brotherly empathy, the desire "to experience what my brothers and sisters are experiencing in the South," steered him toward Winston-Salem. But there is strong evidence that race had nothing to do with Walcott going to Winston-Salem. Instead, he was courted by two Boston students who went there and wanted it to have a stronger presence from their hometown, especially in sports. He was also wooed by Archibald Morrow, who had started Winston-Salem's track program and was then a graduate student in Boston. On top of that, the track scholarship he received from Winston-Salem (which was really more of a work-study program than an outright grant) was, especially for a poor black from lower Roxbury, irresistible.[10]

Attending Winston-Salem surely opened Walcott's eyes to hard-core segregation and up-front racism. During an eight-hour layover between southbound trains in Washington, D.C., while en route to college, he decided to see a film. As he approached the theater's ticket booth, employees and patrons standing outside looked at him strangely. He first checked his pants to make sure his fly was up. Then, asking for a ticket, he was told, "We don't sell tickets to niggers."[11]

Winston-Salem, a small city of ninety thousand at the time, wasn't in the Deep South, but it was far enough below the Mason-Dixon Line that Walcott quickly had to learn new shadings of demeanor. Unlike the arrangement in many other southern towns and cities, Walcott didn't have to sit in the back of a bus since the blacks of Winston-Salem had their own bus company, called, appropriately enough, the Safe Bus Company. But Woolworth's did have separate water fountains for blacks and whites. A few times, Walcott drank from the "white fountain" while whites "glared at him" and a college roommate tried to ignore what was going on. Once, while traveling beyond Winston-Salem, he had to use a men's room. He was told to go to the courthouse, where he found the "Negro rest rooms" in the "sub-basement." Since the ladies' room did not have a door, one woman would have to stand in the doorway while another used the toilet.[12]

Sportsmanlike behavior in Winston-Salem assumed a new meaning during practice for the college track team, for which Walcott ran the 440- and 880-yard relays and the 100-yard and 220-yard dashes. The teams for the teachers' college and for the recently relocated Wake Forest University both practiced at a track in Hyde Park, next to a local high school. Not only did Wake Forest practice first because it was a white school, but Walcott and his black teammates were instructed not to socialize with Wake Forest athletes, especially with females.[13]

At Winston-Salem, Walcott was a good, not a great athlete. According to his coach, he was "better than average, but no record setter." But he excelled in other, less predictable ways. Because of the housing shortage caused by the millions of ex-soldiers on the GI Bill who had been flooding college campuses since the end of World War II, Farrakhan and twelve other young men had to share a room in the college library, which had been commandeered for a makeshift dormitory. On weekdays Walcott had a hard time getting up on time for his 8:00 A.M. classes. Often a roommate, Clarence Jones, had "to shout, 'Get up, Gene. Get out of here. Go to class, Gene.' Sometimes, I had to 'steal' food out of the dining room for him so he could have some breakfast."

But on weekends, he rose by 7:00 A.M., then went to an empty classroom building where, for three or four hours, he practiced his violin. He also organized a calypso band that gave concerts around the state or sometimes wandered around the campus on Sunday afternoons, serenading students with their music.[14]

For the school's annual Freshmen Talent Night, a friend from Roxbury, imitating the hotel bellhop used in the Philip Morris cigarette commercials of the 1950s, called out, "Telegram for 'The Charmer.' Telegram for 'The Charmer.'" Then out from the wings came "The Charmer," who played some classical music on his violin and a few calypso songs on his ukulele. One song that he wrote and performed, "Why America Is No Democracy" (for which, unfortunately, lyrics are not available), predated the protest songs that would be widely popular in another decade. The title hints at Walcott's pre–Nation of Islam politics: a probable amalgam of Garveyism and black resentment, invigorated by the liberating freedom of being away from home for the first time and fueled by seeing the southern black experience firsthand.[15]

Walcott showed no great promise as a student, relying on his past education to get him through his courses. He seems to have spent most of his time honing his music—and not, as would have been the easy temptation at a college with roughly a seven-to-one female/male ratio, being a ladies' man. In fact, until the middle of his freshman year, when he became fond of Betsy Ross, a young lower Roxbury woman whom he met while on vacation, he seems to have thought little about girls. But soon after meeting Ms. Ross, "It was always 'Betsy, Betsy, Betsy.' He never made time for anyone else and he never looked at anyone else."[16]

During his first summer vacation from college, Walcott played a lot of baseball in Westminster Park, showing off for Betsy, who lived not far from the park. During his sophomore year, the combination of being away from his girlfriend and his hometown was wearing on him, and he began to talk about dropping out of college. He was also grumbling about a new calypso singer, Harry Belafonte, who, at age twenty-four (six years older than Walcott) had a career that was surging forward while Walcott was stuck at a small teachers' college and playing small, infrequent calypso gigs in semi-rural North Carolina.[17]

During the summer of 1953, Walcott decided not to return to Winston-Salem. Instead, he announced that he would marry Betsy, who was pregnant. Walcott's mother was furious, insisting that he finish college and doubting that her virtuous, proper son had fathered the child.[18]

But on September 12, 1953—the same day that a young senator named John Kennedy married a young socialite, Jacqueline Bouvier, in fashionable Newport, Rhode Island—there was a marriage, and it was a "correct" one, held at St. Cyprian's Church, where Walcott had been an acolyte as a boy. The marriage certificate identified both bride and groom as "Colored" and twenty-year-old Walcott's occupation as "musician." Betsy, who was a Roman Catholic and only seventeen, listed her "occupation" as "at home." For a wedding present, the officiating minister, the Reverend Nathan Wright, gave the newlyweds a copy of *The Common Ventures of Life* by a Quaker, Elton Trueblood, a book that, according to Farrakhan, he and his wife occasionally read aloud to each other four decades later as a way to remember their wedding vows. Some of the opening sentences of the first chapter are surprisingly congruent with the theology of the Nation of Islam, a theology that Walcott would soon discover essentially denies God's transcendency, promising deliverance in this plane and not in some unproven afterlife. "According to the Gospel," wrote Trueblood in *The Common Ventures of Life,*

the true function of spirit is not to deny matter, but rather to *glorify* it [italics added]. The Word, we believe, was made *flesh.* The Bible is a highly materialist book beginning with the assertion that man was made from dust, and concerned at all points with what happens to bodies, especially broken and needy bodies. . . .

. . . Angels, if they exist, are pure spirits without bodily needs, but men are not pure spirits. Men are combinations of body and mind and spirit, uniting in a working relationship both hand and brain.[19]

For his minister—and not just any minister, but one with whom Farrakhan stayed in touch his entire life—to give Walcott a book that put the physical on a par with the spiritual would endow Nation of Islam theology with an imprimatur that the later Farrakhan probably did not need: he was invariably dead-certain of himself. But it did confer upon his career in the Nation a certain continuum with his past in Roxbury—and Roxbury, to Farrakhan, always represented some of the most golden years of his life.

In the early 1990s, when Farrakhan returned to St. Cyprian's as a guest preacher to give a Sunday morning sermon, it took him nearly five minutes to pull himself together after he started crying in the pulpit "because I was home now where it all started." This apostle of a strain of Islam, this unrestrained critic of Christianity, "knew that I could never leave the church again. Not that I would adopt all the ways [of the church], but . . . if you learn something valuable, come back and enliven the house so that the house may be more representative of itself."[20]

The chemistry of Roxbury and St. Cyprian's, of the long, unexpected route he had taken from his mother's house on Shawmut Avenue, pulled at Farrakhan that Sunday at St. Cyprian's. No surprise is as potent as one is to someone with self-possession similar to Farrakhan, a man for whom the past, which he thought he had left far behind, may have had a more tenacious hold on the present than he ever dreamed or expected.

With no college degree and a wife and child to support, Walcott resumed his stage career. In the Midwest and especially in New

England, where he was a hometown boy, Walcott sometimes earned as much as five hundred dollars a week. Calmer, less enamored heads laugh at claims that "Calypso Gene," as he now called himself, was bigger than Harry Belafonte in New England, but there's little denying that Walcott stirred up a midsized sensation. He did his own PR, sometimes taking publicity shots of himself in a mostly unbuttoned Caribbean-style shirt to the *Boston Graphic*, a local black newspaper, where he impressed a sixteen-year-old working there as "funny and witty—the only time I *ever* saw him funny and witty." In dance halls on Massachusetts Avenue in Boston, and especially deeper into Roxbury at Butler Hall on Tremont Street, customers got off their duffs and danced to his music. Daisy Voigt, then a teenager living in Roxbury and moving on the edges of an arty scene, remembered that "listening to music was different then. For jazz, you went to bars and clubs and you sat because you were cool. For rhythm and blues and calypso, you got up and danced. You would make out with Johnny Mathis [records], and you would party with Harry Belafonte [records]. There were 'rules.'"[21]

But Walcott seemed to set his own rules. Once, for instance, he gave a free concert long before it was common for musicians to play gratis for their particular community, be it for African Americans in Roxbury, hippies in Haight-Ashbury, or yuppies in Central Park. John Rice was "playing softball in Madison Park when we saw a band coming down Ruggles Street on the back of a flat-bed truck. The music sounded so Cuban, so rhythmic. People started dropping their balls and bats and gloves, and other people started dancing all down the street and then down another street. And then I saw that it was Eugene Walcott. He was a show."[22]

Perhaps the show would have gone on and on. Perhaps Walcott would even have eclipsed Belafonte. That is conjecture, as is the not infrequent comment, "We have Farrakhan now because we had Belafonte then." But there was not enough room in that part of the national psyche reserved for pop culture for *two* light-skinned black calypso singers; nor, apparently, were RCA's pockets deep enough for two contracts to such performers. The signed contract went to Belafonte; the one never signed might have been Walcott's had he not had what record executives called "attitude problems."[23]

The belief among Farrakhan partisans that he was just a step or two behind Belafonte in breaking into the big time—and that Belafonte was better at playing the game than he was—is mirrored in their "recollection" that he was an understudy to Belafonte for the Broadway show *Jamaica*. In reality, Belafonte never starred in *Jamaica*; Ossie Davis and Lena Horne did. The one Broadway show of that era that did star Belafonte was *John Anderson's Almanac*. Records for both shows list neither a "Louis Eugene Walcott" nor any variation on that name as an understudy.

Moreover, *Jamaica* opened on October 31, 1957, almost half a year after Farrakhan, then Louis X, became minister of the Nation's temple in Boston, a time when, surely, the Nation of Islam would not have given him a sabbatical to resume his entertainment career. *John Anderson's Almanac* opened in December 1953. Indeed, it was only after his marriage that previous September that Farrakhan started trying to jump-start his show business career; in all likelihood, the show would have been completely cast by then, even its understudy roles.[24]

Walcott's career frustrations, the growing bitterness, the demands from white executives in the music industry to play the game *their* way, may have primed Walcott for what happened while he was in Chicago in February 1955 for an eight-week tour headlining a show called "Calypso Follies." Riding with his wife and daughter in a cab, Walcott saw an old friend, Rodney Smith, walking down the street. He had the cab driver pull over to the

curb and the two pals began bringing each other up to date
about their lives. Smith, a recent convert to the Nation of Islam,
persuaded Walcott to attend the group's upcoming annual convention at its main temple at 5335 South Greenwood Avenue on
Chicago's South Side. The sea change then occurring on the
South Side—from mostly Jewish to mostly black—was typical of
the ethnic undulations in cities around the country. One talis-
man of the change was the stone replica of the Ten Command-
ments that remained on top of the front facade of the Nation of
Islam's Temple No. 2, a former synagogue.[25]

Walcott had heard that everyone was frisked at NOI events.
So before entering the rally, he hid a marijuana joint in his hat-
band. With his wife and an uncle who was wearing flowing
Caribbean robes, Walcott sat in the balcony, a bit skeptical about
the proceedings. He was impressed by the preaching of the
diminutive man at the podium—Elijah Muhammad—but had
difficulty getting past the gnarled grammar typical of someone
who had finished only three years of elementary school.

"This man can't even speak well," he thought to himself.

Suddenly, Muhammad, who was also known as "the Messenger," looked up toward Walcott. "Brother, don't pay attention to
how I speak. Pay attention to what I'm saying. I didn't get the
chance to go to the white man's fine schools, because when I
tried to go, the doors were closed. But if you take what I say and
place it into the beautiful way of speaking you know, you can
help me save our people."[26]

Walcott was stunned. "That scared me to death. I thought the
Messenger had read my mind." But according to an article about
Farrakhan in 1975 in *Sepia* magazine, "What Louis didn't know
was that a Muslim captain had told Mr. Muhammad where
Louis would be seated and informed the Messenger that Louis
'was a college man who could help us if we get him.' But how the
Messenger knew what Louis was thinking remains a mystery."[27]

Near the end of the meeting, when new members were recruited, Walcott's wife immediately signed up. Walcott stayed in his seat, only budging when his uncle urged him to "Get up. Get up." So Walcott got up and joined, but was far from fully persuaded that this was the right path. Not until a few months later, when he heard Malcolm X speak, was he convinced that he had found the right niche for himself, one that conflated Afrocentric mythology, black pride, black nationalism, economic empowerment, and a certain strained moral rectitude into a vehicle that, he was certain, would liberate his people, long-suffering in what was *not* their Promised Land.[28]

That was what Walcott was moving toward. But what he had moved away from—Christianity—had frustrated him with its "hypocrisy." "I hated the fact that, as a Christian, we talked about the 'love of Christ,' but I didn't feel the love of white Christians toward black Christians. And that the church was unwilling—or unable—to address specific concerns of black people for justice. I went looking not for a new religion, but for new leadership that would address the concerns of black people. And I found Malcolm X and Elijah Muhammad. I was not interested in changing my religion, but they were Muslims and they spoke a truth that I could identify with."[29]

The Chicago Savior's Day speech was not Louis Walcott's first brush with the Nation of Islam. His old neighborhood of Roxbury was a prime target for the Nation in the early 1950s. In 1952, on his release after serving four years of an eight-to-ten-year prison sentence for robbery, Malcolm returned to Michigan to visit his mother in a mental institution in Kalamazoo and to live briefly with his brother Wilfred in Detroit. There he attended his first official Nation meeting at the group's Temple No. 1. That September he traveled to Chicago to hear Elijah Muhammad, whose teachings had persuaded him, even while in prison, that "it is better to be jailed by the devil for serving Allah than it is to be destroyed by the devil to walk free." The Messenger sent Malcolm back to Detroit with a mandate to recruit members, especially younger ones, for the local temple. Malcolm took to his charge with a fierce, humorless enthusiasm whose success and determination threatened the leadership of the local minister, Lemuel Hassan. To preserve his fiefdom, Hassan recommended that Malcolm be transferred to Boston, where the NOI had been struggling to establish a temple.[30]

In some ways, Boston was especially ripe for what Malcolm had to offer. He arrived there two years before the Supreme Court struck down school segregation as unconstitutional and three years before a tired Rosa Parks, traveling home on a bus after working all day at a department store in Montgomery, Alabama, refused to give up her seat and move to the rear. Despite its history of abolitionism, Garveyism, and good-hearted, patrician liberalism, Boston would never be on the center stage of the civil rights movement; that distinction was reserved for cities and towns where more visceral, certainly more visual, dramas would unfold: Jackson and Birmingham and Oxford, cities whose personas would eventually be seasoned with tear gas and police dogs and the brutal force of fire hoses turned against the tender abdomens of black youths. As in the South, Boston's blacks had stored up resentment and frustration. But unlike blacks below the Mason-Dixon Line, those in Boston had an extreme crisis of identity: their numbers were so few, and their power (if, indeed, whatever leverage they exerted on the broader society could be called "power") was so limited, that they did not really know who they were. On top of that, the caste and class of black Boston, ordained by economics, social status, and gradations of skin color, made the stratification of their world even more obdurate. Blacks lived in a culture in which social acceptability was determined by the lightness of one's skin—in effect, by one's "whiteness." Thus the saying, "If you're white, you're right. If you're yellow, mellow. If you're brown, stick around. If you're black, get back." Since being *black*—truly deep, ink-jet black—meant being hobbled and impaired, the incentive was to orient self and community to negate blackness—*real* blackness—in all its forms and shapes and idiosyncrasies.

In Boston, Malcolm looked up some old friends, such as Malcolm Jarvis, whom he had converted to the Nation of Islam while they were both in prison for robbery. The two Malcolms and the handful of Nation members in Boston often went "fishing," Nation argot for recruiting members (and which may have been borrowed from Jesus' injunction to Peter, "Follow me, I will make you a fisher of men"). Stopping blacks on the street, they would lecture about the failures of Christianity and how slavery's ravages could be countered only by Islam, which they claimed had been their ancestors' authentic religion before being kidnapped to America.

In the evenings, Malcolm held classes for potential members, who usually ranged from their midteens to their early twenties. These were customarily held in his apartment at 5 Wellington Street, a four-story, brick row house one block off Massachusetts Avenue in the city's South End. For a while, about fifteen teens met with Malcolm every Thursday night, listening to his eloquent, articulate cadences about "revolution," but uncertain "what revolution meant. Our parents were afraid. They said, 'You better not go. If I hear that you go there, I'm going to kick your ass.'"[31]

Walcott was among the first to hear Malcolm in one of those meetings in the South End. In what must have been a momentary anomaly, his usually extroverted presence made barely a dent on those present. "There were about fifteen brothers there," said Jarvis. " . . . [Walcott] was a very quiet person."[32]

But that evening had not been Walcott's initial encounter with Malcolm—or with the Nation. "The Charmer" had previously run into Malcolm one night on Massachusetts Avenue between calypso performances at a club down the street. Still wearing makeup, which lightened his features even more than usual, Walcott was afraid to shake Malcolm's hands because he had heard the minister was so virulently antiwhite. But shake he did—then immediately dashed into a little restaurant called the Chicken Lane.[33]

Another evening, while Walcott was working in a Boston nightclub, a member of the Nation told him, "Brother, God has chosen a Messenger to lead the black man to freedom, justice and equality." In a foretaste of the self-messianism that would mark so many of his later utterances, Walcott left the club and walked down Massachusetts Avenue, "crying and talking to God: 'Oh God, You know I have always loved my people. Why did not You choose me?'" He later realized that "when God chose His Messenger, I was not even born. And if God had chosen a Messenger, that choice is all right with me. Let me find the Messenger. Then I will serve him as I would serve God."[34]

The Messenger—a.k.a. Elijah Karriem, Mohammed Allah, Elijah Black, Rassoul Mohammed, Elijah Muck-Muck, Ilag Mohammad, Moses Black, Elijah Mut Mut, and Gulam Bogans, among an inventory of 109 wonderfully creative aliases—was born as Elijah Poole on October 7, 1897, in Sandersville, Georgia. The name Poole was the name of the white family for whom his grandparents had been slaves.[35]

Given the fact that Sandersville was fairly close to the Georgia coast, where a crude form of Islam was practiced by descendants of slaves who had been Muslims in Africa, and the fact that Elijah's father's first name, Wali, was an Arabic term for a holy man or saint who performed "miraculous feats," Islam may have appealed to Elijah Muhammad because he was exposed to its vocabulary and concepts as a child. The lure of Islam for Muhammad and other blacks also extended from a yearning for tradition, authenticity, originality—and a desire to rebut the Christianity that whites had enjoined upon their slave ancestors. That *some* blacks had *some* claim on Islam was no fiction: on certain plantations, as many as 20 percent of the slaves from Africa had been Muslims. On that continent, Islam had penetrated the savanna south of the Sahara by the beginning of the ninth century. Not only did some local merchants convert, but in certain zones that became the chief suppliers of human cargo to North America, Islam was the preferred religion of royal courts.

Advertisements in the American South for runaway slaves often cited names that were Islamic-influenced: Mustapha, Bullay (for Bilali), Bocarrey (for Bubacar, whose origins are in Abu Bakr), Mamado (for Mamadu), and Sambo, a corruption of Samba, which means "second son" in the language of the Fulbe, a group spread throughout the West African savanna.[36]

While the United States was not especially hospitable toward the Africans' indigenous religion, some slaves did retain their faith. Salih Bilali, for instance, who was prized for his managerial skills as a head driver in the 1810s on a plantation on the Georgia island of St. Simons, fasted every Ramadan. A contemporary of his, Balali (for Ben Ali), who managed a plantation with about five hundred slaves on the Georgia island of Sapelo, wore a fez and kaftan, prayed daily facing the East, observed the Muslim feast days—and with eighty armed slaves, successfully defended the island from the British during the War of 1812. Balali's contempt for non-Muslim slaves, whom he called "Christian dogs," was common among Muslim slaves. Many Muslims kept themselves apart from other slaves, partly because many had owned slaves while they were in Africa, and partly because some had come from an aristocratic elite, were well educated, and could even read and write, a rarity among slaves.[37]

Given whites' determination to eradicate their slaves' native religions, the minority status that the Muslims had among the original African slaves and their descendants, and the inroads that Christianity made among them, the fabric of Islam frayed until it was a distant memory—if, indeed, it was remembered at all.

Poole never got beyond third grade before he had to help his family full-time in the fields. This paucity of formal education—and the cultural biases prevalent in psychometric tests—might explain the worrisome results of intelligence tests that Poole took while incarcerated in a federal prison in Milan, Michigan, from 1943 to 1946 for violating the Selective Service Act: his IQ was 70 to 79 and his mental age, when he was about forty-six years old, was 10.6 to 11.9 years. [38]

The tests also indicated that Poole was a paranoid schizophrenic who detected persecutions "against himself and his race . . . [and] on numerous occasions . . . has had the feeling he is being followed and that people are talking about him. In general, his attitude was that of his own superiority." As of May 1945, sixteen months before being released from prison, he was still having visual and auditory "visions and communications with Allah." His prognosis for "future adjustment" was "guarded."[39]

As a young adult, Poole worked as a laborer for the Georgia and Southern Railroad and was later foreman for a brick company in Macon, Georgia. In 1923, as part of the largest migration in the history of the United States, he moved with his wife and family to Detroit. Blacks in the South were frustrated by a plantation tenant system that essentially made more than three-quarters of those working in agriculture continually in debt to their landlords. Sometimes earnings were so puny that they faced "long months of semi-starvation." The North's promise of greater equality and better economic prospects pulled roughly five million blacks from their homes to the golden, mythical urban centers about which they had heard so much, especially Detroit and Chicago.

The migration started shortly after 1915, when Henry Ford revolutionized American industry by creating an eight-hour day and a daily minimum wage of five dollars—more than seven times the daily wage of seventy-five cents earned by black farm laborers in the South. Further contributing to blacks' disgruntlement was the experience of the 350,000 black soldiers during World War I. Though fighting for a country that had granted them full citizenship in 1868 with the Fourteenth Amendment, most were detailed as stevedores and common laborers on the assumption that they were not suited for anything more challenging. Only 40,000 were actual combat soldiers, and no officer above the rank of first lieutenant in any all-black division could be an African American.[40]

Almost by accident, one all-black division, the Ninety-third, encountered the pleasures of Gallic egalitarianism. Landing in France on January 1, 1918, the Ninety-third was quickly merged into the French army, which was short of fighting men. "Carrying French rifles and eating French rations, they knew an equality denied them by their own military." In August of that year, the American military, worried by the threat to the racial status quo back home, secretly warned French governors and mayors that "Negroes were prone to deeds of violence and were threatening America with degeneration." Robert R. Moton, who had succeeded Booker T. Washington as head of Tuskegee University, was dispatched to France to advise black soldiers "not to expect in the United States the kind of freedom they had enjoyed in France and . . . [to] remain content with the same position they had always occupied in the United States."[41]

But the greatest catalyst for the northward migration, the one that gave discontent with southern life a firm compass point of exit, was the Great Northern Drive, a campaign begun in May 1917 by the *Chicago Defender*, the country's leading black newspaper, to urge southern blacks to come to Chicago to make money and live in full citizenship. Robert S. Abbott, the *Defender*'s publisher and the wizard of the Northern Drive, clothed the campaign in the aura of a new Exodus: "The Flight out of Egypt" was its slogan, and "Bound for the Promised Land" was its anthem. Abbott probably would not have been displeased if someone had nominated *him* as the new Moses.[42]

Between 1910 and 1920, the black population of Chicago increased by more than 148 percent, to 109,458. In the next decade, it would climb by another 113 percent. The Detroit numbers were even more staggering: between 1910 and 1920, its black population swelled by more than 611 percent, to 40,838. In the next decade, the Detroit black population increased by another 194 percent, to 120,066.[43]

From 1923 to 1929, Elijah Poole worked at several jobs in Detroit, barely earning enough to sustain his growing family: he now had six sons and one daughter. Sometimes the children had to scrounge through garbage cans behind grocery stores for vegetables the shops were throwing away.[44] But come Fridays—payday—their father would get drunk, sometimes spending all his paycheck on booze or gambling before getting home. Once a neighbor went running to Elijah's wife: "Oh, Mrs. Poole! Your husband is out laying on the railroad track. You better go get him because the train is going to be coming soon."

And Clara Poole and one of her many children would dash to the tracks and pull a drunken, sodden Elijah to safety shortly before a train arrived.[45]

While on relief for two years because of the Depression, Elijah came under the spell of a man whose identity is shrouded in mystery and probably always will be: Wallace Fard Muhammad, who said he had arrived to awaken the "Dead Nation in the West" and cleanse it, spiritually and psychologically, for the imminent battle of Armageddon. This ultimate, end-of-days struggle would not be waged at the ancient Israeli city of Megiddo, as the Bible ordained, but in the vast, hostile "Wilderness of North America." Nor would it pit a just, moral, and noble Israel against the sinful, wicked, corrupt forces of Gog and Magog, as the Old Testament's Book of Ezekiel, the New Testament's Revelation to John, and the Dead Sea Scrolls all predicted. Instead, in a fierce, long-overdue millennial triumph, the "so-called Negroes" would vanquish Caucasians, the oppressors of the poor and the evil geniuses of a devious "tricknology" that had kept the true blessed of God in illiteracy and ignorance.[46]

For the eight thousand blacks who joined his group, Fard turned prevailing racial demonologies upside down. Not only did his theological schematic exalt the black man as pure and unalloyed—as Goodness Itself. And not only was the black man the Original Man from whom all others derived. He was also the One True God, the Deity Itself. With Fard's racio-centric theology, what you saw was what you got: there was no "spook" god, no transcendent god. But there was a black god embodied in a black body, and there was no more and no less—no previous life and no afterlife, because "the dead is never to return from the grave." The American Negro was "not physically dead, only mentally dead."[47]

By hoisting blacks to the pivotal fulcrum of the man-God relation—indeed, by melding the two into One—Fard went several leagues further than had other patriarchs of some very successful black cults of his day, such as Father Divine of the Peace Mission Movement and Daddy Grace of the United House of

Prayer for All People. To his followers, Father Divine was God, while the devotees of Daddy Grace essentially forgot about God and worshiped their leader. "Never mind about God," scolded Daddy. "Salvation is by grace only. [Daddy] Grace has given God a vacation, and since God is on His vacation, don't worry about Him. . . . If you sin against God, [Daddy] Grace can save you, but if you sin against [Daddy] Grace, God cannot save you."[48]

Fard was more democratic than Divine or Grace (and not as presumptuous about choosing a name for himself). He leveled the entire divine playing field for anyone who had the single required ticket of entry: black skin. Fard intuitively and eloquently satisfied blacks' hunger for deliverance from a wearying impotence—and bestowed upon them the greatest imaginable authority: the authority of divinity. They may not have been *living* as gods, not with their battered tenements and shabby vestments. But by being indistinguishable from the Lord—by *being* the Lord—they could lord over their earthly impoverishments.

Fard appeared in Detroit's almost 100-percent black Paradise Valley community in the summer of 1930, knocking on doors and weaving a spell with fantastic yarns about the silks he was peddling and the diet he was recommending. As an early follower recalled, the fine material Fard was selling was

the same . . . our people used in their home country. If we asked him to eat with us, he would eat whatever we had on the table, but after the meal, he began to talk, "Now don't eat this food. It is poison for you. The people in your own country do not eat it. Since they eat the right kind of food, they have the best health all the time. If you would live just like the people in your home country, you would never be sick any more." So, we all wanted him to tell us more about ourselves and about our home country and about how we could be free from rheumatism, aches and pains.[49]

Fard advocated more than nostalgia for a nebulous, unnamed "home country" or prescriptive cures and nostrums and bromides; some who met him were certain that he was more than simply a struggling, itinerant peddler—or just another voice in the urban babble of street preachers and sidewalk savants. To them, Fard was different. He was The One—Deliverance Incarnate. He was the black man's true liberator who would impart "civilization, righteousness, the knowledge of himself and the science of everything in life: Love, peace and happiness."[50]

As Elijah Poole told Fard privately after hearing him speak for the first time, "I know who you are. You are God." To which Fard whispered, "Yes, I am the One, but who knows that but yourself, and be quiet."[51]

Soon Poole began evangelizing that Fard was "the answer to the prophesy of the Coming of Christ 2,000 years after Jesus's birth." Disapprovingly, Fard told him, "You can do that after I am gone. . . . Don't talk too much about me." According to Nation of Islam legend, the two of them sequestered "night and day . . . , from [the] early part of the night until sunrise or after sunrise, all night long for about two years or more." Fard taught Elijah "things of Islam and what is to come and what was before" and spoke in oblique parables. Puzzled at first, Elijah soon learned the inner language of his teacher, deciphering meaning, nuance, and import available to no one else.[52]

This was the traditional passing of secret wisdom between mentor and disciple, between sage and initiate. What Poole told Fard and what Fard told Poole was the unvarying message that passes between The Chooser and The Chosen, The Enlightened One and His Apostles. In this case, it transpired not in Gethsemane or on the shores of the Sea of Galilee or in the desert of

Sinai or the Deer Park of Benares. It happened in an impoverished black ghetto at the beginning of the worst depression in
this nation's history. And it transpired between two men who,
by calling themselves "Asiatics," by deifying the downtrodden
and the wretched, by wrapping their message in the exotica of
Islam (a faith largely alien to the vast masses of blacks), tried to
revive blacks' sense of their heritage, their destiny, and themselves. What they didn't tell their followers was that their "Islam"
was largely a brilliant, fictional fabrication. Furthermore, what
Elijah Poole himself almost surely did not know was that Fard's
past may have included travels to Mecca or Medina, but also San
Quentin Prison, where he had been booked, fingerprinted, and
served time for selling drugs.

III

God, Huckster, or Sinner?

One could make of W. Fard Muhammad what one wished: Con man. Crook. Hustler. Savior. Prophet. God. This pliability of identity, though not assuring, was so impressive, and the true identity of Fard was so clouded with uncertainty, that his tale eventually entered the realm of fable, if not myth.

Three competing tales arose about Fard. Each tried to wrest some order from chaos; each imposed a narrative on the events that may—or may not—have constituted his life. The first two were fairly detailed; the last was compressed, succinct, and maybe the punch line to the first two. No one could prove any of them (although many have tried), and each was probably the yield of hunches, desires, yearnings, and the political agendas that produced them.

As Ludwig Wittgenstein wrote, "It is not *how* things are in the world that is mystical, but *that* it exists." The wonder of the perseverance of the Fard myths is simply that they exist—and that they coexist side by side, either amplifying or contradicting the others. Together, they create a blurry, gauzy aura that will probably always envelop this patriarch of the Nation of Islam, the man whose theological foundation Louis Farrakhan eventually inherited and whose teachings he would embellish.[1]

Since its creation, the Nation of Islam has idealized Fard as a man of noble, maybe divine lineage who came on a holy mission to save the blacks of America. A thespian of the highest order, he was waiting for the proper moment when he could unveil himself: "I came from the Holy City of Mecca. More about myself, I will not tell you yet, for the time has not yet come. I am your brother. You have not yet seen me in my royal robes."[2]

Given Fard's Islamic trappings, the Mecca of which he spoke was widely assumed to be the Saudi Arabian city where the prophet Muhammad was born and where Muslims journey on the hajj, their annual pilgrimage. Indeed, Fard's early followers claimed that his parents were wealthy members of the same tribe to which the prophet Muhammad had belonged.

(A few doubters interpret Fard's "Mecca" not as the city in the exotic "East" of Arabia, but as jazz-filled, zoot-suited, numbers-running Harlem, which was not only east of Detroit but was widely considered to be the Mecca of black America.)[3]

Curiously for a man whose theology venerated blackness, Fard had a white mother and a black father. Fard once explained that this interracial coupling was deliberate: "[H]is father went often in the mountains . . . in their country where some Caucasians were living. . . . He said he got one of these women and took her for his wife so he could get a son to live more like this civilization of the whites so as to be able to get among them and they will not be able to distinguish them."[4]

Educated at a British university for a diplomatic career, and later at the University of California, Fard "abandoned everything to bring 'freedom, justice and equality'" to the Negroes "in the wilderness of North America," where they were "surrounded and robbed completely by . . . [whites]."[5]

One variation on this history was that Fard had come to the United States from Jamaica and his father was a Syrian Muslim. Still another was that he was a Palestinian Arab who had been involved in "racial agitations" in India, South Africa, and London before arriving in Detroit. But when Detroit police asked him in the early 1930s about his identity, his answer had nothing to do with terrestrial geography or earthly parentage. It had everything to do with divine destiny: "I am the Supreme Ruler of the Universe." The admission stunned Brother Yussuf Muhammadan, an early follower: "He told those police more about himself than he would ever tell us."[6]

Wherever Fard came from, whatever his origins, his finest, most loyal student, Elijah Muhammad, would variously call him the "Son of Man" or "a God in Person." As Elijah became more adept in some of the fundamentals of Islam, he also called Fard "the Mahdi," the Islamic messianic figure destined to reveal a perfect world where truth and justice will prevail.

Regardless of his true identity, Fard offered a lifeline to a sublime, glorious future and a strategy to even the racial score: after ushering Negroes into heaven, casting whites into hell, and righting the wrongs of the past, "the world will know and recognize Him . . . to be God alone." In the meantime, poor Fard bore a Christ-like burden. According to Elijah Muhammad, Fard had chosen "to suffer three and a half years to show his love for his people, who have suffered over three hundred years at the hands of a people who, by nature, are evil and wicked and have no good in them."[7]

Fard found a ready, eager audience in Detroit. By 1933, the

two back-to-back meetings he was holding weekly in a four-hundred-person capacity hall were jam-packed. Fard had become a preacher to reckon with, a potent voice in a despairing urban wilderness. And like the prophets of old, he became a threat to the establishment. His message about blacks' divinity, whites' evil, and the retribution that lay just ahead was unsettling to the order of the day, especially during the volatile days of the Depression, when insurrection, communism, or other wholesale remedies to the nation's woes were being marketed on campuses and from corner soapboxes.[8]

In his account of Fard's life, Elijah tells that he "was persecuted and sent to jail in 1932, and ordered out of Detroit on May 29, 1933. He came to Chicago in the same year and was arrested almost immediately on his arrival and placed behind prison bars." With divine forbearance, Fard "submitted himself with all humbleness to his persecutors."[9]

But Muhammad craftily omitted from his account *why* Fard had been expelled from Detroit and *why* Chicago police had detained him. Instead, he focused on Fard's holy mission, on his profound wisdom, on his divine sacrifice.

After being detained in Chicago, Fard traveled across the country and surfaced again fleetingly in Chicago before virtually disappearing. The last contact Elijah Muhammad had with him was a postcard mailed from somewhere in Mexico. After that . . . the silence of the Holy One who had come to redeem his injured but worthy flock.[10]

The Federal Bureau of Investigation had a totally different take on Fard. In its usually stone-cold, poker-faced internal files, the FBI in 1943 indulged in a few rare chuckles over Fard: "Allah has proved to be very much of a human being since he has an arrest record in the Identification Division of the FBI."[11]

If Fard was ever God, he was a fallen god to the FBI—to

whom he was also number 56062, an ex-con who had spent three years in San Quentin Prison in California—1926 to 1929—for selling narcotics. To the California Bureau of Identification and Investigation, he was number 1797294. To the Michigan state police, he was number 98076. To Los Angeles police, he was 16448F. Police described him as having a "dark, swarthy" complexion, a "slender" build, and "beautiful, even" teeth. Best of all to those who appreciated the fine, coiled intricacy of a good scam, whenever Fard was arrested, and wherever he was booked, he identified himself as a *white* man. His standard story was that he had been born in 1891 in New Zealand to a Polynesian mother and an Englishman who arrived in New Zealand on a schooner. Occasionally, he claimed he was born in Portland, Oregon, and that his parents, Zared and Beatrice Ford, had both been born in Hawaii.[12]

In either case, he appears to have spent some time in Portland, possibly arriving there from New Zealand in 1913 around the age of twenty-two. In 1918, he headed to Los Angeles, where he opened a café called Walley's Restaurant under the name of either Willie D. Ford or Wallace D. Ford.[13]

Fard's first brush with the law came on November 17, 1918, after a customer, R. W. Gilabrand, balked when Fard demanded a two-dollar deposit before putting the steaks he had ordered on the grill. Fard pulled a gun from beneath the counter, then chased Gilabrand outside, where he beat the customer's head on the concrete sidewalk. Charges of assault with a deadly weapon were eventually dropped.[14]

Eight years later, in January 1926, Fard was arrested for selling a pint of bootlegged liquor in his restaurant to an undercover policeman. While waiting to appear in court, he was again arrested, this time for selling narcotics. In June of that year, he was sent to San Quentin for up to six years for marketing in narcotics. He was also fined $401 for selling illegal whiskey. When

Fard left prison in 1929, he briefly visited the common-law wife with whom he had had a son in 1920, then headed for Chicago and eventually Detroit, where he sold silks door to door and polished his patter that he was a Negro, a biblical authority, and a mathematician who had arrived in America from Mecca on July 4, 1930. His "tremendous gift of gab" earned him a modest following, which pored over his "lost-found lessons," a series of question-and-answer exercises, as if they were a new and long-awaited gospel.[15]

Through contributions and selling "official" note paper, Fard soon had a tidy source of income. This dried up in November 1932 when Robert Karriem, formerly known as Robert Harris, erected an altar in his home at 1249 Dubois Street and invited John J. Smith to be a human sacrifice. Karriem had told Smith that his death would make him "the Savior of the world." At 9:00 A.M., the hour set for the sacrifice, he plunged a knife into Smith's heart. According to police, Karriem also planned to kill two women welfare workers because they were "no good Christian[s]."[16]

The smorgasbord of Fard's "lessons" had inspired Smith's murder. These were part science lesson (the earth's circumference is 24,896 miles; the planet travels at 1,037-1/3 miles per hour); part pseudo-history that moved blacks to the pivotal fulcrum of world events; part hybrid theology that borrowed liberally from several faiths, some traditional, others fly-by-night; and part storefront machinations of a new god on the run.

Overall, the lost-found lessons counseled a patient suffering since the devils' domination had officially ended in 1914. Blacks were now living through their "years of grace," the period during which they would overcome their ignorance and debilitation. The exact number of the years of grace kept shifting in the subsequent theology of the Nation of Islam, but the Nation almost certainly borrowed the specific year 1914 from the Jehovah's Witnesses. From their inception in the 1870s, the Witnesses had predicted that the end of time would begin in 1914. The outbreak of World War I in 1914 reinforced their conviction that they were living through Jesus' prophecy that "nation would rise against nation and kingdom against kingdom."[17]

But negating the patience that the lost-found lessons advised were exhortations for blacks to be as violent toward the white devil as the devil had been toward them:

> Q: *Why does Muhammad and any Muslim murder the devil? What is the duty of each Muslim in regard to four (4) devils? What reward does a Muslim receive by presenting the four (4) devils at one time?*
>
> A: *Because the devil is 100% weak and wicked and will not keep the laws of Islam. His ways and actions are like those of a snake of the grafted type. . . . Muhammad learned that he could not reform the devil, so they had to be murdered. Any Muslim would murder the devil because they know he is a "snake" and . . . if he was allowed to live he would "sting" someone else. Each Muslim was required to bring in four (4) devils, and by having and presenting four (4) at one time, his reward was a button to wear on the lapel of his coat; also free transportation to the Holy City of Mecca to see their brother Muhammad.*[18]

In a way, the "lessons" made it seem that removing the "devil" from the earth through these killings would be a cinch, since whites possessed only a puny fraction of the intelligence and strength of blacks: "The mental power of a real devil is nothing in comparison to that of the Original Man. He has only six ounces of brain while the Original Man has seven and one half ounces of brain. . . . The devil is weak-boned and weak-blooded because he was grafted from the Original. The devil's physical power is less than one-third that of the Original Man's." Ordinarily, whites could overcome these shortcomings with a clever craftiness the Nation of Islam dubbed "tricknology." But ultimately white rule was doomed, since all Caucasians would be destroyed in a single day once blacks attained the requisite level of inner strength.[19]

In an age when blacks and the poor were easy prey for charlatans and flimflam men, it was not necessarily Fard's teachings about race and his misuse of religion that ended his scam: it was the murder that Robert Karriem committed in the name of those teachings. Police arrested Fard, who admitted that his lost-found teachings were "strictly a racket" and that he was "getting all the money out of it that he could." Kicked out of Detroit, he found his way to Chicago, where he became a traveling salesman for a mail-order tailor, worked his way through the Midwest, and arrived in Los Angeles in 1934 "driving a new car and garbed in flowing white robes." After visiting daily with his son and vainly trying to reconcile with his common-law wife, he sold his car and boarded a ship for New Zealand to visit relatives, especially the uncle who had paid the fare for his trip to America in 1913.[20]

On August 16, 1963, eighteen days after the *Los Angeles Herald-Examiner* first ran a story by Ed Montgomery that Fard was a con man named Wallace Dodd, Elijah Muhammad offered to pay the paper one hundred thousand dollars to prove its charges. (Other Hearst-owned papers around the country also published Montgomery's story.)

"If . . . [Dodd] was teaching for money in those panic days in Detroit, he did not get it from us," Muhammad said. "Mr. Dodd, undoubtedly, must have been teaching the white people if he received any money at all, because we did not have any. . . . We could hardly pay the rent of a hall in those days." Muhammad challenged the *Herald-Examiner* to bring Dodd to the United States and prove he was Fard by asking him to speak the sixteen

languages that Fard had spoken, or having him write in the ten
languages in which Fard was proficient. Muhammad claimed
that even the paper's description of Dodd's height and weight
did not correspond to Fard's, and he reminded his followers
"against allowing the devils to trick you into believing their false
propaganda which they are spreading all over the world, . . .
especially among the so-called Negroes who have been the perfect model-slaves for 400 years and yet do not have freedom,
justice and equality from the slave masters."[21]

In later years, Nation of Islam leaders would argue that the
section in the lost-found lessons about murdering "devils" was
only a metaphor designed to rally NOI members to "slay"
whites' psychological and social grip on them. In the early
1980s, for instance, as Farrakhan was trying to reform the Fruit
of Islam, the Nation's paramilitary wing, which had often confused violence with righteousness, he inquired, "Did you know
that every time you save a black man you have . . . killed a devil
. . . because when truth comes in, falsehood goes out? And the
only way the white man has been able to rule our people is
through . . . falsehood and ignorance."[22]

But apparently the poor, often barely literate blacks who
heard Fard in the 1930s could not (or would not) distinguish
between the concrete and the metaphoric. Nor apparently could
some of the better educated blacks who joined the Nation two
and three decades later. In the NOI's Harlem restaurant in the
1950s and early 1960s, there were often murmurings of a Muslim two or three tables over who had just come in with a paper
bag that held the head of a white man. The rumors would
spread a chill—and an envious admiration that someone had
taken the "true" teachings so much to heart.[23]

But to judge from the arrest in 1937 of an NOI member in
Detroit as he was preparing to slay *and* cook his wife and daughter, some members could not distinguish between killing "dev-

ils" and killing blacks, especially if the homicide was couched as an order from Allah Himself, an order no one in the Nation of Islam could refuse. The mother-daughter slaughter in Detroit was intended to "cleanse" the would-be murderer from "all sin." The question is whether the spouse and child would have been martyrs for Allah—or for a con man with a dozen aliases and a greedy, fevered imagination.[24]

Fard had not simply espoused "Islam" to those who had never heard of it: he fabricated much of it out of whole cloth. In an audacious inversion of a bedrock of Islam, he discarded the idea of a transcendent God, which, he said, had been invented by whites to convince blacks to worship what "cannot be seen by the physical eye" and "to make slaves out of all that he can so .. . he can rob them and live in luxury": "Me and my people have tried this so-called mystery God for bread, clothing, and a home, and received nothing but hard times, hunger, nakedness and out of doors; [we've] also been beaten and killed by the ones who advocate that kind of God."[25]

Fard's "Original Man," a black man of Eden, had known only peace and righteousness until Yacub, "the Mighty Scientist of that time," created the devil. Born twenty miles outside of Mecca in the year 8400 B.C., Yacub, even as a small child, was a rebel who yearned to overthrow the established order. He began preaching at the age of sixteen. As his teachings spread and caught on, he created confusion and havoc and was thrown in jail.[26]

The king finally promised to release Yacub if he and his followers went into exile. Yacub agreed, and led 59,999 of his disciples to the island of Pelan in the Aegean Sea, to the west of Turkey. There, after six hundred years of trying to "graft" a new race from the "germs" of blacks, Yacub created a manlike creature—whites—that was really the "devil" in disguise. Yacub was determined that his synthetic progeny would outnumber blacks. So, in a crude, cruel adventure in birth control, he ruled that ministers could officiate only at weddings of whites and that nurses had to kill all "black babies at birth by sticking a pin into the . . . baby's head or feed . . . [them] to some wild beast."[27]

One side effect of the Yacub tale that was apparently lost on Fard's followers was that, by burdening blacks with inventing their worst enemy, he also saddled them with the responsibility for their own woeful condition.

Fard also prophesied that the hereafter would be preceded by cataclysmic worldwide destruction, which Elijah Muhammad later warned would be wrought by a twentieth-century version of "the wheel" that the prophet Ezekiel had seen in the sky. Ezekiel's wheel would "sparkle" and rain fiery coals upon evil; Muhammad's wheel—the "Mother of Planes"—would measure "one-half mile by a half mile" and be "a small human planet made for the purpose of destroying the present world of the enemies of Allah." This Mother Plane could stay in space for up to a year and carry fifteen hundred bombers equipped with "steel drills . . . [that could] take bombs into the earth at a depth of one mile. . . . This explosion produces a mountain one mile high; not one bomb will fall into water." The bombers were so "swift that they can make their flight and return to the Wheel . . . almost like a flash of lightning."[28]

With the devil gone, blacks' basic physical condition would not change. Fard's heaven was no visionary, speculative afterlife. It was *this* world freed of whites. Paradisiacal joy would flourish with the ex-masters gone forever and with blacks finally ruling the world into which they had been born to be kings, relying on their "heart[s] of gold, love and mercy," qualities that whites— nasty "two-headed rattlesnakes"—were forever incapable of knowing.[29]

In a very strong sense, whether or not Fard taught authentic Islam is irrelevant. What his followers lacked was power and identity; what Fard offered was potency and a name. The name of their god. The name of their true religion. The name of their true selves. "Orthodoxy" was not an issue for them, not only because they were largely ignorant about Islam, but also because orthodox doctrines had not necessarily advanced them. Traditional Islam, Christianity, and Judaism had not devoted much effort to liberating them spiritually; Muslims, Christians, and, to a much lesser degree, Jews had enslaved them physically. So to many blacks, the force of religion lay not necessarily in theology and words and ancient narratives, but in the immediacy of the experience; in the piercing, sustaining directness of the moment; in the soul-enriching, soul-rousing thrust of music and the cascading shout-and-call of the Sunday morning sermon, all building to an exciting, almost visceral peak that whites' staid, proper houses of worship could rarely match.

Toward orthodoxy, blacks thus had their own answer, one that often did not correspond fully to "tradition." To some, that answer was Master Wallace Fard Muhammad. Both Elijah Muhammad and Louis Farrakhan, in their efforts to sell Fard's creation to the masses, overlaid "Islam" with a template of the Christianity familiar to African Americans. Their mosques had pews, not prayer rugs on the floor; their sermons referred more to the Bible than the Koran; their theological reference points and imagery were almost reflexively (and often exclusively) Christian, not Islamic. These features were all calculated to make the Nation of Islam an accessible, appealing balance to Christianity. As Farrakhan admitted in September 1995 before a group of black Christian clergy whom he was trying to persuade to participate in his Million Man March, slated for the next month on the Mall in Washington, "The mosque is nothing more than a protest kind of church. The honorable Elijah Muhammad . . . set up a new kind of church. He set up the mosque the way the church should be set up. With discipline."[30]

In September 1993, Warith Deen Muhammad, the son of Elijah Muhammad, disclosed that Fard had never disappeared in a divine burst of smoke—now you see him, now you don't. Nor had he been a con-man, bilking the gullible of their hard-earned Depression nickels and dimes. He was simply a misguided soul who had offered the "brilliant psychology of the Nation of Islam . . . to get away from white man's domination. . . . No matter how much progress there was in America, it couldn't change us because the white man's image had changed our minds and our egos."[31]

Into this blight came Fard, spinning glorious tales of blacks being "rulers" and "wearing silks in Mecca" and "automatically being citizens of other Muslim countries if . . . [they] became members of the Nation of Islam." All this was a balm to damaged egos. But really, scoffed Warith Muhammad, Fard's religious schematic was riddled with "contradictions": how could a mere man, even a man who was "God," reach up and place in the heavens all the planets and moons and billions of stars? Maybe, mused Muhammad, in a rationale sprinkled with a charitable generosity toward his father and the followers he had inherited from him, the contradictions were intentional "so we would think more deeply. As Elijah Muhammad said, 'Look deep. Look beneath the surface.'"[32]

Warith Muhammad's version of the Fard myth completed the circle that had begun with Elijah Muhammad in Detroit in 1930. In Warith's account, the father of the Nation of Islam reappeared late in his life, repented "for what he had done and made an effort . . . to bring about the end of his own work." To help him undo the vastly unorthodox version of Islam that Fard and Elijah Muhammad had foisted upon blacks, Warith Muhammad appointed Fard the imam of the mosque in Oakland, California, where he was known as Muhammad Abdullah.[33]

Despite Warith Muhammad's certainty that the imam was

Fard, Abdullah, who died in June 1992 at the age of eighty-seven, never explicitly admitted he was Fard. This, Muhammad was sure, reflected the man's legendary sagacity: "He wanted me to know he was Fard, but he didn't want to say it with his mouth because he didn't want to be put in a situation that he would have to answer all my questions and be exposed to all my rage. I thought he was very wise to never say to me that he was Fard. ... May Allah forgive him his sins and grant him paradise because his intentions were good."[34]

Somehow, Muhammad still had a peculiar kind of faith in Fard. "I wouldn't want to be a prosecutor against Fard in the Hereafter," he cautioned. "I believe he could pull a few things out of a hat."[35]

IV

Heaven . . .

In 1959, Intervale Avenue in Boston's Roxbury had its share of rabbis. At 8 Intervale, Rabbi Morris Twersky lived above his congregation, Mogaine Emoshia Labeth David. At 32 Intervale was Temple Agudas Achim, whose rabbi, Mayor Zaitchik, lived next door at 34 Intervale. But at 35 Intervale, in what had been the Boston Rabbinical College, a new temple appeared on the block: Muhammad's Temple of Islam No. 11. Next door lived a man whom the city directory, in a deliciously inadvertent gaffe, listed as "Rabbi Eugene L. Walcott." Everyone else called him Minister Louis X.[1]

Gene Walcott had returned to Boston. As an entertainer, he had never fully realized his ambition to attain fame and fortune. For that, he would have to marshal the services of several alter egos named, successively, Louis X, Louis Farrakhan, Abdul Haleem Farrakhan, and, finally, back to Louis Farrakhan. Being in the Nation served Walcott well. It gave him a platform that he relished (for he still had his performer's ego) and it gave him a mission—raising up the black masses—that was not out of line with Roxbury's Garveyite traditions. In time, it also gave him the sort of headlines for which any entertainer would kill.

Implicit in Louis X's assignment in Boston was to do what Malcolm X had never really been able to pull off: put the local temple on a greater par with those in other major cities. Chicago's NOI temple, with 600 members, was the largest in the country. This was probably inevitable, since Chicago, where Elijah Muhammad lived, was the Nation's home base. Next came New York with 350 members. The high numbers there were not surprising: New York was Malcolm's turf. Then came Detroit with about 175 members, Philadelphia with 145, and finally Boston, with 85–100 members. For a large city, these were indeed low numbers, but maybe hip, calypso-singing Louis, who already had a following in his hometown (albeit of a very different kind), was better suited to Boston than the stern, sometimes foreboding Malcolm; perhaps he was the man who could perk up Boston's NOI membership rolls.[7]

For the two years he was in Boston, Malcolm had moved from one makeshift temple to another, usually improvising in small, threadbare apartments: no one was getting rich off the Nation then. But in 1954, Elijah Muhammad transferred him to New York to turn Harlem's fledgling temple into a success. The year 1954 was notable for another reason: the Supreme Court ruled that segregated schools were unconstitutional. To the separatists in the Nation, the *Brown v. Board of Education* decision was almost an affront. And to those not in the Nation (and who had never even heard of it, as, in 1954, the vast majority of blacks and whites probably had not), the ruling was simply a *promise* of change that did not immediately change their lives or their children's schooling.

Louis first went to Boston as a captain in the Fruit of Islam, since Elijah Muhammad decided to delay making him a minister until he had proved how well he could perform under the authority of others. In a few months, when Louis was finally promoted to minister, he decided that there would be no temples in apartments for him. He wanted a *real* temple in a *real* building. After scouting around Roxbury, an NOI member found the right site: an Orthodox rabbinic seminary on Intervale Avenue that was for sale. He told the owners he was searching for a place for a church: "If we said it was for a mosque, they probably wouldn't have sold it to us." A Nation member put up his mortgage as collateral, and the deal went through. To mark the occasion, Louis visited the Reverend Nathan Wright, the minister who had married him at St. Cyprian's Church about four years before, to say he had followed him "into the ministry."[3]

Louis may have been a Muslim, but he had not forgotten his Christian roots. If anything, his visit to Wright made it clear that Louis did not think he had abandoned the faith of his youth by joining the NOI. Rather, he was spearheading a parallel church, a "protest" church, a reform movement that would purge Christianity of its hypocrisy and spiritual sterility. Wright, who within a few years would be active in the Black Power movement, was not unsympathetic to Louis's mission. He gave him fifty chairs that St. Cyprian's was throwing out to use in the unfurnished new temple. Wright also gave Louis a list of young men he had recently compiled whom he knew the church could not reach: "The first twenty of his first twenty-five members I gave him. I knew they would never get the caring they needed in my church."[4]

Helped by Malcolm's occasional trips up from New York to speak at the temple, Louis X began to put Temple No. 11 on the map. By November 1957—six months after Louis took over the temple—Malcolm said that under the new minister, the Nation

was "making amazing strides forward" in Boston. At meetings
on Mondays, Wednesdays, Friday and Saturday evenings, and
Sunday afternoons, Louis or an assistant minister lectured
about current events, discipline, honesty, monogamy, faithful-
ness, sobriety—and, of course, about the sly ways of the white
"devils." In the lecture hall, once the Jewish seminary's main
study hall, was a large photo of a lynching down south: a black
body dangling from a tree above a crowd of pleased and smiling
whites, a few of whom were not just "white" but what one visi-
tor called "shoe-polish white." Temple No. 11 and its new minister knew how to draw the color lines to make them distinct
and inviolable—and how to invoke more anger in those who listened than they had had when they walked in.[5]

People came, more than before. But even Malcolm worried
about Minister Louis's fairly quick success in Boston. Maybe, he
mused, the Nation was running into a trap, since "many had left
beautiful churches to come to learn about Islam at the Boston
Temple and [then] described it as a shack." But maybe, he reasoned, it was "better to go into a shack where there are wise people than [to] go into a palace with fools."[6]

As did most other NOI temples, Temple No. 11 had a high
proportion of high school dropouts and former crooks, pimps,
and junkies. But it also had more college-educated members
than other temples. After all, this was Boston, the country's preeminent college town; Harvard and MIT were in Cambridge
just across the river. Elsewhere in Elijah Muhammad's domain,
despite the Nation's emphasis on education and literacy, a college degree automatically tainted a member: Was he a government agent? FBI? CIA? IRS? But there was much less suspicion
of educated members in Boston, whose many West Indians also
emphasized education.

The proportion of members with bachelor's degrees or better
did not sit well, however, with the former song-and-dance man

Louis X, who realized quickly that being an NOI minister was not about putting on a jive-talking, sweet-talking, make-your-audience-smile-tap-their-toes-move-their-hips-hum-along calypso show. This was the Big Time. Salvation. Deliverance. God's Own Blueprint for Liberation. The Showdown before the Final Battle. Apocalypse *Almost* Now. And Louis began to get the willies: "I was not able to relate to many of the educated persons who joined the Boston Temple as they were much more intelligent than I. And because I couldn't understand their ideas, I thought they were enemies of Islam and"—borrowing a phrase more often used about a rebel who evicted money-changers from a certain temple in Jerusalem two millennia before—". . . I drove them out of the temple." Louis X asked Elijah Muhammad to relieve him of his post and to let him bear the responsibility for "any sins" committed by the ex-members while they were banned from the temple. Impressed by this "display of compassion," Elijah let the dismissed members return to the temple—and kept Louis as their minister.[7]

Gradually, Louis gained confidence. Within five years, he almost tripled the Boston temple's membership, and an aura of invincibility began to surround him and the "Moos-lims," as they were called. They were exotic, disciplined, uncompromising, tough. They took care of their own—and took no guff from whites or from their own. From Chicago, Elijah Muhammad ran the tightest ship in the black community, achieving, said *Sepia* magazine, an "outstanding goal in Negro leadership that has eluded other leaders in the past: He has instilled in his followers an 'unto the death' obedience and discipline that amazes outsiders." "Even [Marcus] Garvey," said one New York black politician, "couldn't control his followers, at least not on the level where Mr. Muhammad operates. His followers believe his teachings more strongly than the 'angels' [members of the Peace Mision Movement] believed in Father Divine."[8]

But what the political operative and most people didn't refer to (or didn't know about—or *said* they didn't know about) were the strong-arm tactics behind the "discipline." Said an ex-member who was close to Malcolm,

> I would have hated to have the Nation of Islam on my case. They would get you sure as hell. They had ways and means by which to teach their methods. They had complete control because of the knowledge they collected on you. How are you doing in classes? They knew that. Who's best in the classes? They knew that. Were you dating? *Who* were you dating? They knew that. Who are your parents and grandparents, and where do they live, and what do they believe in? They knew that—and everything else about you. The FBI should have gone to school with these guys.

Unannounced and completely at random, the Fruit of Islam, the Nation's paramilitary wing, inspected members' homes or apartments "to make sure they were spic and span." If they weren't, word filtered back to the local minister.[9]

The Nation's strict protocol of behavior—no drugs, adultery, sleeping during meetings, or missing meetings; no selling or eating pork or using foul language in front of female members; no weight problems; and always meet your quota for selling *Muhammad Speaks*—was enforced with taunts and threats, sometimes verbal, often physical. Members were ranked by classes: in Class A were proper, upright citizens who fulfilled all their responsibilities. Class C members, lax and delinquent, had to do extra work in the temple or sell more papers. And Class F members sometimes had to sit in designated seats in the temple, "where everyone knew you were in trouble," sometimes nursing a black eye after a member of the Fruit of Islam had taken the wayward brother into the temple's back room. Or he might be suspended anywhere from ninety days to five years, during which time he was barred from all NOI activities and NOI members in good standing couldn't talk with him.[10]

Counterpointing the Nation's flaying of "devils" was an implicit emulation of the "devil's" cozy, bourgeois ways. Maybe the white man had enslaved their ancestors and eviscerated their history, but his economics, his suburbs, his fancy cars were the model for the Nation's aspirations—and for the hook they used when "fishing" among the "lost-found." As one former minister recounted, "We used to say, 'Do you want money, good homes, good friends? Join the Nation of Islam.' And they would come to meetings and see brothers with jobs in suits and ties—and sign up on the spot."[11]

Behind the language of race, behind the heated, apocalyptic rhetoric, behind the claims of being an apostle of God, Elijah Muhammad was another sort of apostle: a disciple of capitalism, a kinsman of John Stuart Mill and Horatio Alger, a black counterpart to the Commerce Department and the Small Business Administration. In Muhammad's economic lexicon, bootstraps had only one color, the same as Henry Ford's original Model T. Black. And the only way to pull them up was under his aegis, his direction, his control. He engineered a small-scale economic statism, a 1950s Brooks Brothers/Madison Avenue/Ayn Rand doctrine for the black masses as American as the A&P or Dun & Bradstreet. By the time Louis X arrived in Boston, the Nation owned a $275,000 temple in Chicago, twenty-three restaurants around the country, a farm in Georgia, and assorted grocery stores and bakeries. Elijah Muhammad himself was doing reasonably well, with a 1956 Cadillac that was fully paid for, a monthly mortgage payment of $265 on his Chicago home valued at $65,000, and a yearly income as high as $11,000. Minister Louis did quite well himself, living rent-free in the house next to the temple on Intervale Avenue and drawing a weekly salary of $110. Plus, all members were tithed $2.95 for their minister's upkeep—meaning that when one hundred members met their obligation, Minister Louis pocketed over $15,000 from tithes and $5,720 in salary, for an income that put him solidly into the upper-middle class.[12]

The relative wealth at the top was tactfully alluded to in C. Eric Lincoln's pioneering work, *The Black Muslims in America*: "[The] ideal of brotherly equality is being modified in its application to the life styles of those closest to the center of power." Left unsaid was that, while the seemingly incessant demands on Nation members meant "the black God never sleeps," capitalism in the Nation of Islam was no different from capitalism in the white world: as the masses toiled, rewards flowed upward in an equation that owed more to turn-of-the-century economic Darwinism than to Elijah Muhammad's call for the self-sufficiency necessary for nationhood.[13]

For many of Roxbury's blacks, Temple No. 11 became a place of curiosity. People who never intended to join came to check it out. They listened to the standard Nation rap, then moved on for their own version of fun, often to bars around the corner on Blue Hill Avenue to listen to jazz. Some bristled at being frisked on the way in, assuming, as did one sarcastic wag, that "it was impossible not to feel that the minister must be a personage of enormous importance, the carrier of some potent message, to be protected so carefully." Others were dismayed that the meetings were so sterile and arid, lacking the music or rhythmic hand-clapping common to black Baptist or African Methodist Episcopalian services.[14]

The atmosphere in the temple was especially surprising to those who had known Louis X as "The Charmer," the music man of Roxbury, and who assumed that wherever he went, music went, too. In fact, some of those already in the Nation also chafed under its proscriptions against music and dancing. In the middle of an interview, Malcolm, who had been a dervish on the dance floor before joining the NOI, began telling "an interviewer about his former ballroom exploits. Then, abruptly, he arose from his chair, grabbed a tall, vertical pipe with one hand, as if it were his partner, and started jitterbugging. His feet were moving a mile a minute. Suddenly, he stopped short, returned to his seat and began to sulk."[15]

Even Farrakhan's own mother had difficulty restraining herself. While working as a domestic for a Jewish family in suburban Boston in the late 1950s, she walked into the living room just as her employer put on a calypso record. She started dancing, the three children in the family began dancing behind her, everyone's feet flying and everyone smiling. Suddenly she turned to her boss, pleading, "Don't tell my son, Minister Louis. We Muslims are not supposed to dance."[16]

But sporadically, Minister Louis acted as if he had a formal dispensation from the Nation's ban on music and other entertainment. In the middle of a meeting at his temple, he might break into song; after at least one meeting, he gave an impromptu concert on a violin belonging to a young Nation member. And he cut a record that became the Nation's anthem: "A White Man's Heaven Is a Black Man's Hell," a title borrowed from the name of a weekly series on the teachings of Elijah Muhammad that was carried in some black newspapers.

"White Man's Heaven," which was set to a subdued calypso beat, was not the most subtle of songs. One first had to overcome its length: about ten-and-a-half minutes. Split over two sides of a 45rpm record, it was much too long for the Top 40. Then one had to wade through its lyrics, a somewhat heavy-handed catalog of whites' injustices against blacks and of the triumphalism of

. . . a divine messenger
One prophesied to come
His name is Elijah.
We now can stand up
The whole world to tell
Our God has come to give us heaven
And to take the devil
into hell.[17]

"White Man's Heaven's" lyrics were a bit clunky and pedantic, presaging none of the poetry common to the musical agit-prop—black or white—that would proliferate in the next decade. Composed of equal part sermon, lecture, and polemic, "White Man's Heaven" begins with Minister Louis speaking, much as he might at an NOI meeting:

Why are we called Negroes?
Why are we deaf, dumb, and blind?
Why is everybody progressing, yet we
seem to be lagging so far behind?
Why are we mistreated?
Why are we in this condition, stripped of our names,
our language, our culture, our God and our religion?[18]

The minister then partly blames blacks' condition on "the preacher" who

told us of a Heaven way up
in the sky
That we can't enjoy now
But rather after we die. . . .
The Bible speaks of a Heaven filled with
material luxury

Which the white man and the preacher
have right here, so we see.
So my friend, take it for what it's worth:
Your heaven and your hell are
right here on this earth.[19]

After inventorying whites' "raping, robbing, murdering everything in his path," the minister finally begins to sing, first about
blacks "living in luxury" along the Nile, wearing "silken robes
and slippers of gold," where they were "the wealthiest and the
wisest of people." But whites, who plundered America from
Native Americans and were "too weak . . . to work the land," then
"committed the world's most grievous sin": they bought and
sold slaves, burned them at stakes, hanged them from trees.
They impregnated women and emasculated men. The suffering
and dying of Negroes worldwide suffered and died at the hands
of whites was about to end because

. . . The black man everywhere
is on the rise.
He has kicked the white man
out of Asia
And he's going fast out of Africa.
With every ounce of strength and breath
His cry is "Give us liberty or
give us death."
The whole black world has
their eyes on you.
To see what the so-called Negro
is going to do.
So, my friend, its easy to tell
Our unity will give the white man hell.[20]

As a coda, Louis X alludes to the fifteenth chapter of the Book of Genesis:

> *God made a promise to Abraham.*
> *His seed would be a stranger*
> *   in a foreign land.*
> *They would suffer and be*
> *   afflicted for 400 years.*
> *But He would come and wipe*
> *   away their tears.*
> *Our God and Savior Allah has come*
> *He has declared the white*
> *   man's day as done.*[21]

Judgment was nigh, but not for the Egyptians, upon whom God had unleashed His wrath for enslaving the Israelites. This time, God had sent a new Moses to liberate a new people—and whites would face his fearful wrath.

The record, which sold well, was played on jukeboxes in NOI restaurants around the country and served as an effective recruiting tool. In 1959, Lonnie Cross—later to become Abdul Alim Shabazz—drove through Buffalo with two friends. At a restaurant, they heard a catchy tune on the jukebox. The song's words "made sense to me and my friends instantly. They told the truth."

"Waiter, waiter," Cross called, "who's that on the 'box?'"

"That's Minister Louis X."

"Who's that?"

Cross got a copy of "White Man's Heaven" when he returned to Atlanta, complete with a thumbnail sketch of Elijah Muhammad on the album jacket. The next year, when Elijah Muhammad spoke in Atlanta, Cross joined the Nation. Three years later, he was the minister of the temple in Washington.[22]

"White Man's Heaven" was also the Nation's calling card to the rest of the world, a musical signal of its gripes and its vision. Around 1960, for instance, when the journalist Nat Hentoff, arrived in the NOI's luncheonette in Harlem for his first meeting with Malcolm X, "White Man's Heaven" kept playing, again and again, on the jukebox: "Since I was the only white person in the place, I assumed the instructive message was being directed at me. The singer had a high, flexible, attractive voice. Though the lyrics were decidedly hostile to all Caucasians, the voice was curiously—indeed, rather ominously—serene. The style was lyrical, sunny."[23]

Louis X even "electrified" the audience with the song at an NOI-sponsored New Year's Day celebration on January 1, 1958, according to a contemporary news item in the *Amsterdam News*. Held at the Wayside Casino in Harlem, the Boston minister "brought the gathering to its feet." After the performance, Malcolm told representatives from black nationalist groups and Harlem churches and civic groups, "We must forget our organizational, political differences by realizing that the same vicious dog has bitten all of us."[24]

Louis X followed the success of "White Man's Heaven" with "Look at My Chains," which for several years was beamed to blacks in the United States from a Cuban radio station. He also wrote two plays that incorporated music: *The Trial* and *Orgena* (the latter title is "A Negro" spelled backwards). Both toured on the same bill, playing in cities where there was fairly strong Nation sympathy—New York, Washington, Chicago, Detroit. And both, quite predictably, enshrined blacks and bedeviled whites.

Orgena, which features the song, "Black Gold," portrays black women selling their bodies and satirizes Negro junkies, alcoholics, educators, and nattily dressed businessmen: all the end product of blacks being "kidnapped . . . from their ancient cultures." In *The Trial*, an all-black jury finds whites guilty for their sins against blacks after being denounced by the prosecutor as "the greatest liar[s] on earth," "the greatest drunkard[s] on earth," "the greatest gambler[s] on earth," "the greatest peace-breaker[s] on earth," "the greatest adulterer[s] on earth," and "the greatest trouble-maker[s] on earth."

Especially in *The Trial*, the playwright's disgust with whites, as well as his loathing for plodding do-gooders, is barely contained. As the doomed white man is dragged off to his death, he shouts about all he has done "for the nigra people," four condescending little words often associated with social workers, welfare counselors, and suburban liberals. Of course, in both *Orgena* and *The Trial*, Islam (and particularly the teachings of Elijah Muhammad) restores blacks to their former dignity, intelligence, and high moral plane.[25]

Eventually, Elijah Muhammad put a stop to Louis's entertaining diversions. "Brother," he asked, "do you want to be a song-and-dance man or do you want to be my minister?"

"I want to be your minister, dear Holy Apostle," replied the dutiful minister from Boston.[26]

There is speculation that Elijah Muhammad reined in Louis X's entertainments not because, as a "song-and-dance man," he had been committing any major apostasies, but because, as "bait to grab unwary blacks," his performances may have outlived their usefulness. With his unblinking rhetoric, Malcolm, who was promoted to Elijah Muhammad's national representative in 1957, had given the Nation unprecedented notoriety and publicity, especially after a television documentary hosted by Mike Wallace in July 1959, "The Hate That Hate Produced," introduced the Nation of Islam to millions of Americans, black and white. And Louis X's songs and plays, while valuable in mainstreaming the Nation's message, also detracted somewhat from

Elijah's Muhammad's overall message of sobriety, restraint—
and what was frequently seen as emotional asceticism, if not
emotional repression.[27]

Overall, the late 1950s and very early 1960s were a time of
consolidation for the Nation, a time when it could enjoy its
unexpected success and calculate how to sustain its momentum.
By the end of the 1950s, membership had grown to somewhere
between forty thousand and five hundred thousand. (The
Nation has never released exact membership numbers,
although Mike Wallace, on "The Hate That Hate Produced,"
said, "Negro American Muslims are the most powerful of the
black supremacist groups. They claim a membership of one-
quarter of a million Negroes, and our search indicates that for
every so-called card-carrying black supremacist, there are perhaps ten fellow travelers.")[28] Some of Elijah Muhammad's advisers were cautioning him to muffle some of the Nation's anti-
Caucasian bravura and funnel its energies into more economic
ventures—partly to defuse criticism that the Nation was an
organization with but one issue, hating whites, and partly to
deprive the FBI and other police agencies of ammunition
against the Nation. In such an inward-looking atmosphere,
Louis X's "entertainment outreach" had become obsolete. It was
time to "build a nation."

DOCUMENT NO. F 971605

THE CITY OF NEW YORK

DEPARTMENT OF HEALTH
VITAL RECORDS
CERTIFICATION OF BIRTH

This is a certification of name and birth facts on file in the Bureau of Vital Records, Department of Health, City of New York.

DATE OF BIRTH	MAY 11, 1933	CERTIFICATE NO.	06301	
BOROUGH	BRONX	DATE FILED 05-20-33	DATE ISSUED	06-08-95
NAME	LOUIS EUGENE WALCOTT ***			
SEX	MALE			
MOTHER'S MAIDEN NAME	MAE MANNING			
FATHER'S NAME	LOUIS WALCOTT			

Earlene Price
EARLENE PRICE
CITY REGISTRAR

Do not accept this transcript unless it bears the raised seal of the Department of Health. This reproduction or alteration of this certification is prohibited by Section 3.21 of the New York City Health Code.

The man listed on Farrakhan's birth certificate as his father, Louis Walcott, was his mother's lover—not his biological father. His actual father, Percival Clarke, was his mother's estranged husband. Briefly returning from his extramarital wanderings, Clarke got Mae Clarke pregnant. When efforts to abort failed, she gave birth to Louis, apparently not telling her lover about the newborn's pedigree.

Photo by Craig Terkowitz

In the early 1940s, young Louis Walcott sang in the choir at St. Cyprian's Episcopal Church in Roxbury (second from left) and played violin at church concerts on Sunday afternoon.

Photo courtesy of Amelia D. Winston

TRACK TEAM
STATE CHAMPIONS and CO-NEW ENGLAND CHAMPIONS

1st Row: (left to right) Edward M. Griffin, Augustus J. Calkins, Eugene Walcott, Gerald F. O'Lea Robert C. Sargent, John Cuoco, Jr.; Paul V. Thomas, Pasquale A. Lochiatto, Captain; Lewis Prout, Eugene Washington, Howard J. Shelton, Edward A. Griffith, Alan T. Howe, Albert S. Ho ard, Jr.

2nd Row: (left to right) J. Clifford Ronan, Coach; Francis D. Arnao, James G. Hennessy, Da Brody, Laurence E. Babb, William A. Kowles, William A. Brown, Herbert Stone, Kenneth Coff Harris I. Akell, Harvey L. Sinman, Gregory M. Sarkisian, William C. Welch, Joseph E. Fitzgere Richard T. Francis, Theodore H. Howes, James F. Ettridge, Walter F. Downey, Head Master.

3rd Row: (left to right) Robert H. Howard, Manager, Asgier Asgiersson, Richard A. Plunk William L. Antoine, George K. McKinney, Gerald Hill, Isiah R. Engerman, Richard M. Long, Ste en J. McCabe, Morgan T. Ryan, Neil L. MacKinnon, Arnold T. Howe, Norman S. White, Cullen Si Angelo R. Buonopane, Stephen E. Holeman, Robert M. Simonette, Robert L. Abruzzese, Manac

4th Row: (left to right) David Sault, William D. Tatem, Edmund S. LaMarre, Donald C. Nichols George A. Fowler, Edward Allen, Eugene R. Ellis, Lafayette L. Thomas, Leonard Singer, S ley P. Monteiro, William B. Wharton, Albert J. Braga, Arthur J. Sullivan, Joseph M. Rosen, My Cooper, Willis Powell.

In 1950, Farrakhan (third from left), then still Louis Walcott, helped English High's track team become th state champions.

Photo from 1950 English High yearbook. Photo courtesy of English High Scho

In May 1949, sixteen-year-old Farrakhan (left) played his violin on "The Ted Mack Original Amateur Hour." A decade later (below), as Minister Louis X, he sang at Nation of Islam rallies in Harlem, accompanying himself on ukelele.

Photos by Craig Terkowitz from "For the Love of Music" videotape

Farrakhan will always be linked with Malcolm X, who helped bring him into the NOI and with whose assassination Farrakhan has always been implicated. Below, Malcolm and Farrakhan in Harlem, 1963.

Photo © 1983 by Robert L. Haggins

The top Nation of Islam leadership, May 1963, Phoenix, Arizona: the Honorable Elijah Muhammad (cen ter) and his wife, Clara; (back row, left to right), son Elijah Jr.; son-in-law Raymond Sharrieff, head of the Fruit of Islam; grandson Hasan Sharrieff; and son Herbert.

Photo by Gordon Park

The true identity of Master Fard Muhammad, who founded the Nation of Islam in Detroit in the 1930s, will probably forever be shrouded in mystery. He has been called a charlatan, a con man, a mystic, and a reincarnation of God.

Nation of Islam rally, Chicago, 1967. At the podium is the Honorable Elijah Muhammad. Seated at the fa[r] right on the stage is Farrakhan, who had recently been given Malcolm's X's title as the NOI's national repre[se]ntative. Malcolm had been assassinated two years before.

Photo by AP/Wide World Photo[s]

Farrakhan crying at 1975 NOI Savior's Day, Chicago, 1975. The day before, the Honorable Elijah Muhammad had died.
Photo by Craig Terkowitz from videotape of 1975 Savior's Day

Farrakhan in 1985 announcing plans to create "Power," a new line of cosmetic products financed with a $5 million loan from Libya's Muammar Khaddafi. Farrakhan blamed "Power's" failure on Jewish bankers. Behind Farrakhan is Khallid Abdul Muhammad, whose late 1993 speech at Kean College attacking Jews triggered one of the worst black-Jewish crises of the 1990s.

Photo by UPI/Bettmann

In 1993, Farrakhan's performance of the Violin Concerto by Mendelssohn, who had been born a Jew, convinced some people he was making a musical "overture" toward Jews. Jews called the concert a publicity stunt.

Photo by Brian Jackson

The Million Man March in Washington on October 16, 1995. The very successful march was Farrakhan's idea; the three-hour speech he delivered there was generally deemed a failure.

Photo by Reuters/Theiler/Archive Photos

V

. . . And Hell

Self-sufficiency and a separate state for blacks were the chief planks in the NOI's manifesto, but the Nation never abandoned the American Dream: hard work, discipline, virtue, humility, they all had their rewards—and all in this lifetime. For blacks, the rewards would be quicker, more certain, and less stymied in a black-dominated economy. Malcolm X's conversion, for instance, was the classic stuff of the Dream mythology. From a hustling, foul-mouthed, small-time crook to a clean-cut, clean-living, clean-talking "disciple" of a strict, straightlaced father figure, Malcolm showed that "success" and redemption came from confessing past sins, becoming educated, putting one's shoulder to the wheel, and pushing, pushing, pushing. Faith in the Dream wasn't dissipated, even for the lowly Negro. The Nation just wanted to make sure that Negroes got their fair share of the pie.[1]

But as NOI-owned farmland was being plowed and super-markets were being opened and the foundations of the physical "nation" of the Nation of Islam were being solidified, all was not well within the House of Muhammad, the Nation's royal family. For years, Elijah Muhammad had been fulminating against dating and marriage between whites and blacks and urging faithful, monogamous sexual relations only within marriage. Black men, he said, treated black women like worthless chattel. "Even animals and beasts, the fowls of the air, have more love and respect for their females than have the so-called Negroes of America." Interracial sex diluted racial purity and was especially denigrating to blacks: "When the devil man decides to marry her [a black woman], the so-called Negro press and magazines will make it front-page news. The daily press will not print a so-called Negro man marrying into their race, but you seem to think it is an honor to your own nation when your daughter goes over to your enemies."[2]

Almost against the collective will of the Nation, however, rumors of sexual permissiveness, if not of outright lechery, surfaced to become the most morally corrosive timebomb in the organization. They proved that the seeds of the Nation's own destruction lay within itself, in Elijah Muhammad's fierce instinct to control and rule, in his self-ordained messianism, and in his rationalizations that his own pleasures were neither folly nor random but divinely prescribed.

In April 1960, Wallace Muhammad, the youngest of Elijah Muhammad's sons, was sentenced to prison for three years for failing to report to a hospital where he had been assigned to serve as a conscientious objector to the military draft. Although his father eventually spent twenty thousand dollars on legal fees to have the decision reversed, Wallace went to jail on November 4, 1961.

Of Elijah's six sons, Wallace and his brother Akbar (who would soon study Islamic law at Al Azhar University in Cairo) were perhaps the most serious about studying Islam—and about challenging their father's version of it. Before entering prison, Wallace, whom Fard Muhammad had predicted would succeed Elijah, had begun to doubt his father's rendering of Islam. He especially doubted his father's insistence that Fard was Allah. Wallace used his almost eighteen months in prison to meditate, study Islam, and compare notes about his findings with certain members of his family and with Malcolm X.

By the time he left Sandstone Correctional Institute in January 1963, Wallace was convinced that much of the Nation's theological underpinnings were a sham. With that came a readiness to believe other suspected failings about his father, especially reports about the "explosive situation" in his father's "private quarters" that were confided to him after his release from prison.[3]

Some top NOI leaders had harbored these suspicions of Elijah for five years or more; a few of the more spiritually serious also had their doubts about the veracity of what Elijah was calling "Islam." But Wallace had the guts—and the stature as a member of the "royal family" and a favored son of his father—to speak out publicly, at least about what was truly Islamic and what wasn't, even in classes he taught at the NOI's University of Islam in Chicago. Wallace later obliquely attributed the very source of his heresy to his father and to Fard: "W. D. Fard and Elijah Muhammad taught me to be truthful and not to lie."[4]

But Wallace's actions could just as easily have been motivated by his family's peculiar patriarchy, which left little room for any of the other males in the home and under which filial piety was equivalent to divine loyalty. In the Muhammad household, Elijah was not just a father or a religious leader or a social prophet: he was a god. "My mother put him before all of her children and put in us the same [sense of] mystery for him that he had for all [the members of the Nation]."[5]

Yet Wallace saw Elijah in the flesh: in his bathrobe; at the breakfast table; ordering his wife around; cutting discussions short with dictates and decrees. And Wallace squirmed at his father's ignorance about the very basics of Islam: "Fard had told my father to pronounce the name he gave him"—Muhammad—"as 'Mack-mahd.' We were embarrassed to say our own names. One of my brothers changed his name to 'Bogans' [one of Elijah Muhammad's many pseudonyms]. Finally, in 1950 or 1951, a professor from Jerusalem told my father how to properly say his own name."[6]

The man Wallace lived with was all too human, not divine, as he might have seemed to NOI members (and ministers) in its temples in Boston and other cities. Knowing the man behind the throne lent credence to reports circulating among the NOI's top officials about Elijah's less than godly infidelities. As early as the mid-1950s, one young woman after another working as Elijah Muhammad's secretary became pregnant by him: Rosella in 1955, Lavita in 1956. Eventually, six "wives" produced thirteen children. Around 1960, four of these former secretaries met in Chicago and discovered that Elijah Muhammad had fathered each of their children; each woman repeated Elijah Muhammad's claims that he was a divine prophet and that she was his wife. By 1962, two of them were telling blacks in Chicago about Elijah's peccadilloes. Around the same time, Elijah was thinking about buying a house on the West Coast that could be used as a nursery for all his illegitimate children. Moreover, there was considerable "domestic strife" between Elijah and his wife Clara, who had learned about the infidelities.[7]

The FBI, too, heard about Elijah's progeny, mostly through informants. Adding this information to evidence it had already accumulated about Elijah's high-priced cars and homes purchased on the backs of his impoverished followers, the bureau suddenly realized it had been handed the biggest monkey wrench it could have hoped for to throw at Muhammad: "Any successful attack on his character or his reputation might be disastrous to the NOI. . . . Further study should be given to this matter with the view of instituting a carefully planned campaign to discredit Muhammad in the eyes of his followers."[8]

The next year, one secretary told Wallace about his father's infidelity; Wallace passed this news on to Malcolm. Deeply troubled because the rumors he had been hearing for eight years seemed to be confirmed, Malcolm confided them to one of his oldest friends in the Nation of Islam, Louis X. He then asked the Boston minister, "Brother, what do you think?"

"All praise is due to Allah," Louis told Malcolm.

Stunned that Louis's faith in the Messenger was not shaken, Malcolm asked him to be silent about Elijah's indiscretions.

"I wouldn't tell anyone except the Honorable Elijah Muhammad," answered Louis.

Further stunned, Malcolm asked Louis to give him some time. "Would you please let me write a report to the Honorable Elijah Muhammad? It will take me some time to prepare my thoughts before I write my letter."[9]

Louis agreed. Instead of writing a letter to Muhammad, Malcolm flew in April to Phoenix, where Elijah was spending most of his time to relieve his severe asthma. Elijah not only admitted that he was the children's father, he raised the stakes: he was now an incarnation not only of *all* the prophets, but of an entire cast of other Old Testament characters.[10]

"I'm David," he told Malcolm. "When you read about how David took another man's wife, I'm that David. You read about Noah, who got drunk—that's me. You read about Lot, who went and laid up with his own daughters. I have to fulfill all of those things."[11]

Publicly, Malcolm began backpedaling from speaking about morality, replacing it with politics, current events, and social doctrine and trying to engineer an exit for himself from the Nation, or at least from Elijah Muhammad. He could not represent Elijah after losing faith that the Nation stood for moral reformation. In August, when the NAACP, the Congress of Racial Equality (CORE), and the Southern Christian Leadership Conference (SCLC) pulled off the civil rights movement's monumental achievement of having 250,000 people march on Washington to hear about Martin Luther King's "dream," Malcolm began calling for a "united black front" with these groups. But a few weeks later, Elijah Muhammad tightened the noose by embracing Malcolm in front of several thousand Nation members in Philadelphia and declaring him "my most faithful, hardworking minister. He will follow me until he dies."[12]

It became increasingly apparent that Malcolm had no place to go: the white world, obviously, was closed to him. Despite all his talk of death to Caucasians, neither he nor what passed for the Nation's "mainstream" had much tolerance for actual violence, so more militant black nationalist groups were off-limits to him. On the other hand, he was anathema to the less militant black groups, especially since the March on Washington the previous August had etched civil rights into the national agenda—and the national imagination—as never before. As Malcolm said, with poignant self-awareness, "For Muslims, I'm too worldly. For other people, I'm too religious. . . . For militants, I'm too moderate. For moderates, I'm too militant."[13]

In a few months, Malcolm had no choice but to leave the Nation: his mind was essentially made up for him. Shortly after John F. Kennedy was assassinated on November 22, 1963, Elijah Muhammad privately issued a directive that all NOI ministers be silent about the murder. As one former minister said, "This was done for our own benefit to prevent any violence against *us.*" All ministers observed the gag rule—until December 1, when near the end of a Nation rally in Manhattan, a reporter asked Malcolm about the assassination. Accusing Kennedy of "twiddling his thumbs" at the killing of South Vietnamese President Ngo Dinh Diem and his brother, Ngo Dinh Nhu, Malcolm admitted that he "never foresaw that the chickens would come home to roost so soon. Being an old farm boy myself, chickens coming home to roost never did make me sad. They've always made me glad."[14]

Judging from the grin on Malcolm's face after saying these forbidden words, he seemed delighted to have broken Elijah's decree about silence on JFK. His words may have been his revenge on the Messenger for not being a moral paragon; his declaration of disillusionment and independence; an assertion that he would not cower before any man, especially Elijah, because, as he would say six months later, after going to the press with details about the Messenger's many "wives" and out-of-wedlock children, "Muhammad was nobody until I came to New York as his emissary. If they had left me alone, I would not have revealed any of this."[15]

One order to be silent was replaced by another. Within two days, Elijah had told Malcolm he could not speak publicly about anything. But Malcolm persisted in talking to reporters or overtly feeding them information about the nascent battle inside the Nation. As a consequence, Elijah removed him in late January as his national representative and as the minister of the Harlem temple, making him essentially a minister-without-portfolio and one of the country's most polished public-speakers-without-a-podium.

In early March, after repeated efforts to be reinstated to his former posts and after hearing about several plots within the Nation to kill him, Malcolm resigned from the organization, telling journalists he would return to the fray in ways that would "make his previous efforts pale by comparison." Announcing that he was forming a new group, the Muslim Mosque, Inc., he implied that he had left merely Elijah Muhammad, not Elijah Muhammad's ideas about the ultimate desirability of a separate state: "I still believe that Mr. Muhammad's analysis of the problem is the best solution, and that his solution is the best one. . . . I, too, believe the best solution is complete separation. . . . [But we] need better food, clothing, housing, education, and jobs *right now*."[16]

A few weeks later, in a phenomenally ecumenical statement given the parochialism of the group he had been in for the past fourteen years, Malcolm made it clear that the Nation of Islam did not have a monopoly on "black nationalism." "Black nationalism means that the black man should control the politics and the politicians in his own community; . . . Black nationalism is being taught in the Christian church. It's being taught in the NAACP. It's being taught in CORE meetings. It's being taught in SNCC meetings. It's being taught in Muslim meetings. It's being taught where nothing but atheists and agnostics come together."[17]

The Nation widely denounced Malcolm as a turncoat whom "we should destroy." Loyalties were tested; brother literally turned against brother, father against son. Philbert X, Malcolm's older sibling who had written to him so glowingly about the Nation when Malcolm was in jail in the late 1940s, denounced him at a press conference as a "wayward," "cunning" schemer who would "do anything" to remain in the limelight and who was possibly suffering from the same mental maladies that had afflicted their mother.[18]

In January, Elijah excommunicated his son Wallace for allegedly influencing Malcolm's theological thinking and giving him inside information about the Messenger's style of living.

Furious, Wallace soon started his own group, the short-lived
Afro-Descendent Society of Upliftment, and wrote to his father
that the Nation had become shallow and morally and religious
bankrupt: "I find your helpers, your followers and the family
withering like dying flowers, and the righteousness that you
projected to us so beautifully and so purely and so plentifully is
no more the chief ingredient in the activities of your administration."[19]

Next came the expulsion of another son, Akbar, because he
had praised the teachings of Wallace and Malcolm. A few
months later, after the battle between Malcolm and the NOI's
leadership in Chicago really heated up, Wallace, who had been
groomed to succeed his father, told the *Chicago Defender* that
NOI "officers" in Chicago had threatened his life. He believed
the threats because "I know they are fanatics," and he
denounced certain relatives and members of his father's staff as
"guilty of some or all of those evils [banned by the Nation, such
as adultery or drinking]. There have been beatings, lies and
hypocrisy; they have presented my father as a holy image, and
misused thousands of dollars. . . . They are just as bad as the
Belgian devils who once ruled the blacks of the Congo. . . . Perhaps they are as bad as the whites who now rule our people of
South Africa . . . because their crimes are against their own peo
ple." Asked about his father's ultimate goals, Wallace replied, "To
be the strongest black man on the face of the earth."[20]

One of Elijah's grandsons, Hasan Sharrieff, didn't wait to be
excommunicated: he resigned, issuing an open letter describing
his grandfather as a "fake and a fraud" and accusing his "two-
faced relatives" of skimming off hundreds of thousands of dollars that had been collected for the poor. "It makes me want to
retch," Hasan exploded.[21]

In an extraordinary turn of events, some members fleeing the
Nation turned for protection to the FBI, which had always been

portrayed as their archenemy (and which suddenly saw the Nation imploding before its eyes). Wallace told the FBI about the threats against him—and that seemed to send his would-be assassins into full retreat. On June 11, 1964, seven members of the Chicago temple—Elijah's flagship—walked into the local FBI office asking for protection from threats from within the Nation to beat them up or possibly kill them. They still admired Elijah but were fed up with pressure to sell the Nation's paper, *Muhammad Speaks*, and with top officials' greed, expensive living, and "superior attitude." Twelve days later, Elijah's grandson called an FBI agent in Chicago, notifying him that he had also left the Nation and implicitly asking for protection.[22]

The battle intensified after Malcolm returned to the United States from two trips. The first, which started on April 13, lasted six weeks and included half a dozen African countries and a hajj, or pilgrimage, to Mecca; the second, starting on July 9, lasted eight weeks and included numerous African countries. The hajj in particular changed Malcolm. After embracing "the brotherhood of man" that he had experienced by seeing the many hues of skin color in the Muslim pilgrims from around the world, he condemned Elijah Muhammad as a "faker" who had hawked his "distorted religious concoction" and "racist philosophy" as authentic Islam, intending "only to fool and misuse gullible people."[23]

"Fed up with strait-jacket societies," Malcolm defended "every man's right to believe whatever his intelligence leads him to believe is intellectually sound" and pledged to "never rest until I have undone the harm I did to so many well-meaning Negroes who, through my own evangelistic zeal, now believe in [Elijah Muhammad] even more fanatically and blindly than I did."[24]

The lines were drawn, and the battle was to the death: Malcolm was concerned for his life, while the Nation, which had lost about half its membership, was worried about its very existence. In Detroit, the birthplace of the Nation, at least 150 brothers quit. In Boston, Minister Louis X saw his temple lose more than 60 percent of its 250 members until fewer than 100 were left. Fearing the destruction of his work of seven years, during which time he had more than doubled the Boston temple's membership, Louis unleashed against Malcolm—the man who had convinced him that the NOI was the right path for him, who had called him "little brother" with fondness and respect—the same strain of apocalyptic, blood-drenched rhetoric that both ministers had learned from Elijah Muhammad. For Farrakhan even more than for Malcolm, this style would eventually become his trademark for a country accustomed to niceties and civilities from its public figures.

In a three-part series he wrote for *Muhammad Speaks*, Minister Louis attacked Malcolm's "cupidity," "lying," "jealousy," "treachery," and "defection." Malcolm was to Elijah what Judas was to Jesus or what Moseilma, a false prophet in Islamic lore, was to Muhammad. A cheat and a scoundrel, Malcolm "had benefited and profited most from [Elijah's] generosity" and had "played the hypocrite on both sides," against the white man of America and against Muhammad, too. Consorting with heathens, Malcolm had "made the foolish and ignorant mistake . . . [of saying] his best friends were among such non-believing people as Hindus . . . , Jews, Christians, Catholics, and even 'Uncle Toms.' He really made a fool of himself. . . . No Muslim is a Muslim who accepts such people as his brothers."[25]

And then these words that have haunted Farrakhan ever since: "Only those who wish to be led to hell, or to their doom, will follow Malcolm. The die is set, and Malcolm shall not escape. . . . Such a man as Malcolm is worthy of death, and would have met death if it had not been for Muhammad's confidence in Allah for victory over his enemies."[26]

Speaking to an audience of upper-middle-class blacks fifteen years later, Farrakhan totally glossed over his indictment of Malcolm: "When Malcolm was on fire, how many of us burned with him? Or how many of us burned at him? When the public policy of the United States government said, 'Let's ostracize him,' how many of us were a party to that? Were you there when they crucified my Lord?" No mention of "worthiness of death" or of "dies being set." Just a tongue-lashing of "pitiful people" who sat on the sidelines as their leaders were butchered and slandered.[27]

Others were calling for Malcolm's death, some using more vehement language than Louis X. At a closed-door Fruit of Islam meeting, for instance, Elijah Muhammad Jr. said, referring to the house in East Elmhurst, New York, from which the Nation was trying to evict Malcolm and his family, "All you have to do is go there and clap on the walls until the walls come down and then cut out the nigger's tongue and put it in an envelope and send it to me. And I'll stamp it 'approved' and give it to the Messenger."[28]

But no one dared mention death and Malcolm in the same breath as publicly as Louis X, and aside from the three men eventually convicted for Malcolm's assassination, no one would be haunted by Malcolm's murder during the rest of their career more than Farrakhan. Farrakhan has persistently denied rumors that he was somehow involved in the actual assassination. He was in Newark the day of the assassination—"on rotation," he has said, "to handle the preaching or the teaching of that day" because James Shabazz, the Newark minister, was filling in for Malcolm in the New York temple. One of Malcolm's convicted assassins, in fact, hailed from that mosque. Farrakhan's diatribes against Malcolm in *Muhammad Speaks* ("Is Malcolm bold enough to return and face the music?") stirred its readers into an anti-Malcolm frenzy more than any other article about Malcolm in the paper—more even than one by

Clarence X Gill, the FOI captain in Louis's temple who wrote that his "constant prayer to Allah is that I never turn on my heels and deviate, or because of my weakness, turn hypocrite as others have done. May Allah burn them in hell." But Minister Louis wasn't using such cautionary imagery. He was talking about the death that Malcolm deserved and about the saintliness of the man Malcolm had maligned and disobeyed: Elijah Muhammad, "the only prophet divinely raised up to gather into the fold the lost-found tribe of Shabazz."[29]

In recent years, Farrakhan has tried to moderate his public furies about Malcolm. On ABC's *20/20* in 1994, he told Barbara Walters: "Today . . . Malcolm would be so much more valuable to us alive." But more privately, his anger at Malcolm is still as copious, as roiling, as palpable as when he wrote about him in *Muhammad Speaks* three decades ago. A year before the Walters interview, with only the tape recorder of a print journalist rolling and no TV cameras transmitting his image and words to millions of households, Farrakhan blasted Malcolm's insidious treachery:

Look at what Islam and the teachings of Elijah Muhammad did for him. Malcolm was a pimp, a thief, a hustler, a dope user, a dope seller, a disrespecter of women. He was this before he met Elijah Muhammad. That's when the world became acquainted with Malcolm X. Was Malcolm the deceived one? Was he gullible? Did he became the great Malcolm X because somebody tricked him? I don't think so. What did Malcolm X have that somebody could trick him out of? He didn't have money. He didn't have fame. He didn't have sense. When he left Elijah Muhammad, he wasn't wealthy, but he certainly was famous. And he certainly had plenty of knowledge. He only went through eighth grade, but no college graduate of white America could defeat Malcolm in argument or debate. So Malcolm didn't come out a loser.[30]

But didn't Malcolm imply that the NOI's "Islam" was bogus when, upon returning from Mecca, he said he had experienced the "true Islam of the East?"

"In Mecca and Arabia," said Farrakhan,

Malcolm met the broad world of Islam, which is a world of many races, many colors, many tongues. He *knew* that world when he was still a follower of Elijah Muhammad. Nineteen sixty-four was not the first time he went to the Middle East. He went there in 1959. He had been invited to go to Mecca but felt that honor should first go to Elijah Muhammad. Instead, he was in Egypt, Jeddah, the Sudan, and he saw Muslims who were white, black, brown.

Did it take him from 1959 to 1964 to say he was being deceived? When he left his base in the Nation of Islam, he needed a base. So what was the best way of finding a base, particularly among the civil rights movement? When he said he had seen in Mecca people "whose eyes were the bluest of blue, whose hair was the blondest of blond, whose skin was the whitest of white," . . . he was appealing to the civil rights movement.[31]

Yet Farrakhan's comparison of Malcolm's 1959 and 1964 trips, and his negation of the latter trip, does not preclude what is certain: 1964 was a major juncture for Malcolm. Within weeks after quitting the Nation, Malcolm was seeking a cause and allies. When Christian clergy asked him whether he was still critical of their faith, he said, "I don't care what I said last year. That was last year. This is 1964." To other moderates, he said, "I'm not out to fight other Negro leaders or organizations. . . . As of this minute, I've forgotten everything bad that the other leaders have said about me, and I pray that they can also forget the many bad things I've said about them." In late March, he flew to Washington to watch the debate on the 1964 civil rights bill from the Senate gallery, deliberately "running into"

Martin Luther King in a Senate hallway. The next day, several papers around the country carried a photo of Malcolm and King—whom he had once called "a chump"—shaking hands. And at meetings of Malcolm's new Organization of Afro-American Unity (OAAU), songs were sung by the integrationist-oriented Freedom Singers, who had appeared at civil rights rallies throughout the South, and speeches were given by Fannie Lou Hamer, a leader of Mississippi's Democratic Freedom Party, which had unseated delegates from that state's regular Democratic Party at the party's national convention the previous August in Atlantic City. Malcolm, the former militant, was either losing his ferocity—or was desperate for a place to call home.[32]

Farrakhan's quasi-mea culpas three decades after Malcolm's death do not mitigate the fact that *his* diatribes against Malcolm may have distorted the Koran's teaching that Muslims never punish apostates. Allah, not man, judges them in this life and the afterlife. Even the translation of the Koran distributed by the Nation of Islam clearly states that Muslims should not seek revenge on those who leave the faith:

> *Whoever of you*
> *Turns back from his religion*
> *Then he dies*
> *While an unbeliever—*
> *These it is*
> *Whose deeds go*
> *For nothing in this*
> *World and the Hereafter.*

In the introduction, the translator Maulana Muhammad Ali deplores as a "misconception" the idea "that the Quran provides a death sentence for those who desert the religion of Islam."

"Anyone who takes the trouble to read the Quran will see that there is not the least ground for such a supposition. The Quran speaks repeatedly of people going back to unbelief after believing, but never once does it say that they should be killed or punished."[33]

Shortly after 2:00 A.M. on February 14, 1965, Molotov cocktails were thrown through the living room window of Malcolm's house in East Elmhurst. Others landed in his bedroom and his children's bedroom. All were frightened, but no one was injured. An NOI minister claimed that Malcolm himself had firebombed the house "to get publicity." At a meeting of the OAAU the next day, Malcolm shouted to the five hundred people in the audience, "I've reached the end of my rope. . . . My house was bombed by the *Muslims*," a "criminal organization" led by "a senile old man interested in nothing but money and sex."[34]

The next Sunday, February 21, Malcolm was scheduled to speak at an OAAU meeting at the Audubon Ballroom on West 166th Street in Harlem. Introduced as "a man who would give his life for you," Malcolm took to the podium, gave the usual greeting, "*Aslaikum*, brothers and sisters," saw some scuffling in the front rows as someone yelled, "Take your hand out of my pocket!" and asked for calm. As two men rushed the stage, he was shot with sixteen shotgun pellets and revolver slugs. About ninety minutes later, he died at Columbia Presbyterian Hospital.[35]

Malcolm died shortly after Minister Louis X had finished his lecture at the Nation's mosque in Newark. The minister was sitting at a table at an NOI restaurant across the street from the mosque when he heard about Malcolm's death over the radio. According to him, he immediately left the restaurant and walked the streets, "reflecting on this man who was my teacher, my mentor. Though I disagreed vehemently with Malcolm's characterization of the honorable Elijah Muhammad, I was not happy that such a man was murdered."[36]

The possibility that, in some way, he may have contributed to the atmosphere leading to Malcolm's death does not seem to have crossed Farrakhan's mind until much later.

Three members of the Nation were arrested and eventually convicted of the murder: Talmadge Hayer, Norman 3X Butler, and Thomas 15X Johnson.

Five days after the murder, the Nation held its annual Savior's Day celebration in Chicago. About 3,750 people attended, filling half the sports coliseum rented for the event. A repentant Wallace Muhammad, Elijah's son, asked to be forgiven for siding with Malcolm: "I want to make a confession of guilt for having made public a dispute which I should have taken up privately with my father. I judged my father when I should have let God do it. I regret my mistake." Malcolm's two brothers, both NOI ministers, vowed their fealty to Elijah:

> Where he leads me, I will follow. . . . We have never had a guide or a leader who will work on our behalf like the honorable Elijah Muhammad. . . . I told our leader that if you can get a hold of . . . [Malcolm], you might be able to make something out of him. And he said, when he comes [out of prison], bring him. And that's what we did. In a short while, Malcolm was a man recognized throughout the country because of Allah and the teachings of the honorable Elijah Muhammad.[37]

Then Elijah Muhammad, protected by a phalanx of guards, gave his version of a eulogy to Malcolm: "For a long time, Malcolm stood here where I stand. In those days, Malcolm was safe, Malcolm was loved. . . . We didn't want to kill Malcolm and didn't try to kill Malcolm. . . . I am not going to let the crackpots destroy the good things Allah sent to you and me!"[38]

Regret mixed with pique. Sorrow mixed with triumphalism.

And rage suppressed on all sides—except from Minister Louis X, who shouted from the podium, "Put the light on him! Let the world see him!" when he spied Benjamin Holman, a black journalist who had infiltrated the Nation for news reports he had written for the *Chicago Sun Times* and a local TV station. Hundreds of Muslims ran toward Holman, crying, "Uncle Tom! Kill him!" The mob was finally reined in by the man who, two months earlier, had demanded that Malcolm's tongue be sent to the Messenger and was now a calming and sensible presence. "Go back, brothers!" reasoned Elijah Muhammad Jr. "Go back!"[39]

The brothers went back, but Louis X went forward, supplanting Malcolm once and for all. Three months later, he became minister of the New York temple. Two years later, he usurped Malcolm's other title and became the Nation's national representative. If there had been an heir apparent at that point to Elijah, it would have been Farrakhan, except that Elijah Muhammad's family had learned its lessons from the slain "hypocrite." Despite internal jealousies, familial bickerings and distrusts, despite snickerings over the Nation's intellectual and theological acrobatics as it tried to masquerade as true Islam, the Muhammad family cohered as never before, suspicious of interlopers, wary of newcomers, protective of what they—and their father—had accrued. Louis Farrakhan may have had pretensions about assuming the throne, but as far as the Muhammad family was concerned, the former calypso singer would always be a commoner.

VI

"The Miraculous Transformation of Thugs"

In the years since Malcolm's assassination, the furthest that Farrakhan has gone in accepting some responsibility for the murder is acknowledging that he "helped to create an atmosphere [that led to the assassination]. I was very angry with Malcolm. . . . I was hurt by his assassination. I can't say that I approved and I really didn't disapprove. I was numb."[1]

Perhaps one reason Farrakhan was "numb" was that he had never clearly understood the relation between rhetoric and action. In some ways, his instincts were still those of an entertainer, one who draws his audience into fictions and fantasies. Farrakhan underestimated the connection between the true meaning behind words and their power to move audiences. If

91

words were merely vehicles to amuse and divert, not a spur to concrete action, then to say that "such a man as Malcolm is worthy of death" was not to *sentence* him to death: it was just engaging in gross theatrics.

Despite his demurrals about being directly involved in Malcolm's death, Minister Louis could never claim he was a total stranger to violence. Violence was indispensable to the culture of the Nation of Islam. It was not only in the environment: it *was* the environment. Anyone who spent a week in the organization knew that its structure, its discipline, its very internal momentum, hinged on violence. In Boston, for instance, just eight weeks before Malcolm was killed, one of his aides, Leon Ameer, was severely beaten twice by four members of Louis's temple. Three weeks after the assassination, Ameer was found dead in a hotel room in Boston's Back Bay. The medical examiner said he had possibly died from an epileptic fit; his wife said Ameer had never had epilepsy.[2]

An ex-addict named Clarence X Gill ensured that Temple No. 11 was a hotbed of brutality, retribution, and fear. "Do not whip the men," Clarence once ordered the lieutenants under him in the temple's Fruit of Islam. "Only *I* have the right to whip the men." With each brother being suspected of being an informant, no one was safe, not even relatives of Minister Louis. When Captain Clarence heard that the brother and brother-in-law of the minister's wife were regularly taking karate classes at the local YMCA, "as out-of-bounds as a Muslim can get," he concluded that they were studying the martial art to use it against other NOI members. One evening while a temple meeting was in session, the two were

hustled down to the basement of the mosque for questioning. Instead of confessing, . . . they insisted that they had only been trying to find out whether karate was worth teaching to the rest of the FOI. Clarence didn't believe them and had his lieutenants beat them. When one of the two men, Richard X, began to cry out in pain, he was ordered to be quiet. Clarence pointed out sternly that since his cries could be heard in the temple, they indicated a lack of respect for the minister—Richard's own brother-in-law. And so Richard submitted to the pummeling without any further outcries. He really didn't want to disturb the mosque meeting.[3]

In another incident, members of the temple revolted against a new policy concerning sales of *Muhammad Speaks*. Members around the country had to make bulk purchases of the paper with their own money—and then sell them on the street. In Boston, each member shelled out sixty dollars a month for two hundred papers. One temple officer was "distressed" when he visited fellow members who "were struggling just to put food on the table" and found "unsold newspapers stacked in their closets and in their cellars and in the trunks of their cars."[4]

In 1962, NOI headquarters raised the price of *Muhammad Speaks* by a nickel to twenty cents per issue; as an incentive for members to sell the paper, each Muslim could keep three cents from the cover price for himself. Almost immediately, Clarence X announced that those three pennies had to be returned to the mosque; pressure to sell the papers rose to new heights. Members of the FOI's "terror squad" would visit a delinquent member at night. If he couldn't fork over the money, they drove him to a nearby park and worked him over.[5]

Minister Louis was proud that fifty-two businessmen belonged to his temple. But it was the businessmen who rebelled at the new newspaper quotas. So in the fall of 1962, Elijah Muhammad Jr. flew from Chicago to Boston to quell the revolt. The man who, two years later, would call for Malcolm's tongue to be sent to his father, only made the situation worse. "The Messenger fulfills all," he warned. In the language of the Nation,

that meant that Elijah Muhammad would ensure that past policy would determine future retribution. The businessmen in the
Boston temple interpreted this as meaning that they would be
summarily killed.[6]

Within a few days, forty-two businessmen quit the temple. By
November, membership had shrunk to forty-five. A shaken
Minister Louis issued a general amnesty to all who had left,
telling them that Clarence X had been dismissed from his post.
Almost everyone who had quit attended the next Friday night
meeting, at which Louis promised that newspaper quotas would
be dropped and discipline would be eased. But Clarence quickly
told the NOI leadership in Chicago about the minister's
leniency—and the following Wednesday, the minister, who had
"folded completely" after hearing from Chicago, mounted the
rostrum, ruefully announcing, "Some of you seem to have mis-
understood me." The quotas were back—and so was Clarence.[7]

In November 1963, Aubrey Barnette, the secretary of the temple's Fruit of Islam who had recently left the Nation, had only
harsh words for the organization: "a moneymaking proposition
which bleeds its followers dry." "A peculiar quackery [that]
resorts to terror, violence and extortion." "A hate movement." In
a devastating article for the February 27, 1965 issue of the *Saturday Evening Post*, "The Black Muslims Are a Fraud," Barnette
blew the cover on the Nation's scams, brutality, and hypocrisy.
The only official for whom he showed any sympathy was Minister Louis: "To me, Louis X is a tragic figure. He had the talent
to become a leading figure in the entertainment world. He put
aside all personal ambition because he believed the Muslims
were trying to instill in the Negro a sense of pride and a hope
for accomplishment." Barnette implied that Louis was being
hoodwinked, conned, and scammed and was no better off than
the ordinary NOI members: all were victims of their own high
hopes for Elijah Muhammad's homemade brew of religion and

black nationalism. Weary of being victimized by whites, they were now being victimized by their own kind.[8]

While no evidence exists that Minister Louis ever ordered anyone's murder or beating, there is also no evidence that he (or almost any other Nation leader) ever spoke out *against* violence while serving under Elijah Muhammad. That silence gives him a different sort of culpability, but one that may be no more honorable, no less complicit, than that borne by those who actually pulled triggers or administered beatings. There's also a strong chance that Elijah Muhammad, increasingly feeble, had little idea of the degree of the brutality inside his Nation. Said Wallace, one of Elijah's sons, "I don't think my father was aware of the full extent to which these things had developed. I think he was deceived. He was told that nobody was getting whipped, except those who attacked us."[9]

But Elijah, as infirm as he may have been, knew something of the violence and the crime—and tried to wean his followers away from it. "Take *nothing*," he ordered, when asked about taking somebody's property. "Just take that which God has given to you and make something out of it. You take nothing! You go to war with no man! No! You go to war with yourself. . . . Stop looking at other people's property [or] looking for them to give you theirs. You don't take anything."[10]

Yet even an appeal from the Messenger himself could not staunch the whippings, beatings, and shakedowns that were surely not the Muslim way but had become the Nation's way. The NOI's violence emanated from Elijah's own rhetoric, which was saturated with end-of-time retribution against whites— floods, famines, and pestilence, all of vast biblical proportions. It came from Malcolm's rhetoric, which, while less biblical, was more eager to kick white ass "by any means necessary." It came from the NOI's core constituency, the troubled urban poor. By setting its sights on ex-addicts, ex-alcoholics, ex-convicts, the

Nation could demonstrate its power to rehabilitate and reform and could take considerable, often well-justified pride in its success. "Many of my followers and ministers," said Elijah Muhammad, "were once criminals, but I changed all that by giving them knowledge of *self*. Once they discovered who the devil was and who God was, their lives were changed." Malcolm—the former pimp, thief, and jailbird—had been the convict-turned-Muslim par excellence. But violent habits are hard to suppress, and by recruiting so assiduously from the lower depths, the Nation endowed itself with an underclass with instincts gleaned on the streets, not from the Koran. Backsliding was not just an outside chance: it was a constant, daily threat to the civil facade of the Nation and to the broader black community. "In too many cases," wrote the black columnist William Raspberry, "the miraculous transformation of thugs into white-shirted-bow-tied gentleman has been less than complete."[11]

While only a small segment of the Nation's members engaged in violence, everyone knew about it. They worried either that they would be prey to it or that they would not be part of it when it did occur. Askia Muhammad, a San Jose, California, member who was then named Charles 67X, had the usual crammed NOI calendar: meetings in San Francisco on Wednesday and Friday nights and Sunday afternoons; more meetings in San Jose on Tuesday and Thursday nights; Fruit of Islam classes in San Francisco on Saturday mornings. And he always wondered, "I gotta figure out what they do on Monday nights. Monday must be the night they pass out the guns and when they look at the maps for when 'the thing' goes down."[12]

Finally, the lieutenant of San Jose's Fruit of Islam invited Askia to his house for dinner: "I thought, 'This is *it*!' And all he did was make ice cream. It wasn't about 'duty.' It wasn't about being 'official.' It was just about ice cream. It taught me that if someone says said, 'Let's rob a bank,' as desperate as I might be, it was not right. As Mr. Muhammad said, 'Don't break any laws. Don't even jaywalk.'"[13]

But starting in the early 1970s, the virus of violence thoroughly infected the Nation, cultivated by a combination of the sort of men who had joined the Nation; by emerging fringe groups that were challenging Elijah Muhammad's version of Islam; by Muhammad's top aides refusing to give younger members a voice or a stake in financial policies; and by an erosion of muscle at the very top of the Nation's power pyramid. Forced by severe bronchial asthma to spend most of his time in the salubrious air of Phoenix, Arizona, Elijah Muhammad was losing his grip on the organization. Palace intrigue and schemes began developing over who would succeed him. With three physicians caring for the seventy-five-year-old Muhammad, "the worst [was] expected . . . at anytime."[14]

Violence inside the Nation began swelling in late 1971. In October, Raymond Sharieff, Elijah Muhammad's son-in-law and chief bodyguard, and the president of the Nation of Islam, Inc., was injured when he was shot at five times while walking near the offices of *Muhammad Speaks*. Three months later, in apparent retaliation, Donald 7X Veira and Freddie 5X Webb, two members of a dissident group, were found murdered in their homes. In December 1972, a guard at the Nation's Salaam Restaurant in Chicago was killed.[15]

These incidents were virtual child's play compared to what transpired in 1973, the high-water year for NOI violence. In January, seven Hanafi Muslims, part of a breakaway group from the NOI, were murdered in their home in a fairly prosperous black section of Washington, D.C., dubbed the "Gold Coast." The Hanafis' leader, Hamaas Abdul Khaalis, the killers' probable target, was not home when the murders occurred. So, instead, they drowned two infants in a bathtub and another, a nine-day-old son, in a sink; killed Khaalis's ten-year-old son with two bullets to his head; and killed his twenty-five year-old son with three shots to his head. A young Hanafi member also died after being shot twice in the temple. Also shot in the head several times were the mother of the slain infants and Khaalis's twenty-three-year-old daughter. Both somehow survived the shootings.[16]

Police speculated that the killings were in revenge for Khaalis calling Elijah Muhammad a false prophet, and they eventually convicted seven NOI members from Philadelphia for the crimes. But there was a major snag on the route to conviction. The day before James Price, one of the assassins, was to testify against his fellow conspirators, Farrakhan delivered a chilling radio broadcast that employed some of his most incendiary language since writing in *Muhammad Speaks* eight years earlier that Malcolm was "worthy of death":

> Let this be a warning to those of you who would be used as an instrument of a wicked government against our rise. Be careful, because when the government is tired of you, they're going to dump you back into the laps of your people. And though Elijah Muhammad is a merciful man and will say, "Come in," and forgive you, yet in the ranks of the black people today there are younger men and women who have no forgiveness in them for traitors and stool pigeons. And they will execute you, as soon as your identity is known.[17]

Price reportedly heard Farrakhan's radio broadcast and refused to testify. The next day, he was found hanging in his jail cell.[18]

In May, at least five blacks brandishing pistols and automatic rifles killed the head of the Malcolm X Foundation in his home in Roxbury. Local police attributed Hakim Jamal's murder to an "ideological rift among a local Black Muslim sect," and one police sergeant called Jamal's killers "an execution squad." A local black leader said that Jamal's "loose-lipped" scathing criticism of Elijah Muhammad had signed his death warrant.[19]

In September, the Newark temple looked like a war zone. On Tuesday, September 4, James Shabazz, the fifty-two-year-old minister of Temple No. 25, was fatally gunned down by two young black men as he exited in his driveway from his Cadillac. The next day, three members of Shabazz's temple briefly kidnapped Andy Wingate, a black off-duty police officer, from whom they tried to pump information about the investigation into the minister's murder.[20]

The following weekend, Farrakhan gave his regularly scheduled Sunday sermon in his New York temple. As usual, the sermon was broadcast on WLIB-FM. What made this sermon different from most, however, was its title—"The Murderer of a Muslim"—its fury, and its reliance on Koranic passages that allegedly sanctioned homicide to revenge the assassination of Minister Shabazz.

"When a Muslim, a righteous man, is murdered," said Farrakhan,

> this is a very serious thing. Serious in the eyes of almighty God, Allah, because he has not too many righteous servants in the world. Therefore, when one who submits to do His will is murdered, you not only offend the family, you not only offend the righteous community, but you offend of the God of the righteous. And He is very swift, the holy Quran teaches, at taking retribution of a murderer of a Muslim. . . .
>
> Our brother minister, James Shabazz, was murdered a few days ago. . . . He was cleaning up black men and women in that city, making them respecters of the divine law of God and man.
>
> . . . What is the duty of the Muslim in regard to his death? Or in regard to the death of any Muslim? . . . It is written in the holy Quran that whosoever kills a Muslim, he must be killed. We are not trying to say . . . [we are] taking the law into our own hands. No, we are not permitted to do that. But we are taking the law of

God into our hands that God has put into our hands. . . . You have a duty to a man who was murdered in your city. And we also have a duty . . . to our brother who was murdered in your city.

The holy Quran teaches us—"investigate." And we are investigating. And the holy Quran teaches us, murder him who murders you. Well, we're gonna carry out that law whether the law likes it or not.

. . . We are not an evil people. We are lovers of life and we respect the sacredness of life. But he who did not respect the sacredness of the life of a righteous person and a teacher of righteousness . . . what right do we have to respect a life like that?

The holy Quran said, "Make examples of them." It even goes so far as to teach you how they should be killed: smite them at the back of the neck. Take off their heads since it is in their heads that the thought of evil was hatched. . . . Cut off their heads, roll it down the street and make the world know that the murderer of a Muslim must be murdered. . . . You will find this coming to pass.[21]

(The congregants in Farrakhan's temple enthusiastically applauded for a full fifteen seconds when he mentioned that heads literally would be rolling. The imagery was identical to that in an editorial cartoon in the January 15, 1965 issue of *Muhammad Speaks*, which depicted Malcolm X's head bouncing down the street. The cartoon appeared a month before Malcolm's assassination.)[22]

The section of the very translation of the Koran that Farrakhan was using as the basis for his speech does not mention seeking revenge for the murder of a Muslim. One who has unintentionally killed a "believer" is obliged to free a slave who is a Muslim and pay "bloodmoney" to the "people" of the deceased. If the murderer cannot afford the compensatory payment, he should fast for two months. And "whoever kills a believer intentionally," states the translation, "his punishment is hell, abiding therein . . . and Allah . . . has cursed him."[23]

Thirty-four pages after this passage, the same translation of the Koran states that "the only punishment of those who wage war against Allah and His Messenger . . . is that they should be murdered, or crucified, or their hands and their feet should be cut off on opposite sides or they should be imprisoned."[24]

Again, no mention of beheadings.

On September 18, two weeks after the Shabazz murder, two twin twenty-five-year-old members of the Newark temple were shot to death in their car. A month later, a high school boy jogging through Newark's Weequahic Park came across the decapitated bodies of two former members of Shabazz's temple. Their heads were found in a vacant lot about four miles away, one block from Shabazz's home. Shabazz had been shot through the left eye; one of the decapitated men had been shot in the right eye, the other through the left eye.[25]

In another six days, Newark police, anxious to stem the succession of gruesome killings, rounded up about eleven members of a group that called itself the New World Order of Islam. All had belonged to Temple No. 25. The Order had been feuding with Shabazz, whom they scorned as too conservative. The apparent reasoning of the police was that the violence could not be squelched by arresting members of the Nation of Islam: it had too many members and was much too powerful. After linking the New World Order to the Shabazz murder, the killings ceased.[26]

In December, to round out this year of trouble, the *New York Times* concluded that the Nation of Islam was in "deep trouble." Its $70 million "business empire"—twenty-five thousand acres of farmland in eight states; poultry and dairy farms; ware-

houses; a bank; apartment complexes; wholesale and retail businesses throughout the country; a newspaper printing plant—
was

> in jeopardy of crumbling for lack of cash, and its many small
> business had never really thrived, primarily because the Nation
> did not possess the financial shrewdness to properly manage
> them, especially with so many members coming from the streets
> and prisons. When a campaign to recruit educated, business-
> savvy blacks failed, pressure to keep the businesses afloat—com-
> pounded by the quotas on each member for sales of *Muhammad
> Speaks*—drove many back to the crime from which they had
> supposedly been weaned.[27]

Efforts to get help from Arab countries in the Middle East
were a fiasco. Negotiations for aid from Muammar Khaddafi's
Libyan government, which had loaned the NOI three million
dollars the previous year to purchase a Greek Orthodox church
in Chicago for a mosque, finally failed. So, too, was the year of
shuttle fund-raising waged by John Ali, the Nation's national
secretary, who spent most of the year traveling from one Middle Eastern country to another, begging cup in hand. These
countries, faithful to the traditional Islamic belief that all races
could embrace Allah, were not pleased with the Nation's teachings about whites. Ali was on the verge of a deal with two countries—cash in exchange for the Nation relaxing its racial philosophy and moving closer to traditional Islam—when the
October war in the Middle East broke out. These countries were
probably relieved that the papers were never signed since, upon
landing in the United States in November, Ali showed his true
colors by referring to Arabs as slave traders. The reference
"greatly upset" some Arabs, who were very sensitive to the issue.
Saudi Arabia had banned slavery as recently as 1962, and it persisted in several other Arab countries. But publicly reminding

the world about Arab policy toward slavery tainted Ali as an ingrate, if not an inept fund-raiser.[28]

Strangely, just two or three years before NOI members were killing each other off, the FBI had consistently minimized the group's reputation for violence, especially violence directed against whites. In one internal memo after another, FBI agents around the country made the same basic comments about their local NOI temples: they were peaceful and law-abiding and less of a threat to society than other black groups it deemed "extremist," such as the Black Panthers, Philadelphia's Revolutionary Action Movement, and the Student Nonviolent Coordinating Committee. The FBI even lumped Martin Luther King's Ghandian-influenced Southern Christian Leadership Conference into the same category as these other groups, which were all headed by younger, more impetuous men who flirted with violence in their rhetoric, if not in their actions.

If Elijah Muhammad had hired a crack public relations firm (and if he had been privy to the FBI's files, which have since been released under the Freedom of Information Act), he could have parlayed the bureau's clean bill of health for the Nation into effective recruiting slogans:

"Muslims believe in non-violence and do not carry guns or believe in or sanction the formation of racial unrest."

"It is not believed that [Pittsburgh's] Temple No. 22 presents any potential for racial violence. In fact, . . . [it] acts as somewhat of a stabilizing influence in the Negro community."

"The NOI's propensity [in Buffalo] for violence . . . is minimal. . . . [A local NOI leader said] it would be better to be out of town when trouble breaks out in the ghetto."

"It is not believed that the NOI in South Carolina is a serious threat as far as violence is concerned."

"[In San Diego, the NOI is] following a docile policy opposed to violence and bearing of arms. . . . Recently, the Minister of Mosque No. 8 and the Captain of the Fruit of Islam . . . actually appeared at the San Diego Police Department and reported two members of the mosque who they said were in possession of firearms. They said it was not the policy of the mosque to bear arms or to participate in such activity. . . . Muhammad's Mosque No. 8 . . . is a stabilizing influence on the Negro in San Diego."[29]

While Farrakhan was its minister, there was hardly any violence at the New York temple, but that didn't mean it was free from corruption—or at least, the *appearance* of corruption. Farrakhan, his wife, and seven of their nine children lived in a nine-room house in East Elmhurst, a predominantly white suburb in Queens. They had a maid. He drove a Cadillac El Dorado and a Mercedes convertible and was partial to fine, tailored, expensive clothes. Farrakhan's style can partially be attributed to Elijah Muhammad, who had once urged him to tone down his flashy manner of dressing. After once seeing the New York minister wearing "a bell-bottomed suit, tapered in the waist, a wide tie and a handkerchief sticking out of the jacket's breast pocket," Muhammad said, "When the devils [Caucasians] see you, brother, they'll say, 'Muhammad got his body, but *we* got his mind.' Brother, don't dress in those flashy kinds of clothes. I want you to dress in a certain way. Look at the mohair suits those Jewish rabbis wear. This is the kind of suit I want you to wear. Dignified clothes. Don't wear those straight ties. Put on a bow tie like you see me wear."[30]

Farrakhan sang calypso no more, but neither did he sing the blues. He had money; he had style; he had power.

In August 1967, as part of its COINTELPRO program to "expose, disrupt, misdirect, discredit or otherwise neutralize the activities" of "black extremist" groups, FBI agents in New York cooked up a scheme to "enlighten the NOI membership as to how well their leaders live on the hard-earned cash of their followers." Simple arithmetic had convinced the FBI that a bonanza was flowing into Temple No. 7: each month, every member had to give the temple about $144—$48 in dues and about $96 in newspaper sales. (Members meeting the monthly quota of *Muhammad Speaks* sales of six hundred copies at twenty cents an issue could keep six dollars for themselves.) From its five hundred members, then, about $72,000 flowed into the temple every four weeks, or roughly $864,000 a year. More income came from collections taken at the temple on Sunday, Wednesday, and Friday nights, from every member's obligatory $100 donation on the annual Savior's Day, and from fifteen NOI-owned restaurants, bazaars, and bakeries. "Admittedly," acknowledged the FBI, "a good portion of this money eventually finds its way to Elijah Muhammad in Chicago. However, it is felt that the leaders of the NYC mosque take care of themselves before any funds are sent to Muhammad."[31]

In April 1968, the FBI anonymously mailed to 273 members of Temple No. 7 a twenty-page booklet it produced detailing the mosque's finances and local leaders' high living. The booklet, with a comic-book style designed to "appeal to a generally uneducated audience," had two goals: To "point out to the [New York] membership that they are being swindled," and to convince the temple's top officials that other local NOI leaders were trying to "to take over the NOI in NY for themselves."[32]

With tidy handwriting and simple math, the booklet itemizes the funds flowing to the temple, commenting that this income makes Farrakhan and other officials "very, very happy," even though "the good Muslim . . . and his family" have to deprive themselves of "necessary food, clothing and good times." Childlike illustrations show Farrakhan sitting in an auto outside a prim suburban home, thinking to himself, "This sure is a beautiful and big car," while his wife waves to him from the doorway, shouting, "The maid will be ready at ten. Pick her up for sure." The punch line comes on the last two pages, where the reader is asked, "When the Honorable Elijah Muhammad leaves us, will the thief with the biggest pile win the pot?" The answer is implied on the next page: "Boy, have we all been suckers" (for Farrakhan and the temple's other top leaders).[33]

The comic book didn't work as expected. Farrakhan and other leaders were not deposed, and members of his temple did not leave en masse. The only tangible results were a discussion at one NOI meeting in New York about local officials skimming money from funds earmarked for Chicago; a letter from Elijah Muhammad's office requiring receipts to be issued for all contributions and sales; and an in-person dressing-down of Farrakhan and other New York officials by the supreme captain of the Fruit of Islam, who flew to New York especially to investigate rumors of embezzlement.[34]

As the brutality escalated and the financial empire tottered, Elijah Muhammad still held court in Chicago (on the rare occasions when he was not in Phoenix) in his nineteen-room mansion, where, if we can believe his modesty, he lived reluctantly. Criticized once for living lavishly and owning expensive cars while most of his followers were poor, he said, "Negroes place a high value on things like this. Personally, I prefer any little old car . . . but if I did so, Negroes would say, 'Islam made him poor.'"[35]

In his declining years, Muhammad continued to condemn civil rights leaders as puppets of their slave-masters and tools of the power brokers. In 1972, four years after Martin Luther King Jr. was assassinated, Muhammad "dare[d] Christian theologists to try to prove that the Rev. Martin Luther King Jr. went anywhere else than hell. Good man that he was, Rev. Martin Luther King Jr. was deceived and frightened to his very heart by the enemy," whom he had tried to "satisfy. He gets no credit for all of the work that he did for his enemies, and his enemies know that. . . . Self first. You must put self first. . . . You cannot serve two masters."[36]

Muhammad's character assassination of King was not new. Twelve years earlier, in 1960, he had ridiculed King's Christian love of the oppressor as part of the "slave philosophy" that could only retard, never advance, the black cause: "How long do you think we'd last if the white man thought we'd all bow our heads and present our necks to the axe? About long enough for him to get the axe!"[37]

But by 1972, Muhammad had actually met with King at a semi-secret meeting at his Hyde Park mansion. This was on February 23, 1966, when he had labored to stiffen the Baptist preacher's backbone: "I tried my best to put fearlessness in him. Rev. Martin Luther King Jr. admitted to me that I am teaching right. He admitted that the white man is the devil, but he was afraid to take a stand and preach that the white man is the devil."[38]

King, wobbly and weak, had sold out to the white man's riches: in exchange for the fifty thousand dollars King received for the 1964 Nobel Peace Prize, "the devil" took King to hell, which was a sorrow to Muhammad, not because the world lost a fine man, but because if King had lived, he would have forsaken integration and "been in the same corner with me."[39]

The Messenger met with King just a few hours after the civil rights leader had seized control (a "trusteeship," in King's words) of a slum building in the name of three civil rights organizations. Tenants' rent would be used to clean and renovate the building. The meeting also occurred as King was reassessing the wisdom of totally eschewing nationalism and weighing the benefits of adopting more militant language. Within days after arriving in Chicago in January to lead the slum campaign, he said he was "appalled that some people feel that the civil rights struggle is over because we have a 1964 civil rights bill with ten titles and a voting rights bill. Over and over again, people ask, 'What else do you want?' They feel that everything is all right. Well, let them look around at our big cities," especially at Chicago, where an entrenched "internal colonialism" flourishing in the slums "was not unlike the exploitation of the Congo by Belgium."[40]

In Chicago, King's morale hit an all-time low. He had come to the city confident of success. Its white liberals, who had supported his battles in the South, would surely help him; even Lyndon Johnson, the general of the new War on Poverty, would sympathize with him from the bully pulpit of the White House.

But King underestimated the cynicism of Chicago's blacks, who had long had the voting rights for which King had fought in the South yet had gained little from them. Nor had he appreciated the shrewdness of Chicago's Mayor Richard Daley, who eagerly welcomed him to town, agreeing politely with his goals but doing little to advance them.

In the nine months he was in Chicago, King gained little but a sad pessimism about the virulence of racism in the United States, especially when the howling white mobs he confronted while leading a demonstration in Gage Park exceeded in "hostility" and "hate" anything he had seen in the South. He concluded that slums could be ended only by challenging entrenched economic interests. But contesting America's fiscal engine meant "getting on dangerous ground because you are messing with folk then. You are messing with Wall Street. You are messing with the captains of industry. . . . [White backlash was] a reaction to questions being raised by the civil rights movement which demand a restructuring of the architecture of American society."[41]

By the time he left Chicago, King's verdict on the American

system was not that distant from some of the NOI's more cutting analyses in the 1990s—minus, of course, their anti-Jewish overlay.

Another notable who met with Muhammad at his Chicago mansion, James Baldwin, was struck by the Messenger's confidence that every black is, at heart, a Muslim. When Baldwin told Muhammad that he had left Christianity twenty years before, practiced no faith, and didn't "think about it a great deal," Muhammad parried to those assembled at his dinner table that Baldwin "ought to think about it *all* the deal."[42]

"There was nothing malicious or condemnatory in . . . [Muhammad's comment]," Baldwin realized. "I had the stifling feeling that *they* knew I belonged to them, but knew that I did not know it yet, that I remained unready, and that they were simply waiting, patiently, and with assurance for me to discover the truth for myself. For where else, after all, could I go? I was black, and therefore a part of Islam, and would be saved from the holocaust awaiting the white world whether I would or no. My weak, deluded scruples could avail nothing against the iron word of the prophet."[43]

Meanwhile, in New York, Louis X, whose name Elijah Muhammad had recently changed to Farrakhan, was keeping an ear out for the jealousies about him swirling within the Chicago royal court, which called him "Velvet Mouth" behind his back. Some of Elijah Muhammad's sons were envious that the New York minister could attract seventy thousand people to a Black Family Day Bazaar at a stadium on Randall Island in New York City. They whispered to Elijah what some of them had also whispered about Malcolm: "He's trying to take your glory." "He's trying to take your followers." And some coveted the tough reputation Farrakhan had earned in April 1972 when he headed off a police assault on the Harlem mosque. Police, he said, "came charging into our temple like criminals and were treated like criminals."[44]

Responding to what proved to be a false call from a "detective" claiming to be "in trouble" on the mosque's second floor, two policemen rushed to the mosque and dashed up the stairs, where they were beaten by members trying to evict them. A policeman sent three warning shots through a window of the temple to "shock the people into letting him in through the portals, which were locked," according to a police explanation.

Police returned with reinforcements wearing bullet-proof vests and armed with automatic weapons. None gained entry to the mosque, but their presence triggered a three-hour disturbance outside the facility, where a crowd of more than one thousand people gathered, yelling obscenities, throwing bricks and bottles at the cops, and setting one unmarked police car on fire. Police helicopters wheeled around in the air as the mob below yelled at the white police and press, "I hope you die, you pigs. I hope you drop dead."

At some point, Farrakhan jumped on top of a parked car and shouted to the crowd, "This is our community and we're minding our own business. But every brother and sister here, just be cool. Don't let anyone provoke you."

Order was eventually restored to the corner of 116th Street and Lenox Avenue, and Farrakhan got the credit. In the Nation, people thought Farrakhan "had valor. This wasn't facile. This wasn't entertainment. He was no jive dude. He was committed to 'the struggle.'" And credit even came from the *New York Times*, which reported that "both the mosque and the minister had long before gained reputations for dependability in Harlem."[45]

But there was another struggle going on. Elijah Muhammad entered Chicago's Mercy Hospital in late January 1975. As it became apparent that the seventy-seven-year-old "most power-ful black man in America," as a recent poll had tagged him, was dying, accolades poured in from the mayors of Oakland, Berke-ley, Newark, Atlanta, Gary, and Chicago, not all of whom were black. Suddenly, the man who had painted Caucasians as "liars, drunkards, swine eaters, murderers, robbers, deceivers, trouble-makers and two-legged rattlesnakes," who had become the bogeyman of much of the black establishment, who had said he had known Allah in the flesh, and who had been denounced as a "rogue and a charlatan"—suddenly this man was praised, hailed, applauded, and commended by some of the very people he had censured over the years as blacks' worst foes.[46]

Possibly one reason for the acclaim was that Muhammad had been softening his stance toward whites, particularly during the previous year. At the 1974 Savior's Day, he had preached a form of interracial cooperation that later followers of his son, Warith Deen Muhammad, would use as proof that he had been revamping his separatism and his insistence that Caucasians are irrevocably satanic.

In a remarkable turnaround in this last sermon, Elijah preached that racial insularity was silly in a society as complex, as interdependent, as dominated by whites as the United States. Blacks had to finally live up to the Nation's promise of their self-proclaimed piety: it was time to move beyond rhetoric. Maybe Muhammad had finally appreciated the mischievous cul-de-sac embedded in the Nation's theology. Through Yacub, the rene-gade scientist, blacks may have created whites, but by denigrat-ing their own creation, they were shaming themselves, their ingenuity, their creativity: "Since you say now you are righteous, then prove it; and if you say . . . [the white man] is not right-eous, he will say he was not his maker. That will stop your mouth. He did not make himself; it was our kind that made him. So if you want to make mock of that which you have made, he could easily tell you that 'I am not responsible for my make. You made me yourself.'"[47]

In a peculiar digression from tradition, Muhammad implicitly conceded that whites were masters, at least in the United States, and their might demanded deference: "If God gave a way to them to rule, then you're honoring a ruler; as long as they are in power, then you respect them." Then, in an even more conservative vein, Muhammad argued that the onus for blacks' condition lay not in how whites treated them, but with themselves:

> The fault is not on the slavemaster anymore; since he say you can go free and we say today he is not hindering us. It is us hindering ourselves. . . . He don't deserve us charging him with all the fault because you are free, and to make it clear to you Allah came and give to you and me a flag representing freedom, justice and equality. . . . Do something to make them . . . accept us their equal. We can't set off over here on the curbstone and tell him to come sit down with us. No! We are a lazy people. We want something for nothing. That is the way we are: We are lazy.[48]

If Muhammad had had the energy and stamina to steer the Nation toward his vision in the last sermon, the NOI might have been able to move beyond its reputation for racism and supremacy. The sermon's embrace of Islam's racial diversity echoed Malcolm X; its touting of self-reliance was thoroughly Emersonian. It resonated with Babbitt. (Would he next ask for Nation of Islam chapters of the Rotary and the Elks?) And its wrestling with the irony of the Yacub myth—since blacks created whites, they should respect whites—was poignantly, refreshingly honest after decades of white-bashing.

On February 26, 1975, exactly one year to the day after the last sermon, Elijah died of heart congestion at 8:10 A.M. That evening, the Nation of Islam announced that Wallace Deen

Muhammad would replace his father. Louis Farrakhan, the presumptive heir, was stunned. But as rumors flew about death threats to anyone opposing Wallace, Farrakhan knew he had to dutifully fall in line—or be felled himself.

The passing of Elijah cast a pall over that year's Savior's Day. In the weeks before Muhammad's death, a panicked Farrakhan—who never visited the dying Messenger in the hospital—made many late-night calls from New York trying to decipher who would succeed Elijah. Being in New York put Farrakhan at a tactical disadvantage, but he may have had the wrong contingency plan. He seemed to have allied himself with the wrong Muhammad brother. On a WBLS radio interview just three days before Elijah's death, Farrakhan spoke about the loyalty of one of Noah's sons to his father—and the treachery of another. Some Muslims assumed that Farrakhan was identifying Herbert Muhammad, Elijah's oldest son, as the devoted son, and Wallace—whose father had excommunicated him from the Nation three times (for one year starting in January 1964, for four years starting in late 1965; for several months ending in mid-1974)—as the disloyal son. But a more likely interpretation is that Wallace was the wayward son—and Farrakhan himself was to be seen as the loyal, faithful, devoted son.[49]

It is almost inconceivable that Farrakhan did not know that Wallace was the heir to the throne. While addressing the Fruit of Islam in Farrakhan's temple just six weeks before Elijah's death, Wallace had alluded to his destiny, which had a hint of divine ordination: "When the Honorable Elijah Muhammad dies, . . . the responsibility will fall on me not because he said it, but *because it has been created. . . .* It is time for us to know the truth. It's bad to go wondering what will happen. Don't wonder anymore." Then, turning to Farrakhan, Wallace made what would turn out to be an almost prophetic promise: "The brother will have his position as long as he lives up to the requirements and the demands. But if he fails, . . . I will sit him down."[50]

Savior's Day in 1975 at Chicago's International Amphitheater was unlike any other. Jesse Jackson, the former aide to Martin Luther King Jr. who then headed Project PUSH, praised Elijah Muhammad for "turn[ing] alienation into emancipation" and being "the father of black consciousness." Twenty thousand Muslims chanted, "Long live Muhammad, long live Muhammad," when they heard that "Almighty Allah, in the person of Master Fard Muhammad, the Honorable Elijah Muhammad, and the royal family" had anointed Wallace as their leader. Hyperbole became understatement. Minister after minister from around the country swore his "life," "death," and "undivided allegiance" to Wallace, who had "no equal in knowledge, wisdom, and understanding." The heavyweight champion Muhammad Ali, whom Malcolm had converted to the Nation of Islam eleven years before, said, "[W]hen we look at [Wallace], you are looking at the Honorable Elijah Muhammad." And Wallace, after assuring the crowd that "the house"— the Nation of Islam—"will not be moved by the winds of emotion," parroted his father's most traditional teachings: "Your graveyard is the Christian reading of the Bible. . . . Integration . . . [is coming] apart at the seams. . . . The solution to . . . [blacks'] problem was for something very strange to happen. Allah Himself said, "I'm going to come out of hiding as a mystery god.'"[51]

But there were also hints about what Wallace planned to do with the Nation: "We are not a people who harp upon color or race. I look upon you and see the many colors of the coat of Joseph." Rattling off nationalities and races—Watusi, Egyptian, Chinese, Indian, even white—he said each "could come and see their likeness among you." Confidence came not by denigrating others, but by being comfortable in one's own skin: "This great work has not been done to place a white head on a white body, but a black head on a black body."[52]

The only tears on the podium came from the only other minister who had aspired to be Elijah's heir: Louis Farrakhan. Though he and Wallace had had words earlier that day about Wallace's disbelief that Fard Muhammad was Allah, Farrakhan wanted to create an illusion of unity at the amphitheater because "the devil will be watching—and they'll use anything we say to foment division among the Muslims."[53]

Farrakhan was all encomiums and praise and embraced Wallace's ascension as the "will of God." He swore not to be "unfaithful to the only man I ever knew that was worthy of being faithful to," since Elijah Muhammad had told him that "his son would one day help him. That day has arrived. And I, like all Messenger Muhammad's followers, submit and yield and give of myself and all that I have and within my power to see that the work of Messenger Muhammad is carried on to its completion behind the leadership of his son."[54]

Referring four years later to the death threats supposedly made against anyone who didn't line up behind Wallace, Farrakhan defended his manhood: "I want you to know this ain't no punk talking. . . . Muhammad didn't make me no faggot. I didn't shut my mouth on February 26, 1975, because I was afraid. If you tell me that God revealed to you that I was afraid, I'll tell you to bring your God to me, and I'll kick his butt, because he's a damned liar."[55]

With the speeches over, ministers and family hoisted Wallace onto their shoulders and paraded him around the rostrum. The crowd again roared, "Long live Muhammad, long live Muhammad." The dynasty was intact: Elijah was dead. Wallace ruled. Everything would continue as it was before—or so it briefly seemed.

The next month, the husband of a member of the singing

group the Supremes told Farrakhan that he had heard from Muhammad Ali's lawyer that the minister would be removed from the New York temple because he had been stealing funds. Farrakhan was irate, not so much because of the plotting going on around him, but because "this is a lost-found [a black who was not in the Nation] telling me what's going to happen to me in the Nation for which I worked night and day with my Lord to build."[56]

The final straw for Chicago came in May, when *Sepia* magazine published a five-page article about the NOI's future that called Wallace "passive," "colorless," and looking like a "mild-mannered postal clerk"—and a seven-page article devoted exclusively to Farrakhan, the "miracle man of the Muslims": "He's a better orator than the late Dr. Martin Luther King Jr. He sings better than Marvin Gaye. He's a better writer than Norman Mailer. He dresses better than Walt Frazier. He's more of a diplomat than Henry Kissinger. And he's prettier than Muhammad Ali. . . . A legend in his time, more than surpassing in dynamism and charisma all the claims for the late Malcolm X."[57]

In a further insult to Wallace, an editor's note cited Farrakhan as the Nation's savior: "Many in[side] and outside the Muslim organization . . . see the future growth of the Nation revolving around the man who is considered the most dynamic personality to emerge in its history."[58]

Chicago was not pleased, but Farrakhan was too potent a personality to fire outright. Even worse, getting rid of him barely four months after Elijah's death and on the brink of Wallace's housecleaning of the NOI might have incited mutiny in the Nation's ranks. Instead, Wallace figured out a way to keep a close eye on him, while bringing him down a few notches. In late June, Farrakhan was transferred to Chicago, where he became Wallace's special "ambassador." Two facets of the new arrangement were kept quiet. To show Farrakhan who controlled the money, Wallace gave him fifty thousand dollars, "for the many years of hard work rendered to the Nation." A few weeks later, Farrakhan bought a brick house in Chicago's upscale Beverly neighborhood. And to show Farrakhan who controlled the power, Wallace made him minister of a new temple housed in a "little ghetto walk-up near the Cabrini-Green housing projects with rats and roaches. Wallace was saying, 'Let's see who's top banana here.'"[59]

The almost palpable irony was that Farrakhan, the NOI traditionalist, had been designated to be the mouthpiece for the reformers who were trashing Elijah's creation. Within weeks after assuming Elijah's mantle, Wallace had begun dismantling his father's orthodoxy: No more hate. No more corruption. Not even a dress code anymore. Out went the required jacket and tie for men and the neck-to-ankle dresses for women. Explained Farrakhan, the dutiful spokesman, "It doesn't matter what a man wears or how long his hair is. If he wants to wear a beard, let him wear it. It is what is in his head and in his heart that counts."[60]

For Elijah's end-of-days imagery—the Mother Plane that would vanquish the wicked whites as it saved the blessed blacks—Wallace substituted a nonseparatist vision: there was, indeed, a wheel inside another wheel, but the smaller wheel was the Nation of Islam, while the larger wheel was the world community. Smoking and dancing were allowed for the first time at an NOI event, a $100,000 reception the Nation threw for Muhammad Ali. For the politically loaded term "black," Wallace substituted "Bilalian," in honor of Bilal, a slave whom Muhammad appointed to call the faithful to prayer. He renamed the Harlem temple after Malcolm X, whom Farrakhan had called a cheat, a liar, a hypocrite.[61]

The secrecy shrouding the Nation's worth evaporated when Wallace announced that its assets totaled $46 million. In place of the system whereby each temple set its own salary standards, ministers were put on salaries of $150–300 a week. Alluding to the Nation's business policies that had engendered crime and thuggery among the ordinary members and high living among the leaders, Wallace removed ministers from business operations, where they had become "desperate in their attempts to keep money flowing to Chicago."[62]

Next came blows to the very theological and political heart of the Nation. Wallace dropped demands for a separate state and stopped running the laundry list of the Nation's political demands in every issue of *Muhammad Speaks*: American support for up to twenty-five years for an autonomous, black-only territory seeking to develop self-sufficiency; exempting blacks from all taxes until they were accorded equal justice; and equal but separate schools for blacks.[63]

Wallace demoted his father as "the last Messenger of Allah," for he "had not been speaking in the theological spirit of the Quran and Bible." He put whites on a par with blacks: "From now on, whites will be considered fully human"; "I'm not calling . . . [whites] 'devils.' I'm calling the mind that has ruled those people and you 'devil.' It ruled them for their glory and it ruled you for your shame." Then came the biggest shock of all: whites could now join the Nation.[64]

And finally, on October 18, 1976, the Nation of Islam, under the stewardship of Elijah Muhammad's seventh child, ceased to exist. Christening his organization the World Community of al-Islam in the West, Wallace aligned it squarely within the orthodox, nonracist, non-anti-white world of the broadest current of contemporary Islam: "We're a . . . community that encompasses everybody. We have Caucasians and Orientals who are members and we are all just Muslims."[65]

In Chicago, Farrakhan's name was changed to Abdul Haleem Farrakhan, and he was given a one-hundred-dollar raise above the three hundred dollars he was getting in New York. "But then they stopped me from preaching, thinking I would just sit around until I ran out of gas." Of Wallace's denigrations of his father, Farrakhan privately cautioned him, as one might warn a kid brother: "Malcolm made that mistake. You got a short track record. You just got started. If you attack your father, who everyone's faith is in, the people will go back to the world. Leave your father alone, and go on and do what you have to do."[66]

After Wallace had spoken to the Fruit of Islam at Farrakhan's New York temple in January 1974, the minister had urged the men, "Don't be afraid to reach out for new knowledge. Don't be like the worm that's afraid of the light and wants to keep his head in the darkness." But now, caught between father and son, Farrakhan was becoming wormlike himself, "losing the spirit. Everyday, I'm slipping further, trying to preach what Wallace preached. Maybe this was what the Messenger was leading us to: the practice of the Koran like it's practiced over there [in the Middle East]. I'm trying to reason this out every day. Mean to tell me for twenty years I've been preaching lies? I just shut my mouth."[67]

On the rare occasions when he did talk publicly, Farrakhan did a credible job of explaining Wallace's apostasies, of camouflaging his contempt for them—and of currying favor with Wallace, calling him "the wisest one among us" and scolding unnamed "writers who were amazed and angered at the smooth transition of power in the Nation of Islam. . . . [They] have created a power struggle with their pens. We laugh at their futile attempt like it is a joke."[68]

To explain Wallace's shift toward traditional Islam, Farrakhan told journalists that Elijah Muhammad had

recognized that white America had a serious problem. And that problem was that we had been overtly, systematically and subliminally taught to hate the blackness of our skin, the kinkiness of our hair and our roots and culture in Africa.

So he started where the problem was then, with skin. And he made us proud of our blackness and proud of our heritage. And he made us desire to love ourselves and do something constructive for ourselves. . . .

But Islam is a universal creed. And the Honorable Wallace D. Muhammad realizing that blackness, if taken to the extreme, would turn inward and become self-destructive, brought to us the universal message of the Prophet Muhammad, the universal message of the Quran, which elevated the community from nationalist standpoint to the universal creed of Islam.[69]

It even fell upon Farrakhan to exhume Malcolm, who had been "worthy of death" just a decade before. Now Malcolm was a martyr and a prophet, a true voice of true Islam who "was ahead of his time. . . . [He] began to see that all human beings can become one under Islam. . . . Malcolm died developing the universality of the creed of Islam. . . . Wallace D. Muhammad is moving a community along the same path that Malcolm traveled. . . . Just as we didn't understand Malcolm's growth, . . . many people don't understand the growth and development within the World Community of al-Islam."[70]

In time, Farrakhan endowed Malcolm with a Jesus-like aura. He had died so that others might live and to suffer for their sins, to atone for their trespasses. And Farrakhan, who had beat the drums for Malcolm's downfall, was emerging as a direct beneficiary of Malcolm's assassination, even if he was tardy acknowledging his debt:

When . . . [Malcolm] left the movement and began to . . . attack the moral character of the late Honorable Elijah Muhammad, . . . I turned away from Malcolm. Only later did I learn what Malcolm knew ten years before me: That I had to walk in his shoes to understand where he was coming from. And God has blessed me to walk in the shoes of Malcolm X . . . to be scorned by my own Muslim brothers. To be suspect because of a growing popularity, as was Malcolm. To be undermined and vil-ified as was Malcolm. The only thing I don't want to repeat is the end of Malcolm. And in my last conversation with the late Mal-colm X, he said to me, "Brother, my enemies are going to be your enemies. And I wish it was you setting an example for me instead of me setting an example for you." So if I make it, it will be because Malcolm died that I might live.[71]

But shoved to the sidelines of Wallace's organization, dis-graced and embittered, Farrakhan "began to hate religion. I got so stretched out. I couldn't preach for the father and the son at the same time. I had to make a decision between *that* father and *that* son. It was killing me."[72]

In seventeen months, Wallace Muhammad, in a move as swift and shrewd as that of any CEO, had moved the Nation of Islam from Islam's theological fringe to its center. His business empire was selling off its many properties. He had shifted the NOI from being racially separatist to racially inclusive, and from being a political powderkeg to a political irrelevancy. Wallace's father had fashioned a *political* movement: "It is far more important to teach separation of the blacks and whites in America than prayer." But Wallace—spiritual, apolitical, steeped in the Islam of the Middle East—was fashioning a *religious* movement: "I am a religious man and a religious leader. I try to represent the reli-gion the way the prophets represented religion."[73]

Inevitably, there were deep grumblings about Wallace among some Nation veterans—and even among outsiders. Jesse Jack-son, who had never belonged but had been close to Elijah, told a friend, "Wallace has buried his father too quick and too deep." But as late as May 1977, an increasingly distraught, dissipated Farrakhan was publicly toeing the party line. What Wallace had

wrought, he explained, was part of a logical, inevitable equilib-
rium: "Almighty God had ordained that everything must evolve.
. . . White people were doped up on a high of white supremacy
and black people were doped up on a low of black inferiority.
Elijah [Muhammad] brought it all back into balance. He just
said that the black man is God and the white man is the devil.
So he applied an upper to the downer and a downer to the
upper."[74]

Around this time, Farrakhan needed some "uppers" himself.
He was sleepwalking, going through the motions, inert: "People
looked at me and said, 'That nigger's gone.' Some of the Bilalians
who wanted to kill me . . . said, 'He's already dead.'" In classes in
the Koran and Arabic prayers in Chicago for former NOI ministers, Farrakhan "was in a daze. He appeared to be like a terrified individual." At a conference sponsored by the Congressional Black Caucus in Washington, Farrakhan ran into Askia
Muhammad, the former editor of *Muhammad Speaks*, who was
"talking with Louis Martin, Jimmy Carter's majordomo for black
affairs. I tried to introduce them, but Farrakhan was in a daze. He
wasn't really present. He was really spaced, and he didn't com-
prehend where he was and what's going on. He was out to
lunch."[75]

"Lunch" began to end for Farrakhan in September 1977,
when he preached his last sermon under Wallace. In Temple No.
2 in Chicago, Elijah's old temple and the flagship of the old NOI,
Farrakhan told Wallace to his face, "You got a nerve not wanting
to speak . . . [your father's] name, and *he* built this house. He
gave you everything you have." Three months later, Farrakhan
formally left the World Community of al-Islam in the West and,
once again, stood "proudly on the platform of the Honorable
Elijah Muhammad." Wallace's religious universalism had lulled
him to "sleep." Now God had awakened him, and he was "back
at . . . [his] post," espousing the gospel of separatism, black

divinity, and white deviltry, as if Elijah had never departed. Privately, Farrakhan told a fellow minister, "I won't be a prostitute for anybody anymore. Why should I do it for anybody else when I can do it for myself?"[76]

There are at least two unconfirmed tales about Farrakhan's plans immediately after leaving Wallace. Both involve trying to reenter show business. In one account, he hopped on a westward-bound train, planning to resume his calypso career in Hollywood. En route, he read *This Is the One*, a celebration of Elijah Muhammad by Bernard Cushmeer, who was the Nation's master theologian. Cushmeer's arguments about Elijah Muhammad's divine mission persuaded Farrakhan to revive the Nation of Islam.

Cushmeer disputes that Farrakhan intended to return to the entertainment world, but he does confirm that his book was instrumental in bolstering Farrakhan's yearning to return to Elijah Muhammad's original teachings. According to Cushmeer, he gave Farrakhan the manuscript of *This Is the One* during a meeting with him in the restaurant of a Hollywood hotel in September 1977. Farrakhan took it to his hotel room to read. Cushmeer visited him briefly later that day, twice the next day, and two days later around 11 A.M., when Farrakhan looked "new" and "refreshed. . . . He glowed. He also looked pained. He also exuded determination."[77]

So, just as Jesus had risen two days after his crucifixion, Farrakhan, too, had risen from the hell of Wallace's teaching's on the second day after first meeting with Cushmeer.

The other fable is that, when Farrakhan left Wallace, he initially intended to make a film about Malcolm X in which he himself would have the title role. Financing was almost secured from the Libyan dictator Muammar Khaddafi when the deal fell through—and Farrakhan's only alternative was to resuscitate the Nation of Islam.

Upon hearing that Farrakhan had jumped ship, Wallace sighed that the minister "didn't quit the movement, just the leadership," and that he had been so eager to keep Farrakhan in the organization that he had asked him to head the mosque in Harlem. Of rumored threats on Farrakhan's life, Wallace told his corps of ministers, "We will not act physically against anybody because they don't accept what we represent. If they represent something that influences the minds of this community or seeks to establish the things I've been trying hard to steer them from, then I will attack it."[78]

Despite Wallace's guaranty of physical safety, Farrakhan laid low for about three months. Then, during a speech in March at Baruch College in New York, he announced that he would resurrect the Nation of Islam, physically and theologically. Integration had failed, blacks' condition was worsening, black-on-black crime was rising. If blacks kept "singing the lullaby of integration, [then] we will find ourselves dead under the heels of racism in the United States."[79]

New mythologies were quickly constructed to prove that Farrakhan's resurrected Nation of Islam had been preordained by Elijah Muhammad. Farrakhan recalled that Muhammad had confided to him in 1972 that "the Nation is going to take a dive for the second time. . . . But, don't worry, brother. It will be rebuilt and will never fall again. . . . Go exactly as you see me go and do exactly as you see me do. . . . [Y]ou must practice righteousness or they [the enemy] will piece you in two."[80]

Another time, Elijah reportedly told Farrakhan, "I'm going away to study. I will be gone for approximately three years. What I have given you is just a wake-up message. Don't change the teachings while I'm gone. If you are faithful, I will reveal the new teachings through you on my return."[81]

Later Elijah told Farrakhan, "You can sit over the Nation as the father when I'm gone," and, "As Allah made me to take His place among the people, I am making you to take my place." But Elijah cautioned that Farrakhan would "fall" from grace, only to be redeemed so his rise from disgrace would parallel the rise of the fallen Nation of Islam.[82]

The problem with confirming whether any of these conversations between Elijah and Farrakhan ever occurred is that Farrakhan and others didn't mention them publicly until 1979. But even if they had been videotaped and stored in the National Archives in Washington for posterity, revealing them about eighteen months after Farrakhan left Wallace's group had intimations of being no more than a patently bald strategy to prove that Farrakhan, not Wallace, was the rightful heir to the throne.

Meanwhile, despite Wallace's attempt to lend a patina of civility to the schism between him and Farrakhan, his troops were positioning themselves to prove that *their* man had been sanctioned not only by Elijah but—even better—by Fard Muhammad himself. They recited the NOI's lore that Master Fard had predicted, upon Wallace's birth, that this seventh child of Elijah would succeed the Messenger. Some took this as gospel, some as fable. But all, even Wallace, invested the prediction with a majestic, seductive magic, an allure of the unknown, a taste of preordination. Wallace himself attributed the appeal of the myth to "the power of mystery," although he admitted that

as a child, I didn't take the prophecy seriously. But whenever I was misbehaving, not being the example my mother thought I should be, she reminded me . . . that I was supposed to follow in the footsteps of my father. Growing up, I was quiet, shy. I spent most of my time thinking. My brothers and sisters seemed to be more at ease with their lives. My father used to say, "You know why that boy is different? Because Allah [Fard Muhammad] was really teaching me when he was born. He was filling my head up with wisdom, and it went right into this boy's blood."[83]

Wallace's camp also circulated posthumous dispatches from inside Elijah's mansion suggesting that the Messenger had given his son a mandate to continue the lineage. In 1974, after Elijah reinstated Wallace as a minister, the Messenger gave his son free rein in his preaching, letting him wander from orthodox Nation of Islam teachings toward orthodox Islamic teachings.

"I was free to propagate and preach as my own wisdom dictated," recalled Wallace. "I would actually test the support for me from the Honorable Elijah Muhammad. Nobody else was restricting my movement; I answered only to the Honorable Elijah Muhammad. I would say things I knew were different from some of the things the people had been taught under the leadership of Elijah Muhammad. . . . He never called me in and said what I was teaching was causing problems [or to] slow up or go in another direction."[84]

In 1974, officers of the Fruit of Islam played a tape of Wallace's preaching for Elijah, who had not heard his son at the pulpit. According to Wallace, "He called me over and played it while I was present. He jumped up out of his seat and applauded and said, 'My son's got it! My son can go anywhere on earth and preach."[85]

But Askia Muhammad, then the editor of *Muhammad Speaks* and a witness to that event, remembers it differently:

They played the tape, and Elijah asked me first what I thought of Wallace's lecture. I said it was "food for thought." It was intellectual. I didn't know which way to go with this. I mean, who was I to answer? I was just some employee sitting at the table. A guy who can't get a pay raise. I can't do anything for myself, let alone take on one of the big lions. They went around the table, and there was a big fight between Wallace and one of the ministers, who accused him of deviating from the [official] teaching. Wallace jumped on him immediately, calling him bad names, saying "You never believed in my father's teaching, always undermining him, going against what he teaches." They slugged it out. It was a donnybrook. Each one gave as good as he received.

Finally, Mr. Muhammad said, "Wallace would be a very good spiritual minister if he would only listen to me. If he would only follow me." He didn't take sides. And he didn't indulge Wallace. But he did say he could be better.[86]

The battle lines were drawn: on one side, Wallace, the conservative radical, navigating his father's legacy toward traditions that had eluded Elijah. On the other side, Farrakhan, the radical conservative, cleaving to the ways of the past, the NOI's past. Two disciples professing to be the rightful son of their master, squabbling over their spiritual inheritance, much as Jacob and Esau had squabbled over their birthright from their father Isaac. But at least Jacob and Esau had come from the same bloodline. Amid the collision of truths after Farrakhan's split from Wallace, the one consistent casualty would be truth itself as each camp claimed it was the rightful—and only—heir to the gospel of the Honorable Elijah Muhammad. Each brandished the blessings of the Messenger as enthusiastically as he attacked the other as an impostor.

At the bottom of this religious war, essentially two questions remained: Who was the *true* son of Elijah Muhammad? And was the pretender the equivalent of the anti-Christ? The answers were theologically convoluted, if not downright bizarre. They also bordered on the oedipal. But by laying claim to the middle ground of Islam, Wallace gave himself a broad potential audience: he could recruit from NOI veterans who were exhausted by its bloodbaths and scams, or from those who had never joined the Nation because of its very reputation for bloodbaths and scams—and the peculiar spin it gave to Islam. Farrakhan, on the other hand, with Elijah Muhammad as his guide and Fard Muhammad as his partner, went into the night. Away from Wallace. Away from heresy. First, he had self-resurrected himself from the "grave" into which "Satan"—in the clever guise of Wallace, a "mild-mannered postal clerk"—had sent him. Now he was resurrecting the Nation. By laying claim to the gospel of Elijah Muhammad—word for word and thought for thought—he could cloak himself much as the Messenger had: as the only black man who spoke unpalatable black truths to brutish white power—and in time, as the most fearless black man in America.[87]

VII

One Nation Under Louis

A new nation, which Farrakhan set out to create, needs many things:

Land and Sovereignty

Farrakhan started out with a small parcel by mortgaging his home to buy a funeral home on Chicago's Seventy-ninth Street. Here he established his first temple and the offices of *The Final Call*, the revived and renamed NOI newspaper. The ultimate dream, of course, was the same as Elijah Muhammad's: a separate state or territory maintained and supplied by "our former slave masters" for about two decades "until we are able to produce and supply our own needs."[1]

People

Only two high NOI officials joined Farrakhan when he broke
away from Wallace. Farrakhan traveled around the country, lec‑
turing, and hectoring; launching NOI study groups that even‑
tually expanded into full temples; enticing some veterans of the
old Nation from Wallace's diligently Islamic group, where they
were evidently miserable. By 1981, six thousand people
attended the reborn NOI's first Savior's Day—and Farrakhan's
Nation clearly had a sizable population.

Mythology

An era of miracles and wonders, of new life and rebirth, was
about to unfold, since the twenty-five-thousand-year lifespan of
the Koran would soon expire: "The Messenger was telling us a
new book was coming. We are about to walk out of the Koran.
We are about to fulfill it."[2]

In the new mythology (which matched the old one in sheer
vindictiveness), Wallace was a "cheap hypocrite" who had
plunged the Nation into darkness; a "thief who stole the house
and the affection of the people for his father for himself"; "a
murderer who killed the spirit of life in the people whom God's
messenger had raised to life."[3]

A new trinity was cobbled together. Fard Muhammad was
still Allah—and would never be dislodged from that slot. Far‑
rakhan was either the new Peter—the apostle to whom Jesus
said, "You are Peter, and on this rock I will build my church"—
or a long-awaited prophet. According to Jabril Muhammad, the
NOI pamphleteer formerly known as Bernard Cushmeer who
had encouraged Farrakhan to leave Wallace, Elijah Muhammad
had told him that certain "wise Jews recognize . . . Farrakhan as
the herald of the Messiah as they recognize one of their sons. . . .
The Almighty promised through . . . the prophets that what we

are seeing and experiencing would take place at this time. These promises include the coming and the work of the Honorable Louis Farrakhan."[4]

And Elijah Muhammad graduated from being a mere Messenger (or, on a much more ordinary plane, from being surrogate father to Farrakhan and Malcolm and hundreds of thousands of black men whose true dads had failed them) to being the Son, the Christ, the Messiah. As Farrakhan proclaimed, "The One you've been looking for was in your midst for forty years, and you didn't recognize him."[5]

Elijah had been lifted Christ-like into the heavens, where he tended to his flocks below. "I know you think Elijah is dead," commiserated Farrakhan at his first Savior's Day as prince of the new Nation. "I'm here to tell you that he is as alive as you sitting right down there in that seat. Not only is he alive and well, but he's in power now because I am his witness. You thought you killed him. Now die in your rage because Elijah is back. . . . He and God are together and his return is imminent. . . . I'm telling you that one of your brothers has been exalted to the right hand of God to control the forces of nature."

When Elijah fell, the Nation fell. When Elijah rose, the Nation rose: "If he's not God, *you* can't be. If he's not resurrected, *you* can't be. If he's not raised back from the dead, there's *no* hope. You can't *ever* be raised."[6]

Elijah had not died naturally, Farrakhan revealed, but fell to a conspiracy patched together by the U.S. government, which had plotted to destroy any powerful black leader; by unnamed members of Muhammad's family, whose motives Farrakhan did not explain (but which presumably stemmed from what he had long claimed was their grab for power and wealth); and by Arabs, who had been peeved that Elijah was not an orthodox Muslim—and who were furious when, according to Farrakhan, Elijah turned down a $20-million bribe from them to "send some of his students in the University of Islam to study in Medina and Riyadh and Mecca."[7]

Farrakhan's source for this conspiracy of devils? A black man who had heard about it from a white prostitute who had heard about it from a white doctor who had hired her for an "orgy" in Phoenix, Arizona.[8]

And Farrakhan's proof that Elijah had been resurrected? "Exhume the body and prove me a liar."[9]

There were no takers.

Discipline

The old ways weren't necessarily the good ways. The Fruit of Islam had run amok; the inmates had taken over the asylum. The FOI under Farrakhan would still be an "army," but "not an army of gangsters . . . with the face of a thug." The old Fruit did not consider itself "an army of saviors," but an

> army of killers. And that's why if you didn't have no devil in front of you, several of you turned on each other, threatening each other, jumping in each other's chest. . . . When a brother had fornicated with a Muslim sister, the law said put him out, but the brothers . . . wanted to add some of their own self into the punishment and they met him at the house with lead pipes and beat his head into a pulp because they didn't really respect the mercy in the law of God. They wanted to be a law unto themselves. And before you knew it, . . . it was easy for a brother to kill another brother.

Never again would the Fruit tolerate "little pseudo-cleaned up criminals. We are righteous men, with a righteous purpose. . . . In the name of Allah, we will whip the hell out of any that come against us, short or tall, armed or unarmed. But we got to be right with our God."[10]

Recognition

In some ways, despite his talk about love for blacks, Elijah Muhammad was removed from his own people: he spoke to blacks on *his* turf and on *his* terms. Despite one momentary slip of the tongue in 1966 about forging an anti-slum "common front" with Martin Luther King, Muhammad's centripetal world brooked no alliances and no compromises. In return, much of the black world wanted little to do with him and his Nation, with its image of thuggery and its mythology of supremacy. But to the more polished, more articulate, more chameleonlike, more "presentable" Farrakhan came what rarely, if ever, had come to Muhammad: invitations to speak to mainstream black forums. In such settings, Farrakhan tempered his rhetoric, but not his essential message. He omitted talk of "devils" and Yacub, but rarely wandered from the Nation's doctrine of tribal cohesion, self-improvement, and fierce suspicion of white America.

At a 1979 conference called by the National Black United Fund, Farrakhan scolded "proud, stuffed-shirt, intellectual, . . . bourgeois" blacks who had become "house niggers" in industry or government, where they were so intoxicated with their proximity to power that they couldn't "see the devious deceit, the treachery and the trickery that lie behind a [Caucasian] smile."[11]

Then, in what could have been a white liberal's appeal to guilt and conscience, he scolded his audience for forsaking the "wretched of the earth": "Come down from your false mountain that makes you unjustly proud of your little accomplishments and know that until all have gotten out of the valley, you have not reached the mountain."[12]

In 1983, when invited to speak at the Lincoln Memorial for the twentieth anniversary of Reverend King's March on Washington (which a snickering Malcolm X had called the "Farce on Washington"), Farrakhan metamorphosed, on the same steps where King had spoken, into a tolerant ecumenicist, indeed, almost into the spiritual son of King himself: "No longer can we be separate, you there and me here, or me here and you there, you Muslim, you Christian, you Baptist, you Catholic. We cannot tolerate any longer these artificial barriers that divide us as a people."[13]

By listing faiths and calling for unity, Farrakhan echoed King's similar cataloging in 1963 for "*all* God's children, black men and white men, Jews and gentiles, Protestants and Catholics, . . . to join hands." Farrakhan also honored the fundamentals of America by urging the country to be faithful to its "creed that says all people are created equally," a creed that he didn't bother to say was nullified by the NOI's own theology. Finally, Farrakhan shanghaied the last words of King's 1963 speech—"Free at last! Free at last! Thank God Almighty, we are free at last!"—transmuting them into "Free at last! Free at last! Thank God Almighty, we have united and made freedom a reality at last."[14]

As a speech, it didn't have the rolling majesty and the fine poetry of King's oration; nor could it match the reverend's mighty rhythms and caressing crescendos. As dogma, it may not have pleased Elijah Muhammad. But as strategy, Farrakhan's 1983 speech was a stroke of communal genius, sweeping him into the tribal fold in the guise of an accommodationist and a moderate who belied the image of Nation of Islam members being unstinting, combative ideologues.

Legitimacy

The squabbling between Wallace and Farrakhan put the legitimacy of Elijah's throne into very serious dispute. Just two weeks after Wallace's coronation, Farrakhan had said the NOI's new head was "divinely prepared to do a divine work." Now Wallace's destruction of the Nation made "the work of Malcolm look like baby work. . . . Family don't make you right. Family don't give you no power. It's right that makes you right. Truth that makes you right." And Wallace, ordinarily calm and self-effacing, raged across the gulf between them: "You're trying to get yourself a following. To pay your phone bill. To get a new house. You are against any progress. And [you] lie . . . and pretend to be something you're not and even destroy the truth that I bring to get what you want—[which is] material trash."[15]

To Farrakhan's supporters, Wallace would always be the pretender to the crown. To them, Farrakhan was the Messenger's *sole* earthly apostle. To refuse Farrakhan was to refuse God. To reject Farrakhan was to reject life itself: "I, Farrakhan, have no power to give life. However, the voice of Elijah Muhammad coming through me is giving life to the entire Nation. I warn you that when you turn me down and refuse this truth, you are turning down the Lord, the Savior, the Messiah and the Deliverer that you seek."[16]

But being the voice of Elijah was not enough. Farrakhan cagily surrounded himself with the next best thing to the physical Elijah: the Messenger's six extracurricular "wives" and the thirteen children they had had with the Messenger. Tynnetta Muhammad, one of the "wives," began writing a column on arcane numerology in *The Final Call* and books and pamphlets exalting Farrakhan's "gifts of divine wisdom," "eloquence of Solomon," and "moral purity and uprightness." Kamal Muhammad, a son of Elijah via Ola Muhammad, became the NOI's national secretary. Abdullah Muhammad, a son of Elijah via June Muhammad, became a minister on the East Coast and would be brought out occasionally to lacerate Jews for their "wicked machinations and manipulations." And Ishmael Muhammad, one of the four children Tynnetta had with Elijah, became assistant minister at the Chicago temple. In time, Ishmael's rhetorical flourishes and cadences so well mimicked Farrakhan's that if he was simply heard, not seen, he could be mistaken for Farrakhan.[17]

The final stage in the Nation's rebirth was to resurrect it as Farrakhan said Elijah had been resurrected—physically. So he took advantage of protracted legal bickering over Elijah's estate between Wallace and Herbert Muhammad and Elijah's illegitimate children—and of Wallace's divestment of the old Nation empire. In 1986, Farrakhan purchased Elijah's former Hyde Park mansion to use as the new NOI's "Black House" as well as his own official home—"the equivalent for us of 1600 Pennsylvania Avenue." Farrakhan compared acquiring the mansion to Muhammad's return to the holy city of Mecca. And in September 1988, Farrakhan's NOI bought the flagship of Elijah's network of temples, Mosque No. 2 at 7351 South Stony Island Avenue in Chicago, for $2.1 million.[18]

Enemies

Finally, the prophet was no more in a strange land: he had arrived home, come to God and come to himself. The "dry bones" of the Book of Ezekiel had "come together, bone by bone," clothed with flesh, breathing with life. But these were not the "bones" of the Jews, as Ezekiel had prophesied: forsaking and forgetting their God, Jews had forever lost their place at the front of the line of divine delight to another people—to Farrakhan's people:

> Jews had their day with God and didn't do what they were supposed to do. . . . God loved Jews so well [that] He kept spanking them, sending them a prophet, bringing them back. Spanking them, sending them a prophet, bringing them back. His love for Israel is clear to me. . . . However, it's very important that we study how Jews lived up to their covenant relationship with God.

Jews are the most enlightened community, bar none. They have, however, a duty to enlighten their brethren. If they fail, they break the covenant. . . . Jews had the prophets, so they know the way of God. But they didn't teach us, and neither did the gentiles. When we were let out of slavery, we were not given anything of substance, so we could not make an independent beginning. Now God has intervened to civilize us and help us in the way that we need help. . . . Jews know I don't hate them, but I think they fear what is in my mouth; that it will awaken my people and show why they don't have a covenant with God today. . . .

That's where the real argument is [with Jews and other whites]. It ain't racial. It's theological. . . . We're not chosen because we're black and not because we're righteous. We're black all right, but we're surely not righteous. We're chosen because, as scripture says, "I chose you out of the furnace of affliction." Here's a people afflicted like we've been afflicted [and] suffered like we've suffered [in slavery]. If we purify after suffering like this, I don't believe we could do to white people what white people have done to us. . . . If we fail in that duty, then we've broken our relationship with God—and he finds somebody else.[19]

This ambivalence about Jews was not new to the Nation of Islam. Early on, Elijah Muhammad had admired Jews' "psychology" and business acumen, and the NOI had sympathized with them after being "roasted like peanuts" during the Holocaust. But they were also slick and cunning, draining money from black ghettos with their stores and roach-infested slum buildings, conning vast sums from other whites, because one lone Jew was "smarter than a roomful of 'white men.' He can spend a quarter and make a million dollars. Or he can rob you blind while he's telling you a . . . joke." Malcolm X was especially trenchant about Jews' skills "sap[ping] the very life-blood of the so-called Negro to maintain . . . Israel, its armies and its continued aggression against our brothers in the East. . . . Israel is just an international poor house which is maintained by money sucked from the poor suckers in America."[20]

But Elijah's and Malcolm's gripes against Jews were mostly economic and political. Farrakhan raised their complaints to the rarefied level of theology, a move that further cast him onto the oddball fringe of religion. Even the Roman Catholic Church, for centuries one of the more strident voices of the anti-Jewish New Jerusalem, had retreated from the slander of deicide when the Second Vatican Council issued *Nostra Aetate* in 1965, its landmark statement about relating to non-Christians: "What happened in [Christ's] passion cannot be charged against all the Jews, without distinction, then alive, nor against the Jews of today. . . . The Jews should not be represented as rejected by God or accursed." And Pope John Paul II called Jews the "elder brothers" of Christians and affirmed a "respect . . . based on the mysterious link which brings us close together, in Abraham and through Abraham, in God Who chose Israel and brought for the Church from Israel."[21]

By claiming that Christians worshiped a false messiah, that Muslims venerated the wrong prophet, that Jews were no more God's own people—by declaring his doctrine to be the one solid link in the Abrahamic chain that bound all three faiths and people—Farrakhan alienated in one fell swoop hundreds of millions of people, a feat that should not be underestimated. But it was his fierce, heated bickering with Jews that, starting in 1984, turned into one of the most rancorous, bitter, noisy, and persistent feuds in public life, one that Farrakhan smarted from in a very personal, fatherly way: "You think I liked having my kids walking past the homes of neighbors who have read all those nasty things about me in newspapers?" And one that widened the already broad, deep, increasingly impenetrable chasm between black and Jew—once close allies, now wary sparring partners in a dance from which neither side much benefited.[22]

VIII

"Bloodsuckers" Beware

Two months into 1984—Orwell's year—blacks and Jews, whose once-solid alliance had been sorely tattered since the late 1960s, would be at each other's throats once again. And Farrakhan's fame would far eclipse what he already enjoyed in some segments of the black community. Hereafter, the name Farrakhan would invariably summon—subliminally, if not consciously—an image of a very angry black man clashing with deeply offended, often frightened Jews. Using boilerplate anti-Jewish imagery—"bloodsuckers," "Jews control the media," Israel is "an outlaw" nation, a people "cloaking themselves in the robes of God, but [who] are in fact members of the synagogue of Satan"—all of which Farrakhan presented as irrefutable "truths,"[1] the NOI leader demonized an entire people, while simultaneously denying he was anti-Semitic:

If by "anti-Semite," you mean that I hate Jews and that I work day and night to destroy Jewish efforts and Jewish progress, then no [I am not one]. If by "anti-Semite," you mean anybody who speaks truth that offends the sensitivity and sensibility of Jews in respect to Israel or Jewish involvement in the slave trade. . . . If I'm dealing in truth, don't call me an "anti-Semite," because I speak the same harsh truths about my own people and our own wickedness against ourselves. But I'm not anti-black.[2]

Indeed, Farrakhan did speak "harsh truths" about blacks:

Look at my people. Drive-by shootings. Carjackings. Is that the work of a righteous people? That's the work of the devil. We have fallen short of the glory of God. My people are not dying from skinheads. They're not dying from the Ku Klux Klan. They're dying from their ignorance and self-hatred that has us destroying one another. We can't blame Jews. We can't blame Koreans or Vietnamese who take money out of our community. . . . We have to blame ourselves, because we've been offered the chance to go to the best schools to get an education, but we have not come out and used that education to provide the goods and education that our own communities need.[3]

A creative, if perverse, illogic was undeniably at work here: greedy, clever, tenacious Jews control media, finance, entertainment, sports, slum housing, and ghetto grocery stores—yet blacks "can't blame Jews" for their plight. "Blame" was first ascribed to Jews, then quickly shifted to blacks. It was a shell game of the first order, played for the souls of America's thirty million blacks.

Farrakhan also claimed, soothingly and reassuringly, that Jews had "special" qualities that blacks should emulate: cohesiveness, business savvy, time-tested survival skills—everything necessary for a dispossessed people to maintain tribal affinity in a hostile world. At the same time, he invented or subscribed to new canards, staggering with their bravura, numbing with their effrontery. Jews injected black babies with the AIDS virus. Jews masterminded the slave trade. "International bankers," a classic synonym for Jews, plunged America into World War I by lying about the *Lusitania* being sunk by a German submarine, they financed "all sides" in World War II and later engineered the ever-ballooning federal debt. The fabrications reached their fantastic peak when an NOI spokesman blamed Jews for "the hole in the ozone layer." Just why blacks should emulate a people capable of such deviltry was never explained.[4]

As a defensive reflex, Jews pulled out their worst curse. By equating Farrakhan with Hitler, they elevated him to the ranks of the world's worst mass murderers and obscured, with the infectious ugliness of anything associated with the Third Reich, what Farrakhan was all about and how he could best be met.

Often ignored amid the flak sent up by both sides was that Jews and Farrakhan spoke a different language. Each said they were espousing "truths," but they were truths of different colors. The Jewish truths were linear and historical. Farrakhan's truths, while clothed as historical and verifiable, were emotive truths rooted in the furies of black pain, fueled by the NOI's racial-religious messianism, and stirred by a clever strategy to catapult separatism to the vanguard of the black agenda—and to strike a blow against integration by killing blacks' coalition with Jews, their strongest allies in a world of increasingly fewer allies.

These emotive truths did not absolve Farrakhan of the consequences of the moral fictions he was dispensing, for as James Baldwin wrote in *The Fire Next Time*: "I . . . must oppose any attempt that Negroes may make to do to others what has been done to them. I think I know . . . the spiritual wasteland to which that road leads. . . . Whoever debases others is debasing himself. That is not a mystical statement but a most realistic one

... and I would not like to see Negroes ever arrive at so wretched a condition." But in the end, Farrakhan's framing of his words about Jews as a response to the pain of his people lent him an authority that many blacks interpreted as "integrity," and that others deciphered as outright demagoguery.[5]

Despite the clamor he set off, Farrakhan repeatedly tried to shake off charges that he was engaged in Jew-baiting. Yet the pattern for these attempts was invariably the same: each quickly deteriorated and ultimately did him little good with the very people to whom he said he was reaching out. He would start off being conciliatory, even compassionate, and adopt a stance with which civil rights and human relations commissions could not argue. Then, segueing into his standard repertoire of grievance and gripe, he would demand that whites suffer the same injustices that had been inflicted upon blacks in the past, that they, too, know the pains and the furies of contempt and hate. Farrakhan's was the posture of machismo that was not retractable, of racial bravery that vitiated the original feints of compassion and empathy.

For instance, during a three-and-a-half-hour interview with me in his Hyde Park mansion in August 1994—an interview that ran the full course of Farrakhan's anger and frustrations with Jews and his ostensible yearning for a truce with them—he said appeasingly, "It is improper for any of us to mock your culture or to mock a physical characteristic that you have no control over . . . the shape of your nose or the shape of mine." But then he swung full force into a litany of wrongs against blacks:

Have you ever seen Nigger Brand canned goods? Have you ever read *Little Black Sambo*? Have you ever seen Step'n Fetchit? I have. I read in the *Congressional Record* the words of Georgia Senator Herman Talmadge and Mississippi Senator Theodore Bilbao calling us "burr-headed nigger." . . . The Torah says, "As thou hast done, so it shall be done unto you." How will you know the evil of your own words and actions unless God allows you in another generation to feel and sense and hear some of the same things that your people have put on my people? . . . You should know how we felt all these years.[6]

To Farrakhan, morality obeyed its own physics: to every degradation, there was an equal, reverse degradation. So not only were lessons from his "truths" morally indispensable, they were unavoidable forces of nature propelled by the very energy (this time shifted into reverse) that had been generated by whites' degradation of blacks. But as with most physics, Farrakhan's moral universe was a closed universe, with energy being neither created nor depleted, but simply ricocheting from one sector to another, from an absolute good to an absolute bad, and with hardly anyone having the courage, wisdom, or creativity to deflect it, absorb it—and start anew.

The year 1984 started fairly innocuously for Farrakhan. On January 3, he landed at Andrews Air Force Base outside Washington, back from a successful four-day mission to Syria to free a U.S. pilot, Robert O. Goodman. The trip was organized by Jesse Jackson three months into his campaign as the first black presidential candidate. Goodman, a black navy lieutenant, had been downed while on a bombing run over Lebanon, where tens of thousands of American soldiers were trying to prop up a shambles of a government. Two days into the trip, Jackson met with Syrian President Hafez al-Assad at a villa outside Damascus. The next day, Goodman was released.[7]

Farrakhan's presence on the trip—and his relationship with Jackson in general—was barely noted by the press (although his fluent Arabic had impressed Goodman's captors). He was just a throwaway line in the stories about the Goodman trip. No big headlines. No big deal. No big stink. Just a "Black Muslim" leader tagging along on Jackson's mission of mercy. The trip may have raised Jackson's profile with voters, especially blacks, but it did him little good with Jews, who regarded Syria as Israel's most intractable foe.[8]

For years, Jackson and American Jews had viewed each other warily, holding each other at arm's length while intuitively recognizing the need for some kind of mutual accommodation. Jackson, after all, considered himself the rightful heir to Martin Luther King: a student of nonviolence, he was dynamic and able to command vast audiences while other post-King civil rights leaders could barely fill conference rooms. And Jews, who, for ample reason, had long considered themselves to be the mainstay of civil rights in the white world, still wanted to have some influence on civil rights after the King era—and to be seen as colleagues on the road to racial equality.

But Jackson's credentials with Jews were badly soiled. In the early 1970s, he had inaccurately told followers that four out of five of Richard Nixon's top advisers were Jewish, and he blamed the Nixon administration's insensitivity to the poor on the strategists Bob Haldeman and John Erlichman, two gentiles whom he called "German Jews." On CBS's *60 Minutes* in 1979, he insisted that Jewish-controlled industry was keeping blacks from positions of power in the United States. A few weeks later, photos of Jackson warmly embracing the PLO chieftain Yasir Arafat were splashed on front pages around the country. About the same time, Jackson said that anyone "who does not think Arafat is a true hero does not read the situation correctly."[9]

Most Jews cringed when Jackson gave Arafat a bear hug, interpreting it as emblematic of something deeper, scarier. Ascribing black misfortune to sly, manipulative Jews whose influence was *everywhere*, Jackson seemed to be appealing to a baseness unbecoming to a national leader—and stoking the embers of anti-Jewish prejudice. So on November 3, 1983, Rabbi Meir Kahane, a fiery ultra-Zionist whose frequently apocalyptic language resembled Farrakhan's, led a handful of followers to Washington's Convention Hall, where Jackson was announcing his run for the White House. Shouting that Jackson was "an enemy of the Jewish people," fists flew, fights erupted—and the Jews were expelled from the hall.[10]

Then the phrase that almost halted Jackson's campaign in its tracks was discovered, buried in the thirty-ninth paragraph of a February 3 *Washington Post* article about his rocky relations with Jews: "In private conversations with reporters, Jackson has referred to Jews as 'Hymies' and to New York as 'Hymietown.'" Jackson, who usually excelled at words and whose campaign was implicitly predicated on the courage—the *chutzpah*—of a black man running for the White House, quickly did some of the more agile waffling of his long career. Within one week, he went from denying he ever said the offending words ("It simply is not true," on CBS's *Face the Nation* on February 19) to issuing a reluctant apology ("It was wrong," at a synagogue in New Hampshire on February 26).

Farrakhan had been backing Jackson's White House run after discovering, while reviewing Elijah Muhammad's teachings, that the Messenger had not firmly opposed political involvement. Elijah was just weary of whites taking blacks' votes for granted, then selling them out: "If a politician arose among us who was fearless, who would stand up and plead our cause and would not sell us out, that kind of politician deserved and should get the full backing and support of our entire people." So, on February 9, Farrakhan led one thousand blacks to Chicago's city hall, where he registered to vote for the first time.[11]

But by the time Savior's Day arrived in late February, "Hymiegate" had primed journalists to refer to Jackson's campaign in the past tense; the candidate had received more than one hundred death threats, most of which, Farrakhan believed, came from Jews; and the minister was incensed at a dossier on Jackson published by the B'nai B'rith Anti-Defamation League that portrayed Jesse as pro-Palestinian and anti-Semitic. Convinced that Jews were so poisoning the air that they were encouraging attempts on Jackson's life, Farrakhan warned them from the rally's podium, "If you harm this brother, I warn you in the name of Allah, this will be the last . . . [black leader] you harm. We are not making any idle threats. We have no weapons. . . . If you want to defeat him, defeat him at the polls. We can stand to lose an election, but we cannot stand to lose a brother."[12]

The situation quickly escalated. On February 27, the ADL's executive director, Nathan Perlmutter, deplored Farrakhan's "beerhall demagoguery," an obvious allusion to Adolf Hitler's rabble-rousing in Munich in 1923. The next week, Farrakhan claimed that "Israeli hit squads" had been dispatched to the United States to kill Jackson. And on a March 11 radio broadcast, Farrakhan fumed that the only "similarity" between him and Hitler was that both sought to "rais[e] our people up from nothing," a trait that made Hitler "a very great man." Then, addressing Jews with the same rhetoric of violence that he usually reserved for private NOI sessions, Farrakhan asked, "What have I done? Who have I killed? I warn you, be careful, be careful. You're putting yourself in dangerous, dangerous shoes. You have been the killer of all the prophets. Now, if you seek my life, you only show that you are no better than your fathers."[13]

Jews were not the only targets of Farrakhan's ire on the March 11 broadcast. Milton Coleman, the black reporter from the *Washington Post* who had broken the story about Jesse Jackson calling New York "Hymietown," received a tongue-lashing from the minister:

What do you intend to do with Mr. Coleman? At this point, no physical harm. . . . But for now, I'm going to get every church in

Washington, D.C., to put him out. Put him out. Wherever he hits the door, tell him he's not wanted. If he brings his wife with him, tell his wife she can come in if she leaves him. But if she won't leave him, then you go to hell with your husband. That he's a traitor and [if] you love to sleep in the bed with a traitor of your people, then the same punishment that's due that no-good filthy traitor, you get it yourself as his wife. One day soon, we will punish you with death. You say when is that? In sufficient time, we will come to power right inside this country. One day soon.

This is a fitting punishment for dogs. He's a dog. We don't give the bread of Jesus to dogs. We just throw him out with the rest of the dogs.[14]

The comments about Coleman reinforced the notion of Farrakhan's career (and the entire history of the Nation of Islam) as a peculiar marriage of theology, religion, hypernationalism, and hyperloyalty to a supreme leader—and the notion that any deviance from such fealty was met with death. Farrakhan's reputation in this regard had first become fixed in the public's mind with his words against Malcolm X in 1964. But in 1984, Farrakhan denied that he had actually threatened Coleman, and Jesse Jackson, journalists, and academics familiar with Farrakhan attributed the furor to the "hyperbole" that had always suffused the apocalyptic rhetoric of the Nation of Islam. Nevertheless, Milton Coleman was taking no chances: he took Farrakhan's words seriously enough to notify the FBI and the District of Columbia police that threats had been made against him and his family.[15]

The March 11 radio speech incorporated all the trademarks of classic Farrakhan oratory. He placed himself in fine company by saying that Jews, who had killed "all the prophets," were now targeting him. By assuming that Jews sought to take his life—

although there is no evidence that a single Jew had threatened his life or had yet chanted "Death to Farrakhan"—he ascribed motives to them that perhaps sprang from his own wells of prophetic revenge, perhaps from his own courting of martyrdom. And by melding threats to others with predictions about his own violent end, Farrakhan reminded those in the know (and with a very good memory) that he was indeed a most worthy *rhetorical* heir to Elijah Muhammad. In May 1960, for instance, the Messenger had used the same themes—and almost the same words—that Farrakhan had raised when warning Jackson's foes to keep their distance.

"I have it from the mouth of God," revealed Elijah Muhammad, "that the enemy had better try to protect my life and see that I continue to live. Because if anything happens to me, I will be the last one they murder. And if any of my followers are murdered, ten of the enemy's best ones will be murdered."[16]

The threats in the Savior's Day speech and the March 11 radio broadcast, Farrakhan explained almost a decade later, "were really innocuous and were not intended in any way to harm the Jewish community." Instead, he said, Jews had used them as tools to "derail" Jackson's candidacy: "No words of mine used under other circumstances would ever have made the obituary page."[17]

But when asked at a press conference in Washington a month after the radio broadcast whether he truly thought Hitler was "great," he responded, "I don't think you would be talking about Adolf Hitler forty years after the fact if he was some minuscule crackpot that jumped up on the European continent. He was . . . a great man, but also wicked—wickedly great."[18]

Referring to Hitler as "great" twice in the space of a few weeks sealed Farrakhan's fate as the New Demon, the Great Hater, the Next Fuhrer. Further condemning him was a June 1984 statement that Israel will "never have . . . peace, because there can be no peace structured on injustice, lying, and deceit and using the name of God to shield your dirty religion under his holy and righteous name."[19]

Nine years later, Farrakhan, in an interview with me in a small anteroom just inside his Chicago mansion, apologized for using the phrase, "dirty religion": It was "not appropriate. . . . It was my mistake." Judaism could not be "dirty," Farrakhan explained, "because Islam came from the same God." "Dirty religion" had referred not to Jews' religion but to "specific actions of the Israeli government against Palestinian children."[20]

In fact, Farrakhan had called other people "dirty" when he believed they had strayed from the tenets of their faith: "Muslim sheiks who live in opulence when their people live in squalor are practicing a *dirty* religion"; "Christians [who] preach love, but practice hate and tyranny, use God to cover up their corrupt and *dirty* practices." In the early 1980s, he even used the phrase to describe what some NOI members had done to their own faith. Demanding that the revived Fruit of Islam abstain from the violence that had corrupted the old FOI, he proclaimed,

> The commander-in-chief of the Nation of Islam is the Honorable Elijah Muhammad. We have no other commander. All of us are stand-ins. As long as we recite his commandments, we are worthy to stand in for him. But when we begin to use his name to shield a *dirty religion* and then begin to impose self-made commands in his name, then the FOI must be wise enough to reject such commands because it didn't come properly.[21]

Certainly, the "dirty religion" episode illustrated that the Farrakhan-Jewish clash was more than just another brawl between blacks and Jews. Farrakhan's religious vocabulary was so peculiar, so idiosyncratic, that even most blacks had no idea what he meant by "dirty religion." Yet the currency that he gained from

going head-to-head with Jews—whom some blacks identified as
their chief oppressor— helped propel him into the front ranks
of black leaders. What was important wasn't necessarily his
empirical truths, but his temerity in saying them, especially
about Jews, whose purchase on survival was so terribly tenuous
in the twentieth century. Nerve, in this case, outclassed truth.

Initially, both sides demanded contrition. The ADL would
meet with Farrakhan only if he apologized. And Farrakhan,
casting himself as the aggrieved party because he had been mis-
interpreted—and because he had already apologized to the
Chicago radio host Irv Kupcinet for uttering "dirty religion"—
demanded that Jews apologize. Pounding the small, round table
between himself and me in his Hyde Park home, Farrakhan
inquired,

> Where's . . . [the Jews'] apology coming from? Jews got a hell of
> a nerve asking me to apologize. . . . Good God Almighty, that
> angers me. Jews are too arrogant, too proud of their power. They
> want everybody to bow down to them, and I ain't bowing down
> to nothin' or nobody but God. . . .
>
> I'm not getting down on my knees. If I did, you know what
> Jews would tell me? Too little, too late. Jesse's still apologizing.
> He'll never get finished, because Jews, who have committed sins,
> man, against God, . . . are the most unforgiving people if any-
> body offends them. Why do they want me to grovel before them?
> Who the hell do they think they are that I should bow down
> before them and beg for forgiveness when they helped to bring
> my people into slavery and I have never heard a Jewish rabbi or
> organization apologize to me and my people for what they
> brought my people to?

"I'm no dog!" roared Farrakhan, sitting perfectly upright in his
chair, his secretary and chief of staff—the only other persons in
the room—silently watching yet another fulmination against Jews.

You don't give me no little piece of meat on a hook. I'm not looking for nothing from Jews. . . . You can't give me nothing. You can only get yourself out of the hell you're getting yourself into. . . . You got power. You got juice. And you use it against those you don't like. And for those you like. . . . We either go to the table to deal with truth. Or we don't go at all because I'm going to be a winner. I don't give a damn who comes against me. I'm going to be the winner as long as I stand with God and I stand on truth.

"Through dialogue," Farrakhan conceded, "you might show me I'm wrong. *Then* you get an apology. That's the fitting thing. But," he added, with a fillip that could not possibly endear him to anyone on the other side of a negotiating table, "I'm certainly going to demand something from anyone who demands something from me."[22]

Nevertheless, both sides continued to put out occasional feelers for a truce. The ADL offered to stop knocking Farrakhan if *he* stopped knocking Jews—and if the NOI stopped selling such anti-Semitic propaganda as *The Protocols of the Elders of Zion*, a Czarist-era forgery designed to "prove" that Jews were scheming to take over the world. Or if it stopped selling the NOI's own three-hundred-and-thirty-page polemic that "proved" Jews masterminded the slave trade. Offered through back channels, the ADL deal was nixed: the NOI was dispensing "truths," not peddling propaganda. And "truth" could not be suppressed.[23]

But even if there had been a Farrakhan-Jewish summit, it probably would have settled very little. First of all, in the years after Farrakhan's comments about the "wickedly great" Hitler and about "dirty religion," a peculiar, implicit symbiosis developed between the NOI leader and certain Jewish organizations: a few Jewish "self-defense" groups needed the specter of Farrakhan to help justify their existence (and their budgets). And Farrakhan's sparring with Jews had become a good part of his draw: he specialized in the outrageous. It proved his mettle. Agree with him or not, he was "a man," a rarity among black leaders.[24]

A Farrakhan-Jewish summit would also have failed because Farrakhan's obsession with Jews calcified after 1984. Demands for penance from him only seemed to encourage him to issue further provocations. Racial pride, personal ego, pressure from the NOI's own fringe to remain strong, all simply stiffened his back and quickened his rhetoric. "It's a sign of maturity to say, 'I erred,'" observed one of his confidants, "but sometimes the Jewish community says, 'Nigger jump!' and wants you to take your pants down and say, 'I'm sorry,' before thirty micro-phones."[25]

Instead of putting down the Jewish card, Farrakhan began dealing from a whole deck of them. When he asked several thousand blacks in Washington's Malcolm X Park what to do with black leaders who seek Jewish support, someone shouted, "Kill them." An unfazed Farrakhan quipped, "I didn't say that. I just seconded the motion." Returning to Washington three years later, he blamed blacks' poor self-image on Jews ("Who taught us to hate ourselves? Who writes the textbooks that write us out of history? Who makes the movies that show us as nothing but Toms and bug-eyed dancers?") and dipped into the reservoir of leftover resentment from his childhood when his mother cleaned Jews' homes: "We've been loyal to you. We've cleaned your floors, and when you asked us, 'And you do do windows, don't you?' we said, 'Yes.' We left our homes uncleaned, yet cleaned yours. We left our children unkempt to clean yours."[26]

In Tacoma, Washington, he neatly conflated the "Christ killer" slander, his holy mission, and blacks' divinity into one extraordinary, sweeping statement: "Any black man who stands up for justice will end up like Jesus. . . . The same enemies that hated Jesus hate Farrakhan. Jesus was hated by the Romans, the

Babylonians, the Pharisees, and the Jews. I am hated by the same." In Palm Beach, he touted his own courage for tackling the Jewish question: "Nobody talks to Jews the way they should be talked to. When somebody says something that might upset the Jews, they say, 'Don't say that because it's anti-Semitic.' So you run up a tree and shut your mouth. But Farrakhan ain't running nowhere."[27]

And after reporters wrote that he had bragged that "Jews cannot defeat me. I will grind them down and crush them into little bits," he claimed that they had printed "a gross misstatement of my words. I said, 'I won't be defeated as long as I stand with God,' and I quoted from scripture [Matthew 21:44] that a man of God is 'called a "stone of stumbling," and "whosoever shall fall on this stone shall be broken; but on whomsoever it shall fall, it will grind him to powder." I said, in effect, 'You have fallen on *me*.'"[28]

The battle between Jews and Farrakhan cleared the way for some of the more peculiar political alliances in modern America. In 1985, Thomas Metzger attended a Farrakhan rally in Los Angeles, where he donated one hundred dollars to the Nation of Islam. Metzger headed a white supremacist group, the White American Political Association, and had formerly led the California Ku Klux Klan. Metzger told the *New York Times* that "talks" between black and white supremacy groups had been going on about a year. He did not specify the substance of these alleged talks.[29]

NOI officials denied Metzger's claims that he and nine of his associates had been invited to the September 14 rally. They also denied that Farrakhan had invited Metzger to meet with him after the rally at the private quarters where he was staying in Inglewood, a suburb of Los Angeles. But they did acknowledge that Metzger had informed the Nation in 1984 about "the movements of Jewish terrorist groups that could have caused damage" to Jesse Jackson's presidential campaign. The purpose of such information was "to assure the Nation of Islam that white nationalists generally would not be part of any attacks on the Jackson campaign, and that if it happened it would be a result of somebody else trying to make it look like us." When Abdul Walid Muhammad, editor of *The Final Call*, was asked if the NOI had acted on the information from Metzger, he answered, "We act on all information."[30]

"White nationalists," according to Metzger, appreciated the "similarities" between themselves and Farrakhan regarding Jews. Farrakhan addressed "the exploitation of working people by an elitist group in Washington and by corporations. This man has the courage to stand up and criticize Jews, like any other group should be criticized."[31]

The month after Metzger attended the NOI's Los Angeles rally, he attended a conference of white supremacists on a farm in Cohotac, Michigan, about fifty miles west of Detroit. There, about two hundred white nationalists from California, Connecticut, Florida, Arkansas, Georgia, Idaho, Illinois, Indiana, Ohio, Pennsylvania, and Canada pledged their support for Farrakhan.[32]

"America is like a rotting carcass," the dark-haired, broad-chested Metzger told the gathering. "The Jews are living off the carcass like the parasites they are. Farrakhan understands this." The sentiment was seconded by Art Jones, a white supremacist from Chicago: "The enemy of my enemy is my friend. I salute Louis Farrakhan and anyone else who stands up against the Jews."[33]

The supremacist conclave issued a call to divide the continental United States into a separatist's dream: a "White American Bastion" that would be carved out of the northwestern United States and southwestern Canada. This whites-only territory would include the states of Washington, Oregon, Idaho, Montana, Wyoming, California, Nevada, Alaska, and parts of Utah, Arizona, and Canada. Its capital would be Hayden Lake, Idaho. Jews would be ceded a strip of land along the Atlantic coast from Delaware northward through the southern half of Massachusetts. The capital of this "Zionist Occupational Government" would be New York City. In a surprising gesture of magnanimity, most of the rest of the United States would be ceded to Farrakhan's organization. The capital of this Nation of Islam would be Chicago, which would be renamed New Mecca.[34]

This was not the first time—and would not be the last—that there had been a mutual attraction between the racist right and the Nation of Islam. In June 1961, George Lincoln Rockwell, the "fuhrer" of the American Nazi Party, attended an NOI rally in Washington. Rockwell had often called blacks "the lowest scum of humanity." But during the fund-raising portion of the evening, he suddenly shouted from the audience, "George Lincoln Rockwell gives twenty dollars," and stood with twenty of his storm troopers, all giving a Nazi salute. The next year, Elijah Muhammad invited Rockwell to the NOI annual convention in Chicago. Standing before five thousand blacks and flanked by ten of his brown-shirted storm troopers, Rockwell declared that he was "proud to stand here before black men. . . . Elijah Muhammad is the Adolf Hitler of the black man."[35]

(The distaste that Malcolm X must have had for Elijah Muhammad's flirtations with George Lincoln Rockwell is apparent from this telegram he sent the two-bit fuhrer from Arlington, Virginia, in January 1965. The message was sent just one month before Malcolm was killed:

I am no longer held in check from fighting white supremacists by Elijah Muhammad's separatist Black Muslim movement . . .

If your present racist agitation against our people . . . causes
physical harm to Reverend [Martin Luther] King or any other
black American, . . . you and your Ku Klux Klan friends will be
met with maximum physical retaliation from those of us who
. . . believe in asserting our right of self-defense—by any means
necessary.)[36]

Finally, the Nation of Islam joined forces with another anti-
Semitic group, the Lyndon LaRouche Organization. Previously,
LaRouche operatives had assailed former Secretary of State
Henry Kissinger as a Soviet agent, Queen Elizabeth of England
for "pushing drugs," and Farrakhan for attending a terrorist
conference in Libya in 1986. The LaRouche Organization had
demanded that Farrakhan be arrested on charges of sedition.[37]

But in the late 1980s, LaRouche finally ceased sniping at Farrakhan, apparently realizing the power of combining forces
against the same foe. As a LaRouche follower said in June 1995
while distributing LaRouche brochures and newspapers at
Boston's Logan Airport, "We have a common enemy. And we
both want to bring down the secret government with which the
ADL is affiliated."[38]

One of the favorite targets of this LaRouche-NOI alliance was
the B'nai B'rith and its Anti-Defamation League, which, beginning in the mid-1980s, had highlighted Farrakhan as American
Jews' domestic Public Enemy Number One. Advance publicity
in 1992 for a joint NOI-LaRouche program at Howard University in Washington, D.C., among the nation's premier black universities, announced that the Anti-Defamation League "is historically indistinguishable from organized crime and the
bankers and financiers who operate the $500 million drug trade
known as DOPE, Inc." At a lecture in April 1994 in Baltimore,
one LaRouche speaker said Freemasons had established the
"pro-slavery" B'nai B'rith in the antebellum North as a Confed-

erate spy agency. And Dr. Abdul Alim Muhammad, the NOI's minister of health, declared, "We are . . . at war. Who's fighting us? The ADL. Either we overcome them or they overcome us. Until they kill all of us or we kill all of them, if it comes to that. We must fight them until we crush them."[39]

In the fall of 1992, New York black activist Lenora Fulani said that Farrakhan had assured her he would publicly repudiate any association between the Nation of Islam and the LaRouche organization. LaRouche had already been disavowed by such black leaders as the reverends Al Sharpton and Jesse Jackson.

Fulani was especially distressed at the LaRouche organization's efforts to insinuate itself into the black community by spearheading what it called "a new civil rights coalition." Despite this camouflage, she said, the LaRouche organization was still promoting "a neo-fascistic program," "a racist worldview," "posited that Eurocentric philosophy, culture and education were superior to all others," and "promoted a vision of tanks in the streets to maintain social order."

"There is no place among us for the likes of Lyndon LaRouche," she declared.

Despite Farrakhan's pledge to Fulani, he never issued his repudiation. Moreover, in May, 1995, he praised "the wisdom of Lyndon LaRouche . . . Anybody who will illuminate the masses becomes a dangerous person to those who manipulate the masses to feed their greed."[40]

The frequency—and the fury—of Jew-baiting from Farrakhan and his cohorts seemed guaranteed to keep Jews away from him, not to convince them he was a reasonable negotiating partner. And their verbal assaults on him, especially the chanted demands for his death by members of the fringe Jewish Defense League outside halls where he spoke, seemed guaranteed, from his perspective, to say the same about Jews' stature as negotiating partners.

Equally certain to rebuff Jews were Farrakhan's goals for a summit, which got far less attention than what he was saying publicly to the masses. Both sides would readily agree to the top item on his agenda: to sweep away "the rubbish . . . heaped on each other." Then would come a more important and delicate stage: gauging Jews' role in slavery, then wrangling over Farrakhan's messianic claims for Elijah Muhammad. Farrakhan's criteria to determine that Muhammad was the messiah would be "Torah, Gospel, Quran . . . the revealed words of God. If this man is who I believe he is, then there has to be ample proof in his words, in his work, and in what the prophets predicted. . . . If he's not, then we have nothing to worry about."[41]

(Farrakhan seemingly overlooked that the Jewish Torah and the Christian New Testament agree that the messiah would be a descendant of the House of David; neither Farrakhan nor anyone else in the Nation had ever made such claims for Elijah Muhammad. Also, the Nation had already anointed its founder, Fard Muhammad, as both Allah incarnate and the Mahdi, the equivalent in Shiite Islam of the Judeo-Christian messiah.)[42]

Finally, Farrakhan went one giant step further than other supersecessionist theologies by saying that *he* was Jewish through an "inward circumcision."

"Yes," he said when the talk show host Larry King reminded him that he had said backstage that he was Jewish, "because . . . [one is Jewish] inwardly by the circumcision of the heart. What God demands today is a new Jew and a new covenant. Not the Jew that is the Jew outwardly by rituals. But the Jew that is the Jew inwardly by total submission and obedience to the will and the law of God."[43]

But what if the bickering and name-calling between Jews and Farrakhan continued? What if chants from the JDL for Farrakhan's death bore fruit—and the fatal shot was fired by a Jew?

That, said Farrakhan, would mean the fire—not next time, but *this* time: "My God would destroy America. . . . If you lay your hands on me, you won't have any future. . . . It would be wise to make sure nothing happens to me. Because that would be an act of self-preservation on the part of America."[44]

At one level, talking with Farrakhan, despite his apocalyptic doomsaying, would be just another exercise in interfaith dialogue. But most Jewish leaders were convinced that Farrakhan was insincere about improving relations with them, especially since he would periodically profess to seek amicable relations with them, then either he or a lieutenant would utter something dreadful about Jews. Just two days before the 1995 Million Man March, for instance, Quanell X, the NOI's national youth minister, told a cheering crowd in Washington, "All you Jews can go straight to hell. . . . I say to Jewish America, 'Get ready. Knuckle up. Put your boots on, because we're ready and the war is going down.'" That same evening, the NOI's national spokesman, Khallid Abdul Muhammad, snarled that the Jew was a "parasite who comes into our community and takes out trailer and tractor loads of money on a daily basis." Yet forty-eight hours later at the Million Man March, Farrakhan asked again to meet with Jews—and said not one word about the hate from inside his own organization.[45]

Reinforcing some Jews' suspicions about Farrakhan was the experience of two Chicago rabbis who did meet with the NOI leader. In 1988, Farrakhan initiated the meetings with Robert Marx and Herman Schaalman. Two dinner meetings were held at Farrakhan's home; Marx hosted a third at his home in the Chicago suburb of Glencoe. The rabbis found their dinner companion "friendly," "charming," "receptive." At one point, Farrakhan even asked the rabbis to tell him the specific words that had offended Jews and pledged never again to use them. By the end of the first meeting, both rabbis felt that, "on the Jewish question, he would be honorable."

Between the first two meetings, Rabbi Schaalman detected "a softening of Farrakhan's tone about Jews." But the third meeting in May 1993 was overshadowed by the rabbis' demand that Farrakhan "disavow" the NOI's new book linking Jews to slavery. The three never met again. Farrakhan was insulted that the rabbis wanted proof that he had repented and changed his ways. And the rabbis felt "betrayed" and "disillusioned" by a man who "turned out to be unrelievedly hostile. His leadership is based on blacks' anger that their needs have not been met. But picking on Jews for these grievances is a severe misreading of what most of us know as fact. Demonizing Jews is a game that's been played for centuries."[46]

But Farrakhan had a much more extended private encounter with a Jew than he did with the two rabbis: in 1991, when he decided to resume the violin lessons he had taken as a youth in Boston, he chose as his teacher a Jewish woman, Elaine Skorodin of Glencoe.

Skorodin was "rather taken aback" when she received a call from Farrakhan's secretary asking if she would teach him. She accepted the offer "because he had said that music can transcend differences and he wanted to show his people the beauty of classical music." For the next eighteen months, Skorodin went to Farrakhan's home about once a week to help him prepare for a possible concert. At the first lesson, "he took out his violin"—an eighteenth-century Guadaninni—"and played for me, and it was instantly obvious how talented he was."[47]

Farrakhan practiced "every day for hours." By April 18, 1993, when he played Mendelssohn's Violin Concerto in Winston-Salem, North Carolina, he was good enough for a *New York Times* critic to enthuse, "Can Louis Farrakhan play the violin?

God bless us, he can. He makes a lot of mistakes, not surprising for a man who virtually abandoned the instrument for forty years. . . . Yet, Mr. Farrakhan's sound is that of the authentic player. It is wide, deep and full of the energy that makes the violin gleam. His thrusting sense of phrase has musical power to it, even though some of the erratic movement kept . . . musicians [in the small orchestra accompanying him] scrambling at times."[48]

The symbolism of playing a piece by Felix Mendelssohn, a youthful convert to Christianity from Judaism, was not lost on Farrakhan. But the decision to play Mendelssohn was not political: "This was the first violin concerto I heard and . . . the last concerto I was studying [as a youth]. . . . I got as far as the first movement of the concerto when I went to college, and there were no violin teachers there that I would study under as a black."[49]

After the concert, Farrakhan told the *Times* critic that he had tried "to do with music what cannot be undone with words and try to undo with music what words have done." This comment was widely interpreted to mean that the concert was Farrakhan's overture to Jews. But four months later, with critics carping that the concert had been a cynical way of squirming out of an unpleasant spot, Farrakhan said he had not intended the Mendelssohn concerto to be a musical olive branch: "It was taken as that, and I did not reject that, because I thought great good would come out of it. Jewish leaders said it was a publicity stunt. I don't do things for publicity. Men of God are not like that. I played Mendelssohn because I love Mendelssohn."[50]

Farrakhan related to Skorodin, his Jewish music teacher, in the same way he did with other Jews who met with him privately: he was cordial, friendly, nonthreatening. The discrepancy between his public rage about Jews and his congenial affability toward them in private suggested that he practiced a "pragmatic anti-Semitism": he was obsessed with Jews when he was before TV cameras or vast crowds, but he treated them with respect and dignity when encountering them face-to-face. In the reality of the encounter, all stereotypes, all conspiracies, all machinations collapsed of their own dead weight. It was almost as if Farrakhan, cosseted in his Hyde Park mansion and surrounded by platoons of NOI ministers and the sturdy Fruit of Islam, needed this handful of Jews to remind him that they were not a cardboard, one-dimensional people—just as they discovered, to their surprise, that he was not the cardboard, one-dimensional character about whom they had heard—and whom they dreaded—so much.

A certain choreography evolved: Farrakhan made headlines attacking Jews. They made headlines denouncing him. Columnists and civil rights leaders made headlines trying to figure out how to declare a truce. Then Farrakhan would move on to the next arena in the next city—and the whole dance would be repeated.

But while the steps were new, the underlying sentiments into which Farrakhan was tapping were not. Anti-Semitism—or, at the very least, a profound suspicion of Jews—had long been endemic among African Americans. The South's fundamentalist Protestant culture, whose ambience blacks had absorbed, produced all sorts of justifications for slavery but never encouraged a kind thought for the Savior-killing Jews. As the writer Richard Wright remembered, "All of us black people who lived in the neighborhood hated Jews, not because they exploited us, but because we had been taught at home and in Sunday School that Jews were 'Christ killers.' To hold an attitude of antagonism or distrust toward Jews was bred in us from childhood; it was not merely racial prejudice, it was part of our cultural heritage."[51]

An irascible cunning drove Protestant anti-Semitism. Better for the slaves to hate the Jews than to hate *them*. So the message was taught and the message was sung. Protestant catechism taught young "colored persons" over and over again who had slain the Lord:

> Q: *Who killed Jesus?*
> A: *The wicked Jews.*
> Q: *The wicked Jews grew angry with our Savior and what did they do to him?*
> A: *They crucified Him.*[52]

And slaves sang songs about "De Jews done killed poor Jesus," or that asked, "Were you there when the Jews crucified my Lord?" or that commiserated with the Virgin Mary, who "had one son/The Jews had him hung."[53]

The strategy worked as a device to make blacks complacent with their lot: as bad as many Protestant slaveowners were, Jews *had* to be worse. In 1859, for instance, when a slave was finally found who had disappeared on the very day she was to go to a new owner, she was asked why she feared going to the home of "a good . . . kind mistress" who wouldn't give her "any hard work to do." Her answer: "Ah! But . . . they tell me Miss Isaacs is a Jew. An' if the Jews kill the Lord and Master, what won't they do with a poor little nigger like me."[54]

Once past slavery, the prejudice remained just as deep-seated—on both sides. In 1917, for instance, Horace Mann Bond, who as an adult would be an influential educator, responded to a boy's taunts of "Nigger, Nigger, Nigger," by yelling, "You Christ-killer." Remorse came decades later, when Bond explained that his own bigotry had been nurtured in a family that prayed before each meal, read scripture morning and evening, and attended chapel daily and three times on Sunday. "The thought that Christ had been killed by the Jews," he confessed, "may have had a more ancient basis in my twelve-year-old mind than I can now bring myself to admit." And in 1948, James Baldwin told the readers of *Commentary*, a cultural and political journal published by the American Jewish Committee, that, among blacks, "the traditional Christian accusation that the Jews killed Christ is neither questioned nor doubted. . . . The preacher begins [his sermon] by accusing the Jews of having refused the light and proceeds from there to a catalog of subsequent sins and the sufferings visited upon them by a wrathful God."[55]

Stereotypes of Jews as miserly and greedy reinforced religious doctrine. Black newspapers in the late nineteenth and early twentieth centuries were full of stories that described Jews as "parasitical," "predatory," and "preying upon and devouring the substance of others." Their "sole aim seems to be earning money"; "as a moneylender, . . . [the Jew] holds the purse strings of the world."[56]

To blacks, Jews controlled everything and misused everyone. Blacks' salvation from this scourge might come from their own ranks (from, say, a Elijah Muhammad or a Father Divine). Or as improbable as it might sound, even from such a white protector as a fuhrer. Within a few years after Hitler came to power, the *Dynamite*, a black newspaper in Chicago, proclaimed, "What America needs is a Hitler and what the Chicago Black Belt needs is a purge of the exploiting Jew." Around the same time, the *New York Age* endorsed the Reich's racism: "If the Jewish merchants in Germany treated the German workers as Blumstein's [department store] treat the people of Harlem, then Hitler is right." A survey in the late 1930s found that Jews owned 241 shops in Harlem and Greeks owned 151. (The survey did not mention shops owned by other ethnic groups.) Yet blacks were so predisposed to believe that Jews owned everything around them that a Harlem newspaper reported in 1942 that 95 percent of the neighborhood's merchants were Jewish.[57]

The lingering myth of Jewish evil and avarice said as much about the power of the church as about blacks' desire to identify with the power structure by holding in contempt those whom whites hated (except, of course, themselves—the lowly Negro).

In Roxbury, young Louis Eugene Walcott had, on the whole, seen Jews at a distance. Aside from his Jewish violin teacher or a Jewish pal or two from his high school track team, his world was mostly a black world. But he heard about Jewish shop owners, and from his mother he probably heard about the Jews whose fine suburban homes she cleaned and whose spic-and-span children she cared for. At least once, shortly after Farrakhan became a minister in the Nation, he had to rush to a Jew's home where she was working to calm her down because she thought her employer had slighted her.[58]

Quite possibly, Farrakhan had also absorbed his mother's attitude toward Jews, which had probably hardened in the early and mid-1930s back in the Bronx. There, she and other black women congregated on street corners and bargained with mostly Jewish middle-class housewives for their services as day laborers. Pay ranged from fifteen to thirty cents per hour; a few extra pennies would be thrown in for carfare or for such dangerous work as washing windows. But according to a 1935 article in *The Crisis*, the NAACP's monthly magazine, bearing the combustible title "The Bronx Slave Trade" (but citing no evidence to prove its accusation), "Fortunate indeed is she who gets the full hourly rate promised. Often, her day's slavery is rewarded with a single dollar bill or whatever her unscrupulous employer pleases to pay. More often, the clock is set back for an hour or more. Too often, she is sent away without any pay at all."[59]

That "The Bronx Slave Trade" was published by the ordinarily moderate, circumspect NAACP, which was largely founded and supported by Jews, hinted at the depth of blacks' distrust of whites—and their certainty that black women were being gypped and hustled by bourgeois housewives, Jewish and otherwise, on the street corners of New York.

And from the Garveyite ambience in Roxbury or from his relatives who belonged to Garvey's UNIA, young Louis may have picked up the same ambivalence toward Jews that later marked the Nation of Islam. In the late teens and early 1920s, Garvey admired the early Zionists because their quest for a reborn Zion paralleled, in some ways, his Back to Africa movement: "A new spirit, a new courage, has come to us . . . at the same time as it came to the Jew: When the Jew said, 'We shall have Palestine,' the same sentiment came to us when we said, 'We shall have Africa.'"[60]

But Garvey also believed that Jews impeded blacks' progress. He argued (as Farrakhan would later) against Jews being in leadership positions in the NAACP and urged blacks to open their own shops instead of patronizing Jewish stores. In time, this "Buy Black" campaign assumed an overtly anti-Semitic tone. Indeed, the tone sharpened after 1922, when Garvey was convicted for mail fraud involving a steamship line he helped found. Garvey declared himself the victim of an "international coverup": "I am being punished for the crime of the Jew Silverstone [an agent of the Black Star Line]. I was persecuted by Maxwell Mattuck, another Jew, and I am to be sentenced by Judge Julian Mack, the eminent Jewish jurist [and an NAACP board member]. Truly, I may say, 'I am going to Jericho and fell among thieves.'"[61]

Once Gene Walcott joined the Nation of Islam, his attitude toward Jews became somewhat frozen because of the NOI's self-reinforcing insularity from the white world and even from large sectors of the black world. After resurrecting the Nation and becoming totally unrestricted by either of the Muhammads (Elijah or Wallace), Farrakhan could freely indulge his penchant for the violent, avenging rhetoric he had learned firsthand from two of its best connoisseurs in the country: Malcolm X and Elijah himself. So when he suspected that Jews were coming after Jesse Jackson, he dipped into the Nation's bag of theological tricks and into his own vague memories and impressions of Jews and emerged with several gems aimed at eviscerating the very bedrock of Jewish identity.

Farrakhan's theology was an extension of his separatism—and vice versa. Both sought a black identity that could stand on its own minus the props of white America, Christian America, Jewish America. Both sneered at the lame, insipid integrationists whose picket lines, Freedom Rides, sit-ins, civil rights laws, and goofy notions of equality emanated from a misplaced sense of brotherhood, from a quirky confidence that black and white could live amicably together and prosper—psychologically, socially, financially.

Farrakhan's contempt for the integration of the last half of the twentieth century casually dismissed the tangible good it had accomplished on many fronts: in 1940, there was a four-year gap in median years of schooling between whites and blacks; by 1991, the gap had shrunk to a few months. At the same time, the proportion of twenty-five-to-thirty-four-year-old blacks who had finished high school almost matched that of whites: 84 percent to 87 percent. And a solid, impressive black middle class had emerged from almost nothing. The term had once been used to refer dismissively to those at the top of the bottom economic rung: Pullman porters, headwaiters, small-time funeral parlor owners, successful barbers, and storefront preachers, all dependent on the mechanics of a segregated society. By the middle of the last decade of the century, up to one-third of blacks had joined the same middle class that whites had kept as their private preserve. Farrakhan looked right past such progress to the one-third of blacks living in poverty (a figure worse than the 1969 rate); to an unemployment rate that was twice that of whites; to the one out of every three black males between twenty and twenty-nine who were either in jail or on parole; to the 47 percent of all black seventeen-year-olds who were functionally illiterate; to blacks, who comprise 12 percent of the population, accounting for 47 percent of all deaths by fire.[62]

To Farrakhan, segregation had been a golden era for African Americans, a time when they were self-sufficient because they were *forced* to be self-sufficient, when they created a universe parallel to the white universe, with

> black gas stations, black hotels, black motels, black insurance companies, black bus companies. . . . We pooled our resources, and we began to grow and expand economically. But when desegregation came down, . . . we didn't have to sleep in a black motel anymore. We could sleep in the fine motels built by white people, some of whom are Jews. We don't spend our money with our own; we spend it with Jews and white people. Our motels closed. Our hotels closed. Our bus companies closed. Our insurance companies gone to hell. And the economics of the black South is in ruins. Who benefited? We didn't.[63]

Farrakhan verbally shrugged when considering whether this blow to the black economy was premeditated: "Only God can answer that." But he then proceeded to read God's mind by asserting that the prime beneficiaries of integration had not been blacks but Jews, the very people who had provided most of the white civil rights attorneys, more than half of the Freedom Riders, and two-thirds of the volunteer college students for the 1964 Freedom Summer in Mississippi. Compassion, Farrakhan was convinced, hadn't motivated Jews to enlist in the civil rights movement. They were swayed by the creaky wheel of economic self-enrichment: quite simply, they had put their lives and careers on the line to make a buck, not to advance a higher cause.[64]

"Jews ain't a foolish people," proclaimed Farrakhan.

> They're not a people who don't think and plan. No, Jews are a wise people. And wise people plan effects.... Miami, Jews couldn't go there one time. They got it now. The Cubans that came here, yes, they're Cubans, but they're Jews, many of them. Many of them are rich Jews. Jews are smart, that's all. Look, oh boy, Jews are brilliant. Not all. But the majority have been well taught, well schooled, and by the grace of God, they have benefited, [while] we have suffered.[65]

There was a small kernel of truth in Farrakhan's claim, but one that he distorted and abused. Jews had indeed been "benefiting" at a higher rate than blacks during the post–civil rights years, but not because they had conspired to obliterate segregation so they could appropriate the black economy for themselves. Their lot had improved, quite simply, because the Jewish experience (in America and elsewhere) is in a different league from the black experience. Jewish history, while unique and often tragic, has also been a *Western* history. Jews may have been scorned in many of their Christian "host countries," but Jewish culture and faith undergird much Western culture and faith. Jews have commonalties with the West that would take generations of blacks to establish, if ever. And some commonalties that blacks could *never* emulate. Jews and the white power elite share the same color, and they generally have come willingly and even eagerly to America, while blacks came in chains. As James Baldwin wrote, "The Jewish travail occurred across the sea and America rescued him from the house of bondage. But America *is* the house of bondage for the Negro, and no country can rescue him."[66]

These advantages have long influenced Jewish success and black suffering. According to the Seton Hall University history professor Edward Shapiro,

> On every possible social and economic indicator, . . . blacks have lagged far behind Jews. Jews, who comprise less than three percent of the American population, make up over 25 percent of the names on the most recent *Forbes* magazine annual listing of the 400 richest Americans. By contrast, there was only one black on the list, the entertainer Bill Cosby, even though 12 percent of Americans are black. Blacks are still waiting for one of their number to be selected to head an elite American university, while Jews have already served as presidents of Princeton, Dartmouth, Columbia, Yale, Harvard, the University of Chicago and the University of Pennsylvania. There are ten Jewish United States Senators and 33 members of the House of Representatives. Jews are overrepresented in the Senate by a factor of four and in the House by a factor of three. Although blacks comprise roughly 10 percent of the House of Representatives, there is only one black senator.[67]

So when Farrakhan said, "I know Jews have power," he was not necessarily engaging in paranoid fantasies. Yet no one in polite society could now publicly agree with him about almost anything he has said since. To most whites and many blacks, *he* was now the New Satan. To concede that he had ever made a valid point in his life was to enter into a pact with a very slippery devil. In his efforts to indict the Jews, he violated so many norms of decency and civility—he was so unrelentingly in everyone's face—that he went beyond the pale of civil discourse.

To explain his banishment, Farrakhan took the public person's favored route out of an unpleasant predicament. He blamed the press: "If I am the devil to some, it's not because of something I have done. It's because of the way my words are represented to people through the media."[68]

It was true that, in a few instances, the news media had mis-interpreted Farrakhan's words. But generally, the press treated Farrakhan more gingerly—and surely with more attention—than it treated whites who spouted similar stuff. After hearing Farrakhan speak at the National Press Club in July 1984, where he painted a picture of an America in thrall to "Jewish interests," the veteran columnist Mary McGrory called him "fit, fresh-faced and nattily dressed," as if his sartorial splendor neutralized his message. And Dorothy Gilliam, a black columnist at the *Post*, gushed as if she were reporting on a celebrity event: "Louis Far-rakhan is a man in transition. . . . His style is different. I wanted to know what is changing him and who he is today." Such fawn-ing would have been thrown in the wastepaper basket by the city editor had the speaker been a white man—or a Jew—spreading comparable nonsense about blacks.[69]

And Farrakhan surely had little ground to complain about the media when it came to two notorious episodes: *The Secret Relationship between Blacks and Jews*, a masterful piece of pro-paganda that "proves" Jews were the genius behind the slave trade and to which the press devoted little attention; and the NOI's national spokesman, Khallid Abdul Muhammad, whose vile attacks on almost everyone not in the Nation had been underreported for years. He had blamed the prophet Muham-mad for the terrible shape of today's world; called the very peo-ple from whom the founder of the Nation was said to have descended "rusty, dusty, dirty desert Arabs"; cast whites' sole legacy as "murder, bloodshed, destruction, misery, slavery, colo-nialism, racism, sexism, Zionism, and all forms of madness"; announced that blacks were "tired of a blond-haired, pale-skinned, blue-eyed, buttermilk complexioned cracker Christ or peckerwood Jesus"; and dubbed Columbia University "Colum-bia Jewniversity" in "Jew York City."[70]

Despite the invective—or maybe because of it—Khallid was a Farrakhan favorite: "one of the most brilliant young men I have had a chance to know"; "a stallion, a beautiful black stallion. . . . It takes God to ride such a gifted horse." Perhaps, but the stallion and the NOI's tract on Jews and slavery led the Nation of Islam—and Farrakhan—into its worst PR crisis since the days when it was considered no more than a haven for murder, mayhem, and scoundrels.[71]

IX

Toward the Center

If Farrakhan represented the polished side of the Nation of Islam, then Khallid Abdul Muhammad was the NOI's rough underside: unrepentant, incorrigible, uncensored. Onstage he paced and pranced, tantalizing, titillating, moving swiftly from "ghetto-speak" to "Yiddish-speak" to "whitey-speak" to "politician-speak," a one-man verbal melting pot. His inflammatory speech was offset by the tireless large grin he wore, for he knew that his words, his style, his sheer, naked effrontery could make the blood of some blacks in his audience run fast with pride and anger—and make the blood of some whites (who heard his words through the media) chill with the cold realization that there was a fury abroad that could kill and that whites were its damnable targets.[1]

Khallid's libelous barbs had been tossed about in the media in a somewhat disorganized fashion: he appeared to be a loose gun, dismissable as a quantum of hate without discernible form or shape or agenda. But on January 16, 1994, when the B'nai B'rith's Anti-Defamation League took out a full-page ad in the *New York Times* with excerpts from a three-hour talk Khallid had made the previous November at Kean College in New Jersey, he got premium space in newspapers—and the small college would be ensnared in a trap most academic communities spend their lives trying to avoid.

The ADL ad was a masterpiece of understatement. It had one simple goal: "*You Decide.*" No hard sell. No demands that anyone repudiate Khallid or the man behind Khallid—Louis Farrakhan. Just an appeal to conscience: *you* decide whether Farrakhan really was inching "toward moderation and increased tolerance," as he and others had recently been claiming.[2]

Next in the ad came portions of Khallid's speech. Most of his targets were familiar and time-tested; Khallid devoted most of his attention to Jews, who exploited blacks "on a daily and consistent basis. They sell us pork and they don't even eat it themselves. . . . A wall of liquor keeping our people drunk and out of their mind, and filled with the swill of the swine, affecting their minds."

But controlling the ghettos was just a kick, a lark. Playing for higher stakes, Jews controlled the world: the Federal Reserve. The White House. Libraries ("lie-braries"). TV networks. Hollywood. Newspapers. Jews held black entertainers, athletes, politicians, "in the palm of their hand." They were "stealing rubies and gold and silver all over the earth. That's why we can't even wear a ring or a bracelet or a necklace without calling it 'Jew-elry.' We say it real quick and call it 'jewelry,' but it's not jewelry. It's 'Jew-elry,' 'cause you're the rogue who's stealing all over the face of the planet earth."

The Jew was a fraud, a sham, a deceiver, parlaying an ersatz morality into an even more fraudulent compassion: "The Jews have told us, 'Ve have suffered like you. Ve, ve, ve, ve marched with Dr. Martin Luther King, Jr. Ve, ve, ve were in Selma, Alabama. Ve, ve were in Montgomery, Alabama. Ve, ve were on the front line of the civil rights marches. Ve have always supported you.' But . . . what [the Jews] have actually done, brothers and sisters, is used us as cannon fodder."

Jews had even brought the Holocaust upon themselves:

Everybody always talk[s] about Hitler exterminating six million Jews. . . . But don't anybody ever ask what did they do to Hitler? . . . They went in there, in Germany, the way they do everywhere they go, and they supplanted, they usurped, they turned around, and a German, in his own country, would almost have to go to a Jew to get money. They undermined the very fabric of the society. Now, he was an arrogant, no-good, devil bastard, Hitler, no question about it. . . . He used his greatness for evil and wickedness. But they [the Jews] are wickedly great, too, brother. Everywhere they go and they always do it and they hide their head.

Having dissolved Jews' morality, history, and conscience, Khallid reduced them to the level of savages: "You are the Johnny-come-lately-Jew, who . . . crawled out of the caves and hills of Europe. . . . You are a European strain of people who crawled around on all fours . . . , eatin' juniper roots and eatin' each other."

Jews were cannibals, politically, fiscally and, now, quite literally. Parasites upon themselves and upon all around them. But Khallid's wrath was too ambitious simply to fall into the convenient niche of Jew-hating, and it was here that he truly overstepped the bounds of the NOI's public catechism. Rarely in public had an NOI spokesman, not even Elijah Muhammad or Malcolm X, unleashed such contempt for whites as Khallid did at Kean State. No one was off-bounds, not the pope—"Go to the Vatican . . . [and see] the old, no-good Pope, you know that cracker. Somebody needs to raise that dress up and see what's really under there"—and surely not the whites of South Africa, with whom Khallid hit his full, terrifying stride:

> If we want to be merciful at all, when we gain enough power from God Almighty to take our freedom and independence from him, we give him twenty-four hours to get out of town by sundown. . . . If he won't . . . , we kill everything white that ain't right in South Africa. We kill the women, we kill the children. We kill the babies. We kill the blind, we kill the crippled, we kill 'em all. We kill the faggot, we kill the lesbian, we'll kill them all.
>   . . . [W]hy kill the babies? . . . Because they gonna grow up one day to oppress *our* babies. . . . Why kill the women? . . . [B]ecause . . . they are the military or the army's manufacturing center. They lay on their back and reinforcements roll out from between their legs.
>   . . . Kill the elders, too. Goddamn it, if they're in a wheelchair, push 'em off a cliff in Capetown . . . or Johannesburg . . . or Port Sheppiston or Darbin [*sic*]. How the hell you think they got old? They got old oppressing black people. . . . And when you get through killing 'em all, go to the goddamn graveyard and dig up the grave and kill 'em all, goddamn, again. 'Cause they didn't die hard enough. And if you've killed 'em all and you don't have the strength to dig 'em up, then take your gun and shoot in the goddamn grave. Kill 'em again. Kill 'em again, 'cause they didn't die hard enough.[3]

Khallid later explained that he had gone ballistic at Kean College because several Jews chanting outside the auditorium where he spoke had turned it into "a day of war": "It was not posturing. There were no TV cameras or print media present. But to call for . . . [Farrakhan's] death is very, very serious, and to do it in our face is very serious." So Farrakhan's favorite "warrior" machine-gunned the enemy with his in-your-face, take-no-prisoners rhetoric. In the aftermath, the walking wounded on all sides staggered around, trying to make some sense of Khallid's assault on the country's sensibilities—and carefully watching their political and moral flanks in the meantime.[4]

On the Sunday morning when the ADL's ad appeared in the *Times,* the phones rang at the New Jersey home of Abe Foxman, head of the ADL. First to call was Benjamin Chavis, head of the National Association for the Advancement of Colored People, who thanked Foxman.

"Thanks for what?" asked Foxman.

"Thanks for laying it out," said Chavis. "I did not realize how ugly it all was."[5]

Chavis faxed to Foxman comments he had already inserted into a speech he would deliver that evening at the Smithsonian Institution to commemorate Martin Luther King Jr.'s birthday:

> I am appalled that any human being would stoop so low to make violence-prone anti-Semitic statements. . . . [Khallid's words were] a slap in the face to the memory of Dr. King, Medgar Evers, Malcolm X, Viola Liuzza, Andrew Goodman, James Chaney, Michael Schwerner, and countless others who devoted their lives to the liberation of African Americans and others who have been oppressed. Our struggle for racial justice must never be diverted or derailed by the senseless expressions of anti-Semitism and other hatred.[6]

About two hours later, William H. Gray III, the president of the United Negro College Fund, called Foxman, telling him that he was en route to give a talk that evening to the Philadelphia Baptist Ministers Conference and that he, too, would denounce Khallid.[7]

Pressure built for Farrakhan to respond. Kweisi Mfume, the

Maryland Democrat who headed the Congressional Black Caucus—and who, just three months before, had sealed a "sacred covenant" between the caucus and Farrakhan—equated Khallid's remarks with the "tone of intolerance" endemic to slavery and the Holocaust and asked Farrakhan "to clarify" the situation.

Farrakhan was silent until January 24, when he spoke at the 369th Armory in Harlem. Ten thousand men packed the armory; two thousand were turned away. Farrakhan started on a high moral plane designed to wean the audience from drugs and violence: "Our purpose is to discuss how God intends for a man to act. . . . You don't need a weapon if you have Allah. . . . You are programmed for self-destruction."

About 150 minutes after he began, when Farrakhan finally raised the issue that all had been waiting for, futility and frustration quickly supplanted his previous message of self-respect. All present were victims of the omnipotent Jewish powers: "You'll never succeed because of the Jews. . . . They're plotting against us even as we speak. . . . But I'm not trembling. I'm not afraid. They want to use my brother Khallid's words against me to divide the house. They are terrified. Oh, America, I warn you!"[8]

Farrakhan's attack on Jews—always scheming, always controlling—did not sit well with those who had denounced Khallid. Even Harlem's own congressman, Charles Rangel, said he "would have to believe that anybody who has been associated with the person who made the statement [at Kean State] would welcome the opportunity to dissociate themselves from that statement. We're all doing what we can to talk down hatred and prejudice."[9]

Meanwhile, Jewish pressure to turn Farrakhan and Khallid into a litmus test for blacks' morality backfired as African Americans chafed at the crude double standard. Whites were telling

them what to do, but no black had demanded that whites col-
lectively denounce Louisiana's Senator Ernest Hollings because
the previous December he had compared African leaders to
cannibals. In fact, the rhetorical stance some defensive Jewish
groups took seemed only to persuade blacks that they were the
lesser partner in the relationship. For what was supposed to be
a secret meeting in New York between ADL and NAACP officials,
the Jews were asked by their black counterparts to draft a statement on Farrakhan for the blacks to sign. But one member of the
NAACP board fumed that "we don't need Jews or anyone else
'calling us in' and telling us what to say to or about each other."[10]

Finally, on February 2, the Senate condemned a speech for
the first time in its history. Voting 97–0, it censured Khallid's
comments as "false, anti-Semitic, racist, divisive, repugnant,
and a disservice to all Americans." The same day, Mfume
ended the Congressional Black Caucus's covenant with the
NOI, affirming the "sacred and non-negotiable . . . right of all
people and all religions to be free from attacks, vilification and
defamation."[11]

It was not uncommon to ascribe Mfume's month-long dance
around Farrakhan and Khallid to the same dilemma that hobbled other mainstream black leaders: treading the narrow line
between moral impulses that steered them toward integration
and interracial accord and their community's desperate need to
cement coalitions and unions with *anyone,* even separatists and
nationalists, who might staunch black's misery that was worsening by the year. Between 1985 and 1990, violent deaths among
black teens increased by 78 percent. Fifty-seven percent of black
children lived in single-parent homes—compared with 16 percent of white youths. Twenty-one percent of black babies versus
6 percent of white babies were born to single, unwed teens.
Black men, who made up 6 percent of the country's population,
comprised half the male population in jails, had twice the

unemployment rate of white males, and had a suicide rate that had doubled since 1960.

With 65 percent of African Americans believing that racial equality would not be achieved in their lifetime, if ever, the tactical advantage had swung to Farrakhan, who was masterful at staking out a position for himself as the lone black leader with the temerity to speak black truth to white power. The minister also knew his base was expanding: in 1964, 3 percent of blacks thought the NOI was "doing the most . . . to help Negroes." By 1990, 20 percent said Farrakhan was "very effective" at representing people like themselves.[12]

In some ways, Farrakhan was closer than many black leaders to the more conservative politics not uncommon among ordinary blacks. Most blacks favored prayer in public schools; most black leaders opposed it. The percentage of blacks opposing abortions was three times that of black leaders who favored it. While Farrakhan never presented himself as a Republican or a Democrat, many of his values—discipline, self-reliance, economic self-betterment, even an abhorrence of welfare—were bedrock, country-club Republicanism, although the more reparation-oriented policies he supported, such as affirmative action, were classic Democratic policy.[13]

So when Farrakhan held a press conference in Washington about Khallid, the stage had been exquisitely set: Khallid had been denounced coast to coast as a sick crackpot, and Farrakhan as a flaming bigot. But Farrakhan also knew this was a splendid opportunity to speak to a widening constituency from a magnificent grandstand. He wanted them to know that, from *his* perspective, *he* hadn't been backed into a corner: he had backed *everyone else* into a corner. The greater the attacks against him and the Nation of Islam, the greater his standing among certain blacks. Isolation and vituperation only enhanced his image as prophet, nay-sayer, redeemer.[14]

Farrakhan's February 3 press conference put to shame Washington politicos who thought they'd mastered the art of media manipulation. He announced that Khallid would remain in the NOI but be stripped of his titles. In a "rebuke" more akin to a gentle, avuncular chiding than a public dressing-down of a foul-mouthed insubordinate, he scolded the "vile . . . , repugnant, malicious, mean-spirited . . . manner" in which Khallid had spoken "truths" at Kean State. But Farrakhan disagreed only with Khallid's *manner*, not his substance. Whites, he said, *were* "the beneficiaries of the wealth of our slave labor." The federal government *had* spied on black leaders and organizations, turning one against the other. Catholic popes had *not* "spoke[n] out . . . in blacks' defense when we were being lynched and burned and hung." But worst of all were those crafty Jews, who had owned "75 percent of the slaves in the South. . . . If Brother Khallid had just quoted the book [*The Secret Relationship between Blacks and Jews*, written by the Nation of Islam's anonymous Historical Research Department], nobody would have been able to condemn him or call him anti-Semitic."[15]

But if Farrakhan himself—who had admitted to me the previous August that he was no scholar of slavery, "just a victim of it"—had carefully read *The Secret Relationship*, he would not have said that Jews *owned* three-quarters of the slaves, since such a statistic is not even in the book. He was possibly alluding to the fact reported in *The Secret Relationship*, that in 1820, three-quarters of Jewish households in Charleston, Richmond, and Savannah owned "one or more slaves"; and in 1830, three-quarters of the heads of Jewish households in the South owned "one or more slaves."[16]

The Secret Relationship does not compare these ownership patterns with other ethnic or religious groups. In fact, the book places none of its "revelations" into any context—social, political, cultural, or historical. Nor does it include the following comments, which are in the very study from which it culls statistics about slave ownership in 1820: the proportion of Jews in the United States who owned slaves—about two-fifths— "should not seem abnormal when it is realized that about half the [Jewish] community lived in southern states where slavery was part of the mode of life."[17]

Also omitted is this balanced comment from Bertram Korn, a Jewish historian whose work *The Secret Relationship* otherwise liberally quotes:

> Jewish owners of slaves were not exceptional figures. . . . Jews acclimated themselves in every way to their environment; . . . they followed most of the life patterns of their fellow citizens. . . . The history of slavery would not have differed one whit from historic reality if no single Jew had been resident in the South. . . . But whether so many Jews would have achieved so high a level of social, political, economic and intellectual status and recognition without the presence of the lowly and degraded slave, is indeed dubious.[18]

Implicit in Korn's point is that Jews, a barely discernible minority in antebellum America (fifty thousand out of a total population of twenty-three million in 1850) had little leverage with which to assert whatever misgivings they may have had about slavery—if indeed they had any: "From testifying against Negroes in court, to apprehending a runaway slave, to inflicting punishment upon a convicted Negro, these Jews were thoroughly a part of their society." Trying to assimilate as best they could, some Jews may have been thankful that someone was below them on the social ladder, since "Negroes acted as an escape valve in Southern society. The Jews gained in status and security from the very presence of this large mass of defenseless victims who were compelled to absorb all of the prejudices which might otherwise have been expressed more frequently in anti-Jewish sentiment."[19]

Surely this perspective does not excuse Jews' participation in slavery, but their involvement becomes slightly more psychologically comprehensible if viewed within the wide arc of history. Not only were Jews among the most outnumbered of American minorities, but their foothold in most lands was invariably precarious. After being expelled from England in 1290, from France in the fourteenth century, and from Spain in 1492, the expediency of participating in some aspects of the slave trade may have seemed like the acceptable price of survival in America.

But even if enslaved blacks did provide a buffer against anti-Semitism, that did not necessarily mean that Jews embraced slavery more than Christians did—or even more than some blacks did. In the South in 1830, for example, only twenty Jews were among the twelve thousand slaveholders owning fifty or more slaves. According to David Brion Davis, a Yale history professor and one of the nation's foremost authorities on slavery, "[E]ven if each member of this Jewish slaveholding elite had owned 714 slaves— a ridiculously high figure in the American South—the total number would only equal the 100,000 slaves owned by black and colored planters in St. Dominique in 1789 on the eve of the Haitian Revolution." Davis concluded that "the allure of profits and power transcended all distinctions of race, ethnicity and religion." In Charleston, South Carolina, the percentage of free African Americans who owned slaves "increased from one half to three quarters as one moved up the socioeconomic scale." In Louisiana, black farmers "owned more than 50 or even 100 slaves."[20]

Contrary to the impression conveyed by *The Secret Relationship* that Jews' involvement in slavery was a deep, dark secret, suppressed by censorship and tribal pressures, their participation has been openly chronicled by historians, both Jewish and non-Jewish. David Brion Davis, for instance, has written that in

Suriname, later Dutch Guinea, in the late seventeenth and early eighteenth centuries, Jews established the town of Joden Savanne, where they "extracted labor from African slaves in one of the most deadly and oppressive environments in the New World." The "significant point" to Davis was not that such a history leads to the "often seductive belief in a collective guilt that descends through time to every present and future generation," but that *some* Jews found a "path to their own liberation and affluence by participating in a system of commerce that subjected another people to contempt, dishonor, coerced labor and degradation."[21]

Outside the Nation of Islam and the enclaves of Afrocentrism, *The Secret Relationship*—whose author was possibly an academic and probably not a member of the Nation of Islam—was denounced as a spiteful jumble of misquotes and miscited statistics. On February 8, 1995, in a rare move, the eighteen-thousand-member American Historical Association condemned the book for "violati[ng]" the historical record and being "part of a long anti-Semitic tradition that presents Jews as negative central actors in human history." And Henry Louis Gates Jr., chairman of Harvard's African-American Studies Department, called the book a "massive misinterpret[ation] of the historical record. . . . American Jewish merchants accounted for less than two percent of all the African slaves imported into the New World . . . [and] all the Jewish slave traders combined bought and sold fewer slaves than the single gentile firm of Franklin and Armfield."[22]

But *The Secret Relationship* was a call neither to reason nor was it dispassionate scholarship. Rather, it appealed to the depths of the black psyche that detected secret, genocidal conspiracies against them everywhere. Sixty percent of blacks suspected that the federal government "deliberately makes sure that drugs are easily available in poor black neighborhoods in order to harm black people." Twenty-nine percent thought that the AIDS virus "was deliberately created in a laboratory in order to infect black people."[23]

Farrakhan wholeheartedly subscribed to these theories. During dinner at his home in 1995, he told me he had recently read a book that claimed that one billion units of the AIDS virus had been shipped to Africa after being developed at Fort Meade in Maryland. The intent was to exterminate much of the continent's black population. Spotting what was probably a dubious, if not cynical, look on my face, Farrakhan's chief of staff, Leonard Muhammad, said, "You may think this is conspiracy and paranoia, but Jews say 'Never again,' and no one says they're conspiratorial or paranoid."[24]

Ironically, blacks' embrace of victimhood was occurring at the same time that many Jews were concluding that a new generation needed more than victimhood and guilt to be Jewish. Now blacks were challenging Jews about who was the bigger victim, the weaker victim, the more helpless victim, about who had *suffered* more. As part of NOI efforts to discredit Jews on all fronts, there was certainly a psychic advantage in settling this feud to blacks' advantage. Once again, the Jew was a fraud. Blacks would claim the victimization premium in America and wrest from Jews center stage of redressing past wrongs. Blacks would claim the victimization premium in America and wrest from Jews the center stage of redressing past wrongs.

Behind *The Secret Relationship* was a far-from-secret agenda. As Farrakhan said before fifteen thousand people at the University of Illinois in 1991, the book had been intended to "rearrange a relationship" that "has been detrimental to us." For all its academic pretensions—1,275 footnotes, an editors' statement that they had excluded "a substantial body of evidence ... from sources considered to be anti-Semitic and/or anti-Jewish"—the very impetus of the book had stemmed from Jews' protests in 1984 when Farrakhan attributed slavery to "some Arabs, some Jews, some European whites, American whites, [the] government of America. . . . The Jews came out forcibly denying any involvement and accusing me of being an anti-Semite for even saying it. So . . . we . . . researched it and found not only were they involved, but they were the architects of it, and that's serious."[25]

So *The Secret Relationship* would settle a grudge by demonstrating that Farrakhan had been merely a good student of history, not an anti-Semite. But on the slavery issue, both Farrakhan and Jews were retroactively applying 1990s standards of conscience and culpability. Many contemporary Jews, proud of their compassion for the underclass, which they partly credited to their own bondage in Egypt, were honestly ignorant about their ancestors' involvement in slavery, even though it was frankly discussed by historians. Farrakhan sought to discredit them as traitors to their own twentieth-century identity as promoters of social justice because a minority of their ancestors had owned slaves. But sadly, neither side had much use for nuance. As "history" was mutated into propaganda, the chasm between blacks and Jews broadened into a canyon so wide that the other side could sometimes not even be seen, much less heard.

The Khallid affair didn't seem to hurt Farrakhan. If anything, it brightened his aura of valor. With so many blacks convinced that America had abandoned them, Farrakhan's gall became Farrakhan's allure.

In the next few months of 1996, Farrakhan increasingly dominated black politics. Within twelve days after his February 3 Washington press conference, 70 percent of blacks affirmed that he was saying things the country needed to hear, 63 percent said he spoke "the truth," and 53 percent called him a model for black youth. Only 34 percent considered him "a racist or bigot."[26]

Requests for interviews came from the nation's top broadcasters, all of whom gave him a remarkable opportunity to "mainstream" his message beyond the cloistered NOI. On February 25, Farrakhan appeared on Arsenio Hall's late-night talk show. From the outset, it was obvious that the evening would resemble a brotherly lovefest more than a properly rigorous interview. When a beaming Farrakhan almost bounced onto the stage, Hall embraced him. Hall didn't ask a single follow-up question or ask for clarification, elaboration.

Once, he even let Farrakhan speak up to six minutes uninterrupted, a rare display first of a talk show host showing good manners, and then of Farrakhan spreading interracial joy and brotherhood.

For instance, when Hall asked Farrakhan if he was the "new black hitler," Farrakhan responded: "I have never desired to put another human being in an oven. . . . If I am righteous, I can never hate another person because of their faith." Hall wondered, would Farrakhan "convert criminals and drug addicts . . . [into] an army of hate" for himself? "I will convert criminals and drug addicts to an army of love for ourselves— and if we can find a way to communicate the same love we have for self, it won't stay there. It's for the total human family of the planet earth."

Eight weeks later, Farrakhan sat down with Barbara Walters on ABC's *20/20*. Walters tried to steer the interview where *she* wanted it to go and to not let Farrakhan slide by with facile reasoning or take historical liberties:

FARRAKHAN: When I have to look at a movie and see a black person depicted as a buffoon . . .

WALTERS: You don't anymore. That's changed.

FARRAKHAN: But the image is there.

WALTERS: Society is trying.

FARRAKHAN: But the image is there. When I've got to go to school and read a textbook about Little Black Sambo . . .

WALTERS: It's changed. It's no longer there.

FARRAKHAN: If Brother Khallid is saying that which stings and hurts, then . . . say that's a terrible use of language, and then go back and look at the terrible use of language by your people.

WALTERS: But this is in the present he's saying this. This isn't ten years ago or twenty years ago.[28]

In June, the biggest news about the NAACP's first National African American Leadership Summit was that Farrakhan, the "bogeyman" from the Nation of Islam, would attend. His mere presence so diverted attention from the summit's agenda—to create a "common front" that transcended ideology, personality, and organization—that this granddaddy of all integration groups was accused of disgracing its rich tradition by inviting a nihilist into its historically egalitarian tent.

Farrakhan put his own spin on the invitation:

> By keeping the "radicals" and "extremists" out of the tent, you cannot affect their "radicalism" or their "extremism." Nor can they affect your lethargy or bourgeois attitude. By bringing everybody under a tent, which raises the discomfort level of all those present, because we are all comfortable with those who think and feel as we think and feel, we . . . have a chance to dialogue with many in our community that we never would have dialogued with before. . . . If I am an "anti-Semite," [the Harvard African American professor] Cornel West is not an anti-Semite and Roger Wilkins [a black academic and journalist and grandson of Roy Wilkins, the NAACP's executive secretary from 1955 to 1977] is not an anti-Semite. Those who have traditionally

been members of the NAACP are not haters of Jews or whites. .
. . Sharing ideas and concepts with men like this can affect
change in us as we affect change in them. I don't think that we
can change them for the worse.

But wouldn't some Jews and whites say that Farrakhan might
change the *moderates* for the worse? "Then," reasoned Farrakhan, "some Jews don't have enough confidence in the bril-
liance of a Roger Wilkins or a Cornel West."[29]

The summit didn't change Wilkins (who didn't attend anyway). Or West. Or certainly Farrakhan, who shortly before the
conference defended Khallid Abdul Muhammad's latest attack
on Jews—God should kill the Jewish "bloodsuckers"—by asking
an audience, "Did he lie?" The crowd roared, "No!"[30]

The summit, in fact, *couldn't* have changed anyone, since no
one was willing to shed his or her basic ideology: in a reprise of
the turn-of-the-century arguments between W. E. B. Du Bois
and Booker T. Washington, the three-day summit was a head-on
collision between social activists (NAACP regulars and black
politicians) and economic entrepreneurs (Farrakhan and black
nationalists). As one participant dryly said, "We were debating
which discipline. If *we* could settle that, Du Bois and Washington would have gotten together."[31]

The summit proved that Farrakhan, the reputed bête noire of
the "civilized world," was house-trained: no biting, no fighting, no
mussing. Even moderates could sit in the same room with him
and emerge unscathed. For the NAACP, the epicenter of black cen-
trism, to open its doors to him was as heady and momentous as a
young girl's first date. But the nagging issue was: *Who* was courting *whom*? And did Farrakhan's presence mean that the NAACP
was abandoning its commitment to fair play and a fair world?

In another six weeks, such questions were moot. On August
20, Benjamin Chavis was fired as the NAACP's executive direc-

tor for authorizing the use of $332,400 from the financially strapped organization to pay a woman threatening him with a sexual discrimination lawsuit. Chavis, who had headed the NAACP for only sixteen months, had been Farrakhan's main ally inside the NAACP. With Chavis gone, Farrakhan was gone—or so it seemed.[32]

Farrakhan never lacked for resourcefulness. With entrée to moderates seemingly blocked by Chavis's ouster, he made an end run around them by calling for the biggest march in the nation's history. One million black men. *Only* men, for they needed to repent for sins against themselves and their community. After this "army" proved they could gather in massive numbers without "creat[ing] tremendous havoc," black males would "never again be looked at as the criminals, the clowns, the buffoons, the dregs of society."[33]

To many observers, the call for a march seemed arrogant and futile. Few establishment black leaders or mainstream media outlets paid any attention to it—other than to dismiss it as a crackpot scheme from a man who had defended himself just five years before as "not known to be a nut and . . . not known to be insane." But that was when he was telling editors at the *Washington Post* about a vision he'd had in September 1985: he was being carried by a beam of light from a mountaintop in Mexico into the half-mile by half-mile Mother Plane—or as Farrakhan helpfully translated for the *Post*'s editors, "You call them Unidentified Flying Objects." There, through a loudspeaker in a ceiling, Elijah Muhammad warned Farrakhan that then-President Ronald Reagan and the Joint Chiefs of Staff were planning a war. Muhammad did not specify against whom the war would be waged. Two years later, Farrakhan concluded that the foe was Libya's Muammar Khaddafi, whose capital had been bombed by American warplanes in April 1986.[34]

By 1989, Farrakhan had decided that this attack was a prelude to "an even more significant and consequential war . . . , a war against the black people of America, the Nation of Islam, and Louis Farrakhan, with particular emphasis on our black youth, under the guise of a war against drug sellers, drug users, gangs and violence."[35]

But a Million Man March was a very different ball of wax. By late September of 1995, after black newspapers and radio stations had been steadily beating their drums for the march for months, it was apparent to even the whitest of whites that *something* would happen in Washington on October 16, 1995. Almost overnight, news magazines and TV networks unearthed a "sudden" groundswell for the march. Pundits began talking about "the Farrakhan march." Moralists began to moan that anyone who endorsed the march would be lending credence and respectability to a malignant bigot.

As the date for the march approached, it was increasingly endowed with a religious flavor. Fast, Farrakhan told black America, from sundown the night before the march to sundown the day of the march, borrowing from the Jewish concept of the beginning and ending of the day. Behave as Jews do on Yom Kippur, for "in spite of hatred, in spite of oppression, . . . [they] have managed to survive through all the centuries with dignity . . . *because* of the Day of Atonement."[36]

Jews bristled at the injunction to mimic Yom Kippur: was it yet another slur by the man who had so frequently smeared them and their faith? "Were these words said by someone else who hadn't spread so much hate," said David Friedman, Washington director of the Anti-Defamation League, "it would be easier to accept them as a positive tribute to Jewish observance."[37]

On the evening of October 15 and in the early hours of the next day, the city of Washington, already 66 percent black, began to get even blacker. Black men from around the country began to fill the Mall in front of the Capitol Building. For the 1963 March on Washington, Martin Luther King Jr. had 250,000 blacks and whites face westward toward the Lincoln Memorial, with the Washington Monument behind them. The Washington-to-Lincoln era roughly corresponded to the years blacks were in bondage, so Farrakhan asked them to face eastward, toward a new dawn.

African drums and an ecumenical service broke the silence at sunrise. By 10:00 A.M., the quiet, attentive crowd extended two-thirds of the way from the Capitol to the Washington Monument: men in jeans or suits; men carrying briefcases or knapsacks; men holding young children or carrying aloft pictures of their heroes (Malcolm or King or Noble Drew Ali of the Moorish Science Temple, a possible precursor to the Nation of Islam). A gathering of the tribes. A sea of dreadlocks and bright, round African hats, of sandals and oxfords, sweatshirts and pinstripes. It was a march unlike any other Washington had seen: a march for self-dignity and self-respect. The handful of whites on the Mall, adrift in a sea of at least four hundred thousand blacks, glimpsed how blacks feel every day being outnumbered, eight to one, by whites. The black "army" caught a fleeting glimmer of the joy of being the majority, a benefit lost on most whites who take it for granted.

A cynic could have easily concluded that Farrakhan's separatist wish had been granted: America was *already* bifurcated into two distinct nations: one pale, one dark; both other to the other, speaking different languages, engaging different visions, resonating to different rhythms and cadences. Another cynic might have pegged the march as white America's worst nightmare: hundreds of thousands of *black men* converging at the behest of the black leader who most frightened America's caucasians.

In some ways, there were *two* marches: the march on the podium and the march on the Mall. Each had its own agenda. From the podium a few speakers, including the Reverend Jesse Jackson, gracefully tried to distance the march from Farrakhan.

But the preponderance of speakers from the Nation of Islam—several ministers, a "wife" of Elijah Muhammad, one of Farrakhan's sons—and the presence everywhere of grim, silent, young, bow-tied members of the Nation's Fruit of Islam, gave the march the feel (and the tensions) of an NOI rally.[38]

Yet, for most on the Mall, the march endorsed neither Farrakhan nor the Nation of Islam, but the selfhood and the integrity of the black male. As one forty-seven-year-old writer from Harlem said, "Farrakhan had the idea, but *he's* not important. It's the idea, the community, that's important. Maybe through this whole process, Farrakhan is seeing the world in a new way."[39]

Finally, around 3:20 P.M., the crowd began to lose patience and manners. Many had been on the Mall since dawn. They picked up the chant, "Farrakhan. Farrakhan. We want Farrakhan," drowning out the two men who spoke just before the minister. A cheer rose when Farrakhan finally took the podium, yet when he started to speak, many were visibly let down. Within fifteen minutes, Farrakhan began to lose the crowd, some drifting toward benches to rest their feet, some heading toward the train stations or bus depots for their long rides home. At the pinnacle of his career, before a Mall crammed with men who had been stirred by his improbable vision of such a gathering, and with 2.2 million households watching him on television, Louis Farrakhan, ordinarily a master of oratory, meandered through a loose patchwork of themes that never quite cohered. Even more of a surprise was that from the very person who had called for a "Day of Atoning" came no atonement. Instead, his two-and-a-half-hour "lecture," as he tagged

his oration, was a catalog of evils and infamies visited throughout history on blacks. On this day when he implored black men
to look inward, to repent, to confront their weaknesses and
uphold their strengths, Louis Farrakhan, who professed to be a
humble servant of Allah and the Honorable Elijah Muhammad,
seemed to have forgotten the meaning of introspection.[40]

Not that Farrakhan was incapable of such ruminations. In
vast arenas and in the privacy of his home, he had freely, openly
admitted his failings and faults. For a very public man, he could
often reveal his very private soul. But on this one day when he
had all America riveted to his every syllable, America heard
everything from Farrakhan *except* penitence. This was a significant lost opportunity, because Farrakhan, while cloaking himself in the trappings of prophets and the righteous garb of religion, had never claimed to be a saint. Like all of us, he fell far
from that mark.

As Farrakhan offered up a quilt of Masonic lore and NOI theology, he somehow remembered that the black community is
predominantly a Christian community. He mentioned Moses,
David, Solomon, Nebuchadnezzar, Jesus, and Matthew, cited the
Lord's Prayer and a spiritual ("There is a balm in Gilead to heal
the sin-sick soul"), and quoted or alluded to the Bible at least
thirty times while referring to the Koran only five times. If anyone usually categorized as a black "extremist" had ever tried to
center himself squarely in the psyche of black America, with all
its layers and permutations, it was Louis Farrakhan that day.

Numerology came first in Farrakhan's lecture: the men on the
Mall were surrounded by omens and spells. Adding a "1" to
"555," the height of the Washington Monument in feet, produced the year 1555, "the year we arrived in Jamestown as
slaves." (He did not mention that Jamestown was not founded
until 1607.) Then came a roster of nineteens: the statues of Presidents Lincoln and Jefferson at their respective monuments in

Washington were each nineteen feet tall; the combined order of Jefferson and Lincoln in the sequence of presidents—numbers three and sixteen—was nineteen, which was also the number of the nineteen rays of the sun on the Great Seal of the United States. All these corresponded to the power that the NOI (and Sufism, the mystical school of traditional Islam) had invested in nineteen, which, according to the Koran, was the number of angels hovering over the fires of hell.[41]

But only a small minority on the Mall knew anything about the spiritual dimensions of the number nineteen, and Farrakhan's explanation was far from helpful: "That number 19—when you have a 'nine' you have a womb that is pregnant. And when you have a 'one' standing by the 'nine,' it means that there's something secret that has to be unfolded."[42]

Next came history, a history of resentment (and of some fabrication). "White supremacy," proclaimed Farrakhan, "caused Napoleon to blow the nose off the Sphinx because it reminded [him] too much of the black man's nose." In reality, the Sphinx's eyes and nose were shot off during target practice by Ottoman Mamelukes, the Islamic overlords of Egypt, about eleven hundred years *before* Napoleon landed in Egypt. Napoleon wanted to capture Egypt for strategic reasons, but also to catalog whatever was left of Egypt's ancient civilization before it all vanished. Not only did he order that the Sphinx be dug out of the sand that then covered it to the neck, but he also established the Egyptian Institute, which published, over twenty years, ten volumes that effectively inaugurated the discipline of Egyptology.[43]

Midway through the lecture, Farrakhan discoursed on the day's theme of "atonement": "When you 'a-tone,' if you take the *t* and couple it with the *a* and hyphenate it, you get *at-one*. So when you 'a-tone,' you become 'at-one.' At one with who? The 'a-tone,' or the one God."[44]

Near the end, he issued a call to sit down with Jews: "I don't like this squabble with the members of the Jewish community. If you can sit down with Arafat, where there are rivers of blood between [Arab and Jew], why can't you sit down with us where there are no rivers of blood?"[45]

But Farrakhan didn't say *what* he wanted to discuss with Jews. The widely held assumption was that any Farrakhan-Jewish dialogue would determine whether *he* was anti-Semitic; whether *they* were "bloodsuckers"; whether, indeed, the chasm between him and Jews could even be bridged. This, surely, was on Farrakhan's agenda, but he omitted plans to debate whether Elijah Muhammad was the messiah and, if so, the extent of the duty owed by Jews, Moslems, Christians, and the American government to Muhammad.[46]

At the end of his speech, with the sky finally dark and maybe one-third of his original audience remaining on the Mall, Farrakhan led the assembled men in a seven-minute pledge to help rebuild their community and abstain from violence, drugs, and sexual or verbal abuse.[47]

Unavoidably, Farrakhan's speech would be compared to Reverend King's thirty-two years before at the Lincoln Memorial. King's had been a concise, mesmerizing, soaring piece of poetry; garnished with acute phrasings, stellar imagery, biblical cadences, and a clear, precise vision; furiously, passionately fused together, each phrase building on what preceded it and each foreshadowing what would come. Although King wandered from his prepared text, his message and manner were familiar. In Detroit two months before his march and in Chicago just the week before the march, his "I have a dream" phrase had elicited standing ovations: it was almost as if he were doing a test run for the Washington march.[48]

King thus had proven oratorical passages. Moreover, he was a proven leader of national stature. In 1995, Farrakhan may have been the leader in the black community with the greatest longevity. No one else with his prominence dated back to Malcolm and Elijah and, indirectly, to Garvey. But prominence was not stature, and Farrakhan had amassed only a small portion of King's eminence. Even in the black community, the name "Farrakhan" could produce guffaws, dismay, or disgust as often (if not more often) as it elicited respect and admiration. For all his concern (especially in his Million Man March speech) about black unity, for all the decades he had spent on the front lines of a version of economic black self-empowerment and a version of religious black self-fulfillment, Farrakhan was deemed by many blacks to be an opportunist, a mere dilettante of black harmony.

Not uncommon on the streets of black America, even among some of his oldest and best friends in Boston, were variations on the question: What has Farrakhan really done for us? The answer was slightly less murky in the immediate aftermath of the Million Man March. He was the only person who could so intuit the needs and the frustrations of America's blacks that he could summon hundreds of thousands to the nation's capital to, of all things, atone. The men hadn't come for Farrakhan, they had came for an opportunity to be publicly redeemed, to assert a manhood America had long denied them, to thumb their noses at how they had been treated and at being told who deserved to be crowned a legitimate black leader. They knew there was no one better in the black world with whom to thumb a nose at whites than Farrakhan. He'd been doing it for decades.

The march's indisputable success finally convinced some black leaders that Farrakhan was a force to be reckoned with. Thirty days after the event, the fifth National African American Leadership Summit convened in Washington, headed by Farrakhan. Attending for the first time was Hugh Price, head of the National Urban League, who had boycotted the march because he disapproved of Farrakhan's anti-Jewish statements. But he came to the summit because the march had been "an extraordinary, extraordinary event: The largest family values rally in the history of the U.S."[49]

Farrakhan had at last achieved the goal he had laid out to me for himself two years before: "I've got grandchildren. I'm not getting any younger. I want to leave *something* when I leave the earth." That same afternoon two years before he had also said, gently and quietly, in a small room just inside his Chicago home, "God is not making men today to . . . grovel at the foot of no man. We don't fear the censure of any censurer. We fear God. We all ought to be respectful of God. And we all ought to try to do justice by each other."[50]

There was wisdom in that wish:

> We all ought to try to do justice by each other." Justice from blacks and justice from whites; justice from Jews and Christians and Moslems. But it had to come most forcefully, adamantly, and authentically from those who say they bear the mantle of the Lord, for without such men and women carrying olive branches, the nation was doomed to words of hate and deeds of violence and a hollow authority that mocked the very morality to which it lay claim. The task before Louis Farrakhan and his Nation, despite his huge success at the Million Man March, was to prove he could meet that challenge; that he was not only a prophet of rage who assaulted the social order, but a man of peace and a force for good; that he could indeed harness the love of self and the love of race that he championed into channels of good for "the total human family of the planet earth."[51]

The man who stood before hundreds of thousands of black men on October 16, 1995, was, at heart, not much different from the boy who had played his violin for hours in the locked bathroom at his mother's house on Shawmut Avenue in Roxbury, hearing in his mind's eye the roar of the crowd and watching with careful deliberation his every bow stroke in the mirror, calculating his every gesture, his every movement, every tilt and move of his head. Now his voice was his instrument, his pulpit was his stage—and the world was his mirror. But Farrakhan also had become a mirror, a reflection of the traumas and the hopes that plagued our nation's soul and frayed its fabric, and that still, almost four hundred years since the first black slave was brought to the English colonies in America, tainted and corrupted the very essence of what it meant to have a United States.

Within three months after the march, Farrakhan answered the implicit queries about how he would leverage the massive political capital he had reaped from the Million Man March. Essentially, he would deploy his new claim to power on *his* terms. He would defy expectations, not tempering his rhetoric and outrageousness, but pursue instead the unpalatable "truths" available to him as a "man of God," truths which bruised ordinary mortals—and ordinary nations—but to which he and his "nation" were privy. The "center" still held Farrakhan because the "center" to which he owed allegiance, one impervious to external dictates and norms, *was* Farrakhan.

On a five-week "World Friendship Tour" in January and February through twenty-three countries in both Africa and the Middle East, Farrakhan met with political and religious leaders. At the beginning of the tour, he was moderate and accommodating. In South Africa, Nelson Mandela lectured him on his government's policy of "non-racialism," a policy which Farrakhan told reporters he "agreed with totally. Islam is a religion which, if practiced, disallows racialism, racism, injustice, tyranny and oppression." In Liberia, he said that "the spirit of atonement, the spirit of reconciliation, and the spirit of forgiveness is the spirit we bring to . . . Africa and, really, to the world." In Gambia, he said, "We must submit ourselves to Allah and rid ourselves of ignorance."[52]

The "World Friendship Tour" seemed to be taking the high

road—until Farrakhan began consorting with some of America's worst enemies. In Libya, Muammar Khaddafi pledged Farrakhan $1 billion to mobilize "oppressed . . . blacks, Arabs, Muslims, and red Indians" to influence the outcome of American foreign policy and the 1996 presidential election. In Tehran the next week, Farrakhan pledged that "God will destroy America by the hands of Muslims. God will not give Japan or Europe the honor of bringing down the United States. This is an honor God will bestow upon Muslims. . . . " In another twenty-four hours, he met in Baghdad with Iraqi president Saddam Hussein, then held a press conference deploring United Nations' sanctions against Iraq as a "crime against humanity" and vowed to work "nights and days marshalling the moral force that I believe is in all the American people to bring every pressure . . . on our government . . . that the mass murder of the Iraqi people must cease."[53]

Farrakhan may have been adhering to his thoroughly idiosyncratic moral imperatives, but back home there was broad displeasure, if not outright disgust. The Justice Department readied a letter warning Farrakhan to register with the federal government if he planned to act as a foreign agent for Libya. The State Department accused him of "cavorting with dictators" in Libya and Iran. The syndicated columnist Clarence Page, never one of Farrakhan's favorite black journalists, questioned why Farrakhan "typically turns a blind eye to reports of slavery in Africa," especially in the Sudan, where a thirteen-year-old civil war between the mostly Arab north and the mostly black south had resulted in a thriving, brutal practice of Arabs enslaving blacks. Page also questioned why Farrakhan had not grilled Khaddafi about his own country's role in this servitude. According to a State Department report, women and children from the Sudan had been trucked to unknown destinations in Libya as recently as 1993.[54]

And throughout the nation, there were grumblings that Farrakhan had committed acts of treason, a charge not leveled at
any Nation of Islam leader since 1942 when Elijah Muhammad
had been convicted for violating federal draft laws.[55]

On February 25, three days after returning to the United
States, Farrakhan pulled out what had become his standard
defense when becoming embroiled in yet another controversy.
At the Nation of Islam's annual Savior's Day in Chicago, he told
twelve thousand cheering admirers that if he was asked to testify before Congress about his trip, he would "call the rolls of the
members of Congress who are honorary members of the Israeli
Knesset" and would question the United States' policy priorities:
"Every year, you [the United States] give Israel $4 [billion] to $6
billion of the taxpayer money and you haven't asked the people
nothing. Who are you an agent of?"[56]

It seemed that all Farrakhan was determined to prove by
squandering any good he could have gained from the Million
Man March was that his political and organizational skills were
a distant second to his skills with angry, troubled—and troubling—words. Instead of marshalling the momentum of the
march in the service of a very specific, very detailed, very aggres-
sive political agenda that he could have announced at a press
conference the day after the march, he chose to solder alliances
with some of America's worst adversaries abroad. It made one
wonder about his political sagacity and his bearings in the more
practical, more sensible world outside of the Nation of Islam.

Essentially, the Farrakhan/Tripoli/Tehran/Baghdad axis
posed little strategic danger to the United States. And it surely
did not advance Farrakhan as a man of peace and moderation.
Worse, it dashed the hopes of many blacks that their leaders and
organizations from one end of the political and religious spec-
trum to the other were finally ready to cobble together a broad
united front that could transcend their differences for the

greater good of their community—and the nation. The Million Man March had, indeed, been a high point for blacks: It reminded them—and the rest of America—that a people scorned and depicted as brutal outlaws, as restless, indiscriminate philanderers, as a blight and a burden on the nation and even on their own community had a dignity and a gravity that belied their image. Yet, the aftermath of the march was close to a shambles. And at the center of the shambles stood Louis Farrakhan, ever-defiant and always provocative, his sense of self furiously inflated by the irrefutable success of the march, and who had been persuaded more than ever that he did not need the legitimacy sought by lesser, more ordinary men because *his* legitimacy was unique, special, irreversible: Bestowed upon him by God, it could *never* be retracted by man. With "divine" authority, he would proceed to venture into the world, saying what others did not, infuriating his foes with his temerity and indelibly convinced that *his* way was God's way, that he would never compromise or mince words, that the furies of his people drove his mission and his rhetoric.

But lost in all the heated words and counterwords, in all the verbal jousting, was just what any of this meant in the real lives of real people suffering, as Louis Farrakhan well knew, in the bleak ghettoes of America and who needed more than theatrics on an international stage to relieve them from their despair and their sorrows. Farrakhan may have been a release valve for their wrath, but whether he was the purveyor of a constructive *answer* to their plight seemed increasingly dubious in the aftermath of the March that had appeared to make him the black leader of the decade—and the tour that appeared to make him the political bumbler and maybe even the traitor of the day.

Acknowledgments

Behind the single name on the front cover of this book are dozens of people who provided insights and history, helped with research, and sustained my spirits when they were flagging.

Thanks, first of all, to Minister Louis Farrakhan, whose interviews with me provided the initial impetus for this book. The minister was generous with his time, his hospitality, and his thoughtfulness, occasionally opening a door for me to someone I needed to interview that would not have been open otherwise. Minister Farrakhan was well aware from the beginning of this project that it was not intended to be an "authorized" biography. Deeply appreciated are the risks he took by speaking with me. I also appreciate that he allowed certain members of the Nation of Islam to speak with me and that he encouraged several non-NOI friends to be interviewed.

The veracity and the tenor of a biography greatly depend upon details, large and small, that can be gleaned from contemporaries of the subject. Among those who opened their lives to me, and in the process gave me insights into the life of Minister Farrakhan, were Daisy Voigt, Askia Muhammad, Khalid Lateef, Hasan Sharif, Farid Muhammad, Elaine Skorodin, Rabbi Herman Schaalman, Clarence Jones, Dr. Abdul Alim Shabazz, George Guscott, John Bynoe, Elma Lewis, John Rice, Malik Abdul Khallaq, and Amanda Houston.

Because of the volatility and the sensitivity of this project, many whom I interviewed preferred to remain anonymous. To those, a confidential tip of my hat in appreciation.

James Muhammad, thanks for the fine conversation over breakfast at the Salaam. Brian Jackson, thanks for the thorough nighttime tour of NOI landmarks and, most assuredly, for your trust. Abe Foxman, your honesty and openness, as always, were appreciated. Frank Reid, dinner with you helped crystallize some of my thinking about the minister in particular and about race in America in general. Julian Bond, your comments (not to mention your fine foreword) were invaluable. James Besser and Mustafa El-Amin, you went beyond the call of duty. John Devaney and Sandy MacDonald, thanks for the bed on your top floor.

Encouraging me from the sidelines throughout this project were Robert Kanigel, Helen Whitney, Ira Rifkin, Fiona Lawrence, Robyn Katz, Larry Sandler, Stuart Matlins, Chris Leighton, Joel Zaiman, Charlie Obrecht, Art Abramson, and all my friends at 1501 Broadway. Whoever I left out gets a free dinner.

Computer maven Bert Orlitzky somehow got me up and running on a technology I can only pretend to understand.

Especially helpful on delineating the theological differences between the Nation of Islam and more traditional Islam were *The Religion of Islam and the Nation of Islam: What Is the Dif-*

ference? by Mustafa El-Amin (Newark, N.J.: El Amin Productions), and *The Holy Quran's Condemnation of the Racist and Un-Islamic Ideology of "The Lessons" of W. D. Fard and the Teachings of Minister Louis Farrakhan's "Nation of Islam"* by Imam Khalid S. Lateef (Wheatley Heights, N.Y.: Americans for Justice and Positive Change).

My two researchers, Sarah Rottenberg in Washington and Jennifer McPeak in Boston, were quick and savvy, always able to adroitly maneuver their way around libraries and archives and never tiring until all the pieces of various puzzles were solved. May I be so lucky as to find two more like them for my next project.

Appreciation to Chuck Buerger and Michael Davis for backing my original idea to interview Minister Farrakhan. My agents, Bill Adler and Lisa Swayne, went far beyond the standard obligations of the author-agent relationship. Neither I nor my family could have survived the rigors of this project without their help and understanding. Alan Sultan and Joel Joseph were instrumental in getting this book off the ground. Stephanie Lehrer, Marilyn Mazur, Kerrie Loyd, and Richard Fumosa —all at Basic Books—all did yeoman's work to get this book out. And every reader should thank John Donatich, my editor, for his keen eye and sharp insights.

My parents imparted the sense of racial justice and curiosity that undergird this book. And my family (including all the many pets, except maybe Lady) supported me from the moment I had the idea for *Prophet of Rage*. They tolerated my crankiness, endured my enthusiasms, and gave me countless hours of (relatively) undisturbed quiet and privacy. To them—my wife, Helen, and our daughters, Sarah, Amy, and Molly—my love, affection, and gratitude.

Notes

Prologue

1. Louis Farrakhan, dinner conversation with the author, Farrakhan's home (Chicago), June 21, 1995.
2. Louis Farrakhan, interview with the author, Chicago, August 5, 1993.
3. Louis Farrakhan, speech, Chicago, November 21, 1982.
4. Farrakhan interview, August 5, 1993.
5. Ibid.
6. "Boston Minister Tells of Malcolm—Muhammad's Biggest Hypocrite," *Muhammad Speaks*, December 4, 1964, pp. 11–15; remarks on *20/20*, ABC-TV, April 22, 1994.
7. Amanda Houston, interview with the author, Boston, June 2, 1995.

8. James Baldwin, *Nobody Knows My Name* (New York: Dell, 1961), p. 69.
9. Confidential interview with the author, Maryland, July 5, 1994.
10. Confidential interview with the author, Chicago, June 20, 1995.

Chapter 1

1. Bruce Perry, *Malcolm* (Barrytown, N.Y.: Station Hill Press, 1992), pp. 12–43; Hillel Levine and Lawrence Harmon, *The Death of an American Jewish Community* (New York: Free Press, 1993), p. 105. Other nicknames for the West Indians were "Turks," "black monkeys," "monkey chasers," and "banana eaters." Most of these nicknames came from whites, a few from blacks.
2. Levine and Harmon, *The Death of an American Jewish Community*, pp. 37–38.
3. On desegregation, see Elizabeth Hafkin Peck, *Black Migration and Poverty* (New York: Academic Press, 1979), p. 92; on Coughlin, see Nat Hentoff, *Boston Boy* (New York: Knopf, 1986), p. 18.
4. George Guscott, interview with the author, Boston, June 1, 1995.
5. John Bynoe, telephone interview with the author, June 6, 1995.
6. Guscott interview, June 1, 1995.
7. Ibid.
8. Peck, *Black Migration and Poverty*, p. 94.
9. Malcolm X, with the assistance of Alex Haley, *The Autobiography of Malcolm X* (New York: Ballantine, 1992), p. 41.
10. Ibid., pp. 42–43.
11. Malik Abdul Khallaq, interview with the author, Boston, June 1, 1995.
12. John Rice, interview with the author, Boston, June 1, 1995.
13. Guscott interview, June 1, 1995; Bynoe interview, June 6, 1995.
14. Rev. Nathan Wright, telephone interview with the author, May 26, 1995.

15. Elma Lewis, telephone interview with the author, June 7, 1995.

16. Louis Farrakhan, speech before Christian clergy, St. Louis, September 13, 1995.

17. For description of Farrakhan's mother, see Wright interview, May 26, 1995; on West Indians' expectations, see Lewis interview, June 7, 1995.

18. Louis Farrakhan, talk at Symphony Hall, Newark, N.J., April 28, 1995; New York City birth certificate for Louis Eugene Walcott; on Mae's attempts to abort, see Louis Farrakhan, *A Torchlight for America* (Chicago: FCN Publishing, 1993), p. 110.

19. Farrakhan talk, April 28, 1995.

20. Ibid. Farrakhan also told the white woman who taught him violin in the early and mid–1990s that he may have had some white ancestry. Telephone interview with Elaine Skorodin, June 21, 1995.

21. Ibid.

22. James Davis, *Who Is Black: One Nation's Definition* (University Park, Penn.: Pennsylvania State University Press, 1991), pp. 5, 21. Davis also notes that "in terms of gene frequencies, . . . somewhere between one-fifth and one-fourth of the genes of the American black population are from white ancestors. The national estimates by physical anthropologists have ranged from about 20 percent to 31 percent. . . . The estimates vary considerably for different regions, with Northern blacks having the larger percentages of 'white genes.'"

    Davis further observes that there are estimates that "about one percent of the genes of the white population of the United States are from African ancestors"—a possibility that makes biological and philosophical mincemeat of the "one-drop rule" that *any* black blood automatically categorizes one as black. Or it means that a number of whites who would be classed as black because of their gene composition have been quite successful at "passing" as white.

23. Phillips Verner Bradford and Harvey Blume, *Ota Benga* (New York: Delta Books, 1993), p. 128.

24. On skin color in Farrakhan's family, see Lewis interview, June 7, 1995; on Malcolm's family, see Perry, *Malcolm*, p. 5.

25. On Boston, see Harmon and Levine, *The Death of an American Jewish Community*, pp. 37–38; for street addresses, see *Boston Directory* (Boston: R. L. Polk & Co. Publishers, 1936, 1937); on Farrakhan's father, see Lewis interview, June 7, 1995.

26. Hentoff, *Boston Boy*, p. 21.

27. On defending Jewish friends, see Farrakhan dinner conversation, June 21, 1995; on hitting a white boy, see Farrakhan interview, June 27, 1994.

28. Khallaq interview, June 1, 1995.

29. Confidential telephone interview with former employer of Mae Manning Clarke, June 30, 1995.

30. For date of move to Boston, see "Alvan Farrakhan Dies," *The Final Call*, November 2, 1994, p. 3; for costs of music lessons and music teachers, see Guscott interview, June 1, 1995; for more on music teachers, see Bynoe interview, June 6, 1995, and Louis Farrakhan, interview with the author, Chicago, June 27, 1994; on starting lessons at age six, see "Black Journalism Review," WEAA-FM, October 15, 1995; on playing violin in bathroom, see "Farrakhan: On the Road with the Fiery Black Minister," *Life* (August 1984): 53.

31. Bynoe interview, June 6, 1995; Lewis interview, June 7, 1995; Randall K. Burkett, *Garveyism as a Religious Movement* (Metuchen, N.J.: Scarecrow Press, 1978).

32. Louis Farrakhan, interview with Stephen Barboza, in *American Jihad* (New York: Doubleday, 1994), p. 148; on Farrakhan's uncle's picture of Garvey, see Sterling X Hobbs, "Miracle Man of the Muslims," *Sepia* (May 1975): 28.

Malcolm had so much more Garveyism in his personal history than did Farrakhan that he was the Garveyite equivalent of a "Red diaper baby." His father was a Garvey organizer in Omaha, Milwaukee, and Lansing, Michigan; Malcolm X, *The Autobiography of Malcolm X*, pp. 1, 3, 5. His mother, in a role totally unmentioned in his famous autobiography, was the

Omaha office's branch reporter for the UNIA's newspaper, *The Negro World.* (Ted Vincent, "The Garveyite Parents of Malcolm X," *The Black Scholar* [March–April 1959]: 9.)

Garvey died in June 1940 at the age of fifty-three. Interestingly, his birth certificate lists him as "'Malcus' Mosiah Garvey Jr.": his middle name is a close approximation of the Hebrew word for "messiah," *moshiach.* This nomenclatural endowment was probably lost on most of his followers, who nonetheless considered him and his movement their deliverance from penury and injustice.

33. Burkett, *Garveyism as a Religious Movement,* p. 47. Regarding the "Negro-ization" of Jesus, Burkett states (p. 53) that

> one of the most spectacular ceremonies which took place under UNIA auspices, and the event which probably caused more comment throughout the United States in both the white and the Black press than any other in Liberty Hall, was the divine service "for the canonization of the Lord Jesus Christ as the Black Man of Sorrows, and also the canonization of the Blessed Virgin Mary as a black woman." It is in the [UNIA's] Lesson Guides, however, where one finds Garvey's private assessment as to the paramount themes which would be emphasized concerning the doctrine of Christ: ". . . Show that whilst the white and yellow worlds, that is to say the worlds of Europe and Asia Minor, persecuted and crucified Jesus the Son of God it was the black race, through Simon the black Cirenian [*sic*] who befriended the Son of God and took up the Cross and bore it alongside of Him up to the heights of Calvary. The Roman Catholics, therefore, have no rightful claim to the Cross nor is any other professing Christian before the Negro. The Cross is the property of the Negro in his religion because it was he who bore it.
>
> ". . . Jesus Christ had the blood of all races in his veins, and tracing the Jewish race back to Abraham and to Moses, from which Jesus sprang through the line of Jesse, you will

find Negro blood everywhere, so Jesus had much of Negro blood in him." (p. 53)

. The "black Jew" label pinned on Roxbury's West Indians stemmed not only from their preference for quality education but also from Garvey's nationalism. In a speech in 1920, he declared, "A new spirit, a new courage, has come to us simultaneously as it came to other people of the world. It came to us the same time it came to the Jew. When the Jew said, 'We shall have Palestine,' the same sentiment came to us when we said, 'We shall have Africa.'" (Harmon and Levine, *The Death of an American Jewish Community*, p. 106.)

Garvey may have been a nationalist, but he was not a supremacist. Witness this injunction from Acts 18:26 on the UNIA's official letterhead: "He created of one blood all nations of man to dwell upon the face of the earth."

Chapter 2

1. Hentoff, *Boston Boy*, p. 35.
2. On the percentage of students at English High, see Guscott interview, June 1, 1995. "'The Charmer' in the Fast Lane," a hagiographic account of Farrakhan in the black newspaper *The Daily Challenge* (July 13, 1994, p. 7), states that Farrakhan was a track great at English High, as did some of his old Roxbury friends in interviews with the author. This assertion was contradicted not only by records at English High but by the school's present athletic director in a telephone interview with the author, September 20, 1995.
3. Rice interview, June 1, 1995.
4. Confidential telelphone interview, May 24, 1995.
5. Rice interview, June 1, 1995.
6. Bynoe interview, June 6, 1995.
7. Quoted in "'The Charmer' in the Fast Lane," p. 7.
8. Farrakhan speech, Newark, N.J., April 28, 1995.
9. From NOI-produced videotape, "For the Love of Music." Far-

rakhan appeared on *The Ted Mack Original Amateur Hour* on May 15, 1949.

10. On Juilliard and Farrakhan's reasons for going to Winston-Salem, see "'The Charmer' in the Fast Lane," p. 7; on enrollment at Winston-Salem and alternative reasons for Farrakhan's attendance, see Clarence Jones, telephone interview with the author, June 27, 1995; on Archibald Morrow, see Clarence Gaines, telephone interview with the author, August 27, 1995.

11. "'The Charmer' in the Fast Lane," p. 7.

12. For Safe Bus Company and water fountain incident, see Jones interview, June 27, 1995; on rest room incident, see "'The Charmer' in the Fast Lane," p. 7.

13. On Farrakhan's races, see "Farrakhan: On the Road with the Fiery Black Minister," *Life* (August 1984): 54; on track team incidents, *see* "'The Charmer' in the Fast Lane," p. 7.

14. On Farrakhan as an athlete, see Gaines interview, August 27, 1995; on Farrakhan as a late riser, see Jones interview, June 27, 1995.

15. On the talent show, see Jones interview, June 27, 1995; for the title "Why America Is No Democracy," see "Finding the Nation of Islam," *The Daily Challenge*, July 14, 1995, p. 5.

16. Jones interview, June 27, 1995.

17. Ibid.

18. "Finding the Nation of Islam," p. 5.

19. Elton Trueblood, *The Common Virtues of Life*, pp. 15, 16; for story about *The Common Ventures of Life*, see Wright interview, May 26, 1995; for wedding details, see marriage certificate no. 4662, September 12, 1953; for Betsy Ross's Roman Catholicism, see C. Eric Lincoln, *The Black Muslims in America* (Queens, N.Y.: Kayode Publications, 1991), p. 280.

20. Farrakhan speech, St. Louis, September 13, 1995.

21. Daisy Voigt, interview with the author, Washington, D.C., June 13, 1995.

22. Rice interview, June 1, 1995.

23. Hasan Sharif, telephone interview with the author, July 10, 1995.

24. For dates and cast information, see 1953 and 1957 editions of *Daniel Blum's Theater World* (Philadelphia: Chilton Co./Books Division).

25. Farrakhan mentioned headlining the "Calypso Follies" in a speech delivered at the Philadelphia Civic Center, January 20, 1992; on his meeting Rodney Smith, see "Finding the Nation of Islam," p. 5.

26. Sterling X Hobbs, "Miracle Man of the Muslims," *Sepia* (May 1975): 28.

27. Ibid.

28. For details on Farrakhan and his wife joining the Nation, see "Finding the Nation of Islam," p. 5; on Farrakhan's uncle saying, "Get up, etc.," see Farrakhan speech, St. Louis, September 13, 1995.

29. Farrakhan interview, August 5, 1993.

30. Perry, *Malcolm*, pp. 101–47; "better to be jailed" from a letter Malcolm wrote from jail, January 29, 1950, referred to in FBI files, May 4, 1953.

31. For details on Malcolm's meetings and adult reactions, see Rice interview, June 1, 1995. Rice attended the meetings shortly after he had graduated from high school and while he had a brief career as a singer before going into the army. His high school guidance had told him, "You got straight A's, Rice, but don't plan on going to college. There's no future in it."

This discouragement was not that dissimilar from how Malcolm's eighth-grade English teacher, Richard Kaminska, responded when he asked the boy what he wanted to do with his life. According to Malcolm's autobiography, he had never given the matter much thought. And he never figured out why he blurted out, "Well yes, sir, I've been thinking I'd like to be a lawyer." To which Kaminska, under whom Malcolm had been getting some of his best marks, "leaned back in his chair and clasped his hands behind his head. He kind of half-smiled and said, 'Malcolm, one of life's first needs is for us to be realistic. Don't misunderstand me, now. We all here like you, you know that. But you've got to be realistic about being a nigger. A lawyer—that's not a realistic goal for a nigger. You need to be thinking about something you *can* be. You're good with your hands. . . . Everybody admires your carpentry shop work. Why don't you plan on carpentry?'" (p. 36). (For more information on Malcolm's autobiography, see endnote 9, Chapter 1.)

32. "Farrakhan's Boston Roots," *Boston Globe*, July 27, 1994, p. 16.

33. "'The Charmer' in the Fast Lane," p. 4.

34. Hobbs, "Miracle Man of the Muslims," p. 28.

35. For aliases, see internal FBI report on Elijah Muhammad, October 17, 1969; for details on Muhammad's grandparents, see his statement to FBI, September 20, 1942, Chicago. There is some dispute over Muhammad's original name. Some accounts state that he was first Robert Poole. The name most commonly ascribed to him as the one given to him by his parents is Elijah Poole.

36. Michael A. Gomez, "Muslims in Early America," *Journal of Southern History* 60, no. 4 (November 1994): 685–86; on the percentage of Muslim slaves, see C. Eric Lincoln and Lawrence Mamiya, "Challenges to the Black Church," in *1993 Yearbook of American and Canadian Churches* (Nashville, Tenn.: Abingdon Press, 1993), p. 3.

    Six zones eventually provided more than 73 percent of the exported slaves. Of these, about half came from areas in which Islam was a strong presence. As Gomez, an associate professor of history at Spelman College, calculated: "Given that between 400,000 and 523,000 Africans came to North America during the slave trade, at least 200,000 came from areas influenced by Islam to varying degrees. Muslims may have come to America by the thousands, if not the tens of thousands." "Muslims in Early America," p. 686.

37. Gomez, "Muslims in Early America," pp. 689, 693.

38. FBI report about Muhammad, January 27, 1958, p. 6.

39. Ibid. In *The Autobiography of Malcolm X*, Malcolm recalled that Elijah Muhammad had been "buoyed" while in prison by visions that "Allah had often sent him . . . of great audiences who would one day hear his teachings" (*Autobiography of Malcolm X*, p. 250).

40. Clifton E. Marsh, *From Black Muslims to Muslims* (Metuchen, N.J.: Scarecrow Press, 1984), p. 29.

41. Ibid., pp. 30, 31.

42. For statistics on black farmers and Henry Ford, see Marsh, *From Black Muslims to Muslims*, pp. 32–34; for details on Abbott, see Nicholas Lemann, *The Promised Land* (New York: Vintage Books, 1992), p. 16.

43. Marsh, *From Black Muslims to Muslims*, p. 36.

44. See interview with Elijah's grandson, Wali Farad Muhammad, in Stephen Barboza, *American Jihad* (New York: Doubleday, 1994), p. 273.

45. Ibid., p. 272.

46. Fard gave hope—indeed, he gave a *future*—to his followers by crassly indulging in a peculiar "theodicy," a term that Michael Eric Dyson, director of the University of North Carolina's Institute of African-American Research, has defined as "justifying the ways of God to human beings, especially as a response to the problem of evil." Fard's theodicy sought "to explain the evil of white racism and the suffering of Blacks by reference to an elaborate demonology of whiteness and a justification of the Nation of Islam's superior moral position in relation to white people." Michael Eric Dyson, *Making Malcolm: The Myth and Meaning of Malcolm X* (New York: Oxford University Press, 1995), p. 196.

47. "Lost-Found Muslim Lesson No. 2," in Khalid S. Lateef, *The Holy Quran's Condemnation of the Racist and Un-Islamic Ideology of "The Lessons" of W. D. Fard and the Teachings of Minister Louis Farrakhan's "Nation of Islam"* (Wheatley Heights, N.Y.: Americans for Justice and Positive Change), p. 14.

48. Quoted in E. Franklin Frazier, *The Negro Church in America* (New York: Schocken Books, 1988), p. 66.

49. *Master Fard Muhammad: Detroit History,* text by E. D. Beynon, annotation and commentary by Prince-A-Cuba (Newport News, Va.: United Brothers and United Sisters Communications Systems, 1990), p. 4.

There is a minor dispute over what sort of merchandise Fard sold in Detroit. The usual accounts that he sold silk, which has certain links to the Orient, implicitly corroborate his alleged connections to the Islamic world overseas. But in a radio broadcast, Elijah Muhammad said Fard "was not a peddler of the kind of merchandise that you have heard that he was. He took orders for made-to-measure suits for men folks." Even though this correction came from the Messenger himself, it dilutes some of the aura surrounding Fard. Elijah Muhammad, "Master Fard Not a Peddler" (audiotape), distributed by Secretarius MEMPS, Atlanta.

50. From "Lost-Found Muslim Lesson No. 2," p. 15.

51. Marsh, *From Black Muslims to Muslim,* p. 53; *History of the Nation of Islam,* as discussed by Elijah Muhammad (Cleveland: Secretarius Publication, 1993), p. 2.

52. *History of the Nation of Islam,* pp. 3, 4.

Chapter 3

1. Wittgenstein quoted in Joseph Campbell, *The Masks of God: Creative Mythology* (New York: Viking Press, 1974), p. 676.

2. E. D. Beynon, *Master Fard Muhammad: "Detroit History"* (Newport News, Va.: United Brothers and United Sisters Communications Systems, 1990), pp. 5–6.

3. Ibid., p. 5.

4. Interview with Elijah Muhammad, in Hatim A. Sahib, (master's thesis, University of Chicago, 1951), cited in Martha F. Lee, *History of the Nation of Islam* (Lewiston, N.Y.: Edwin Mellon Press, 1988), pp. 6, 10, 30–31.

5. Lee, *History of the Nation of Islam,* p. 6.

6. For Fard's possibly Jamaican and Palestinian origins, see Eric

Lincoln, *The Black Muslims in America* (Queens, N.Y.: Kayode Publications, 1991), p. 14; for "Supreme Ruler" quote, see Beynon, *Master Fard Muhammad*, p. 6.

7. Elijah Muhammad, *Message to the Blackman in America* (Newport News, Va.: United Brothers Communications Systems, 1992), p. 20, 24–25.

8. On attendance at Fard meetings, see Elijah Muhammad statement to FBI, September 20, 1942.

9. Muhammad, *Message to the Blackman*, p. 25.

10. Lee, *The History of the Nation of Islam*, p. 35.

11. FBI, memo on the Allah Temple of Islam, November 9, 1943.

12. For most law enforcement agency ID numbers for Fard and his account of being born in New Zealand, see "Black Muslims' Founder a Fake; Posed as Negro," *Seattle Post-Intelligencer*, July 28, 1963, p. 1; for L.A. Police Department number for Fard, see "'Prophet' of Muslims Afoul of Law in L.A.," *Los Angeles Herald-Examiner*, July 29, 1963, p. 1; for account of Fard's birth in Portland and physical description, see FBI, memo on Nation of Islam, February 15, 1963.

13. "'Prophet' of Muslims Afoul of Law in L.A.," p. 1; "Black Muslims' Founder a Fake," p. 1.

14. "'Prophet' of Muslims Afoul of Law in L.A.," p. 1.

15. Ibid. If Fard invented his theology, he may not have done so single-handedly. Shortly before appearing in Detroit, another black cult leader, Noble Drew Ali, had died—and some accounts claim that Fard not only arose to take his place, but that he was Drew Ali's reincarnation.

Noble Drew Ali, born as Timothy Drew in North Carolina in 1886, also rested his canon on something he dubbed "Islam." The legend of Drew Ali is that, after encountering some form of Oriental philosophy, he traveled to North Africa, studied Islam, and received a "commission" from Morocco's king to teach Islam to the Negroes of America. To first prove that he was fit for the task, he had to find his way out of a pyramid. Upon exiting, all knew that he was a true prophet.

Preaching in basements and on street corners in Newark starting in 1913, Drew Ali became obsessed with the notion that national identity was the precursor to religious certainty. Blacks were not Negroes: they were "Asiatics," "Moors," or "Moorish Americans." Only by knowing their nation of origin and their true names could blacks achieve fullness and spiritual salvation. As would later follow within the Nation of Islam, there was a strict dress code: males wore fezzes, women wore long dresses that reached to their shoes, and some women wore turbans.

By the mid-1920s, the Moorish Science Temple had possibly as many as twelve thousand members. In one year, Drew Ali pocketed as much as thirty-six thousand dollars, partly by selling "various nostrums and charms he had concocted, among them Old Moorish Healing Oil, Moorish Purifier Bath Compound and Moorish Herb Tea for Human Ailments." He moved his headquarters to Chicago, where he issued "identity cards" stating that the bearer was "a Moslem under the Divine Laws of the Holy Koran of Mecca, Love, Truth, Peace, Freedom and Justice" and "a citizen of the U.S.A." Members believed the card would restrain any white who might harm them. They began insulting whites and pushing them into the gutters while passing them on the street. Drew Ali ordered "all Moors . . . to stop flashing our cards before Europeans as this only causes confusion. We did not come to cause confusion; our work is to uplift the nation."

Eventually, Drew Ali's leadership was contested, chiefly over the profit-making potential of what he had started. Leaders were shot and stabbed; at least one died in March 1929. Drew Ali was arrested for the murder and released on bond. A few weeks later, he died under mysterious circumstances. Some said injuries inflicted by the police during his brief imprisonment caused his death; others said death came from a vicious beating by a rival's followers. Either way, Drew Ali's death left a vacuum in the spiritual life of several thousand blacks, one that

Fard Muhammad may have cleverly exploited to his advantage. Marsh, *From Black Muslims to Muslims*, pp. 43, 49. FBI file on Charles Kirkman Bey, May 19, 1943, pp. 3, 4, 5, 6.

16. Beynon, *Master Fard Muhammad*, pp. 9, 15.

17. Details on Jehovah's Witnesses from *Jehovah's Witnesses in the Twentieth Century* (Brooklyn, N.Y.: Watchtower Bible and Tract Society of New York, 1989) and *Jehovah's Witnesses Unitedly Doing God's Will World-Wide* (Brooklyn, N.Y.: Watchtower Bible and Tract Society of New York, 1986).

18. "Lost-Found Muslim Lesson No. 2," in Khalid S. Lateef, *The Holy Quran's Condemnation of the Racist and Un-Islamic Ideology of "The Lessons" of W. D. Fard and the Teachings of Minister Louis Farrakhan's "Nation of Islam"* (Wheatley Heights, N.Y.: Americans for Justice and Positive Change, n.d.), pp. 12–13.

19. Ibid., pp. 17–18.

20. "Black Muslims' Founder a Fake," p. 4.

21. "Nation of Islam Offers Hearst $100,000 to Prove Charge," *Muhammad Speaks*, August 16, 1963, p. 1.

22. Louis Farrakhan, *The Meaning of FOI* (Chicago: The Honorable Elijah Muhammad Educational Foundation, 1983), p. 13.

23. Confidential interview, New York, April 13, 1995.

24. Beynon, *Master Fard Muhammad*, pp. 9, 15.

25. "Lost-Found Muslim Lesson No. 1 (1–14)" and "Lost-Found Muslim Lesson No. 2 (1–40)," in Lateef, *The Holy Quran's Condemnation*, pp. 10–18. By proclaiming the black man as God, Fard was being heretical to traditional Islam, which taught that only

> *Those who fear Allah;*
> *Who believe in the Unseen,*
> *Are steadfast in prayer . . .*
> *And who believe in the Revelation*

would be redeemed. Even worse, the Koran warned that anyone who worshiped another God was committing a "heinous" sin and would be eternally damned.

26. This Yacub—in one of the several identities assigned to him by Fard and Elijah Muhammad—was the Jacob of the Old Testament, but unlike Jacob, he wrestled not with an angel but with his government. The fight was totally secular, not otherworldly. But the victor, in both cases, was the same.

27. "Lost-Found Muslim Lesson No. 2 (1–40)," pp. 16–17.

28. Ezekiel quoted in *New American Standard Bible* (Carol Stream, Ill.: Creation House, 1973), p. 1167; for Muhammad on the wheel, see Muhammad, *Message to the Blackman*, pp. 290–91. Just how the Mother Plane was powered was never clear. Elijah Muhammad once said it could reach "a height of forty miles above the earth . . . and take on oxygen and hydrogen . . . to permit it to stay out of the earth's gravity until it needs refueling. . . . " At other times, he stated that "she can produce her own power to go wherever she desires to go in space. The Mother Plane is not like your little bullets or cameras which are powered by your limited power." (Elijah Muhammad, *The Mother Plane* (Cleveland: Secretarius MEMPS, n.d.), pp. 16, 33, 37.

    In the introduction to *The Mother Plane*, Nasir Makr Hakim, the president of Secretarius, a group dedicated to distributing material by Elijah Muhammad, gives a psychological, nontranscendent reason for Muhammad's insistence on the Mother Plane: "We have been awe struck by what we have been deceived into believing is power; namely, the white man's ability to drop bombs, shoot bullets and launch satellites. Since we have been raised on such a continued show of destructive force, we believe there is nothing else that is capable of defeating the white race" (p. v).

29. "Lost-Found Muslim Lesson No. 2," pp. 14, 18; for "heart[s] of gold, love and mercy," see Muhammad, *Message to the Blackman*, p. 122; for "two-legged rattlesnakes," see "Go Ahead, Apostle," *Newsweek*, March 31, 1961). After this destruction—the hereafter of the Nation of Islam—life for blacks would not be in another dimension of time or space. The dead would not be physically resurrected, "because the dead is never known to

return from the grave"; the only resurrection was the mental rebirth of the "blind, deaf and dumb" "lost-found" who had been mentally numbed by their masters. This trio of ailments that Elijah Muhammad and Malcolm X were so fond of citing, and that cut to the quick with the black masses they were trying to recruit, was not unique to them: the Koran refers to nonbelievers as those from whom

> *Allah took away their light*
> *And left them in utter darkness.*
> *So they could not see,*
> *Deaf, dumb and blind. . . .*

The Holy Quran, trans. Mushaf al-Madinah an-Nabawiyah (Medina, Saudi Arabia: The Custodian of the Two Holy Mosques King Fahd Complex for the Printing of the Holy Quran, n.d.), p. 10, 2:18.

The Koran's portrayal of the Day of Decision also centers on great cataclysmic destruction: the day will be preceded by the "fold[ing] up" of the sun, by the stars "losing their lustre," by the mountains "vanish[ing] (like a mirage)," and the oceans "boil[ing] over like a swell." But salvation is determined by deeds, not by race: Allah will judge all peoples from all time, with each community gauged by the standards of its own prophets and its own holy books, and each individual accountable for his or her own actions. The righteous will be consigned to the eternal pleasures of heaven, where they will recline "on couches/Encrusted with gold" and enjoy the pleasures of "Companions/With beautiful, big/And lustrous eyes." Meanwhile, the evil will be consigned to the incessant tortures of hell, where pleas for relief will be answered with "Water like melted brass/That will scald their faces/How dreadful the drink!" *The Holy Quran*, Sura 81, verses 1–6, pp. 1904–5; Sura 56, verses 15–22, pp. 1674–75; Sura 18, verse 29, p. 828.

30. Farrakhan speech, St. Louis, September 13, 1995.

31. Warith Deen Muhammad, speech to his followers, Detroit, September 1993; speech to interfaith gathering, Baltimore, August 9, 1995.
32. W. D. Muhammad speech, August 9, 1995.
33. W. D. Muhammad speech, September 1993.
34. Ibid.
35. Ibid.

Chapter 4

1. *Polk's Boston City Directory*, vol. 1959 (Boston: R. L. Polk & Co., 1959), p. 422.
2. For data on membership, see CIA, report on the Nation of Islam.
3. Khallaq interview, June 1, 1995; Wright interview, May 26, 1995; on Farrakhan's arrival in Boston as an FOI captain, see handout at Farrakhan speech, Philadelphia Civic Center, January 20, 1992.
4. Wright interview, May 26, 1995.
5. For Malcolm's remarks, see "Malcolm X in Boston," *New York Amsterdam News*, November 9, 1957, filed in FBI memo, April 30, 1958; Khallaq interview, June 1, 1995; Voigt interview, June 13, 1995; for schedule of meetings, see Aubrey Barnette, "The Black Muslims Are a Fraud," *Saturday Evening Post*, February 27, 1963, p. 25. In addition to attending the four evening meetings and one afternoon meeting per week, NOI members in Boston were instructed to be out on the streets selling *Muhammad Speaks* on Tuesday and Thursday evenings and Saturday and Sunday mornings.
6. FBI memo, April 30, 1958.
7. Sterling X Hobbs, "Miracle Man of the Muslims," *Sepia* (May 1975): 29.
8. According to Bruce Perry, the Boston temple's membership was around 250 in 1964; *Malcolm* (Barrytown, N.Y.: Station Hill Press, 1992), p. 289. For assessment of Elijah Muhammad's control of NOI, see "Can Moslems Capture the Negro?" *Sepia*

(October 1957), filed in FBI memo, November 29, 1957.

9. Khallaq interview, June 1, 1995. While the FBI often succeeded in infiltrating the NOI or in planting disinformation inside it, its efforts were just as often clumsy and transparent. According to Khallaq, whose Roxbury barbershop was a hub of local NOI activity in the 1950s and 1960s, "Some of the FBI guys were so dumb. They would come in here—white guys coming into a black place!—with their nice shirt and nice tie on and sit down and kind of hide behind the newspaper. We knew who they were as soon as they walked in."

10. Confidential interviews with a former NOI minister and a former FOI captain, Maryland April 17, 1995.

11. Confidential interview with a former NOI minister, Maryland, March 20, 1995.

12. On NOI properties, see "Can Moslems Capture the Negro?"; for information on Elijah Muhammad's car and mortgage, see FBI memo, January 27, 1958; for Farrakhan's income, etc., see Barnette, "The Black Muslims Are a Fraud," p. 25.

13. C. Eric Lincoln, *The Black Muslims in America*, p. 94; for "black God never sleeps," see confidential interview with former NOI minister, March 20, 1995.

14. On listening to jazz, see Voigt interview, June 13, 1995; for remarks on "personage of enormous importance," see Barnette, "The Black Muslims Are a Fraud," p. 24.

15. Perry, *Malcolm*, p. 148.

16. Confidential telephone interview with Mae Manning's former employer, July 30, 1995.

17. From audiotape of "A White Man's Heaven Is a Black Man's Hell."

18. Ibid.

19. Ibid.

20. Ibid.

21. Ibid.

22. Abdul Alim Shabazz, interview with the author, Washington, D.C., June 10, 1995.

23. Nat Hentoff, "Farrakhan as a Cultural Hero," *Washington Jewish Week*, August 23, 1990.

24. *Pittsburgh Courier* and *New York Amsterdam News* articles, both dated January 11, 1958, in FBI memo, January 15, 1958.

25. *Orgena* and *The Trial* quoted in Lincoln, *The Black Muslims in America*, pp. 3–4, 280–81; Malcolm X, with the assistance of Alex Haley, *The Autobiography of Malcolm X* (New York: Ballantine, 1992), p. 250; Abdul Alim Shabazz, interview with the author, Washington, D.C., June 10, 1995; Barnette, "The Black Muslims Are a Fraud," p. 26; and Thomas Landess and Richard Quinn, *Jesse Jackson and the Politics of Race* (Ottawa, Ill.: Jameson Books, 1985), p. 105. The symbolic white man in *The Trial* was actually an NOI member in "white"-face.

26. Hobbs, "Miracle Man of the Muslims," p. 29. It seems that although Elijah Muhammad ended Farrakhan's career as a "song-and-dance man," he enjoyed having him privately play his violin for him during the last year of his life. According to Farrakhan, he essentially abandoned his violin in 1951 when he went to college, aside from picking it up briefly "every three or four years . . . I had no instrument of my own until 1974 when Elijah Muhammad began asking me to play for him. When he died a year later, I put the violin away." "Sending a Message, Louis Farrakhan Plays Mendelssohn," *New York Times*, April 19, 1992, p. C16.

27. "The Hate That Hate Produced," WNTA-TV, New York, July 10, 1959.

Chapter 5

1. Some ideas in this paragraph were inspired by Jennifer L. Hochschild, *Facing up to the American Dream* (Princeton, N.J.: Princeton University Press, 1995), pp. 168–69.

2. Elijah Muhammad, *Message to the Blackman in America* (Newport News, Va.: United Brothers Communications Systems, 1992), pp. 59–60.

3. On the "explosive situation," see "Muhammad Son Says Muslims Threatened Him," *Chicago Daily Defender*, July 8, 1964, p. 3.

4. W. D. Muhammad speech, August 9, 1995.

5. Ibid.

6. Ibid.

7. Information from Malcolm X's appearance on the Jerry Williams radio show, WMEX-FM, Boston, June 13, 1964, summarized in FBI memos on NOI, January 23, 1964, and April 26, 1962.

8. FBI memo on NOI, April 26, 1962.

9. Askia Muhammad, telephone interview with the author, December 27, 1995.

10. Most of this account is based on Malcolm's appearance on the Jerry Williams radio show, WMEX-FM, Boston, June 13, 1964, summarized in FBI memo on NOI, January 23, 1964. Perry talks about Malcolm hearing rumors about Elijah's promiscuity "as far back as 1955" (*Malcolm*, p. 230).

11. Malcolm X, with the assistance of Alex Haley, *The Autobiography of Malcolm X* (New York: Ballantine, 1992), p. 299.

12. Perry, *Malcolm*, p. 236.

13. Ibid., p. 338.

14. "Malcolm X Scores U.S. and Kennedy," *New York Times*, December 2, 1963, in FBI memo about NOI, December 6, 1963; and confidential interview with a former NOI minister, June 10, 1995. As the audience chuckled and applauded at Malcolm's comments, he noted that newspapers' persistent efforts to get NOI leaders to comment on the assassination had been intended to trap the organization into a "fanatic, inflexibly dogmatic" statement, but what the press had really been seeking was for someone from the Nation to exult, "Hooray, hooray! I'm glad he got it!" ("Malcolm X Scores U.S. and Kennedy, *Times*.)

Unlike Malcolm, whose "chickens coming home to roost" quip was widely interpreted as gloating over JFK's assassination, Elijah Muhammad's public comments about the assassination, printed in *Muhammad Speaks* shortly after the event, attributed the president's murder to his advocacy of blacks' rights. Comparing the Lincoln and Kennedy assassinations, Muhammad said, "On each one of these occasions where outlaws overruled legal authority, it was in the case of presidents who opened their mouths and said something favorable for the so-called Negro. I am not saying this was the reason why President Kennedy was assassinated, but it seems very strange that every president who says something favorable for the so-called Negro pays for it with his life." [Quoted in Jabril Muhammad, *This Is the One* (Phoenix: Book Company, 1993), p. 243.] Muhammad's presumption of Lincoln's and Kennedy's goodness contradicts the NOI's theology that Caucasians are irredeemably evil.

15. Quoted in "Eighty Guards, Thirty-two Police for Malcolm X," *New York Herald Tribune*, June 16, 1964, in FBI memo about Malcolm Little, January 26, 1965.

16. On Malcolm's resignation, see Perry, *Malcolm*, p. 250; on still being faithful to Elijah Muhammad's ideas, see George Breitman, *The Last Year of Malcolm X* (New York: Pathfinder Press, 1967), p. 59.

17. Breitman, *The Last Year of Malcolm X*, p. 61.

18. For "we should destroy" Malcolm quote, see FBI file on Malcolm Little, January 20, 1965; Philbert Little quotes from "Malcolm X: Make It Plain," PBS-TV, February 1, 1995. Philbert later admitted that the script from which he read his denunciations of Malcolm had been handed to him immediately before the press conference by John Ali, the Nation's national secretary, who ordered him to read from it. Karl Evanzz, *The Judas Factor* (New York: Thunder's Mouth Press, 1992), p. 218.

Occasionally, when Malcolm wasn't being attacked by NOI leaders, there were implicit admissions that the Messenger wasn't all Elijah Muhammad was cracked up to be, witness the title of a speech to New Jersey and New York FOI members: "So

What If He [Elijah Muhammad] Is Not All Pure, Look What He Did for You and I." (FBI file on Malcolm Little, January 20, 1965.)

19. For Wallace's expulsion, see Clifton E. Marsh, *From Black Muslims to Muslims* (Metuchen, N.J.: Scarecrow Press, 1984), p. 79; Wallace quoted in Hobbs, "Miracle Man of the Muslims," p. 21.

20. On Akbar's expulsion, see Martha F. Lee, *History of the Nation of Islam* (Lewiston, N.Y.: Edwin Mellon Press, 1988), p. 58; Wallace quoted in "Muhammad Son Says Muslims Threatened Him," p. 3.

21. Perry, *Malcolm*, p. 308.

22. FBI memo on Elijah Muhammad, October 9, 1964.

23. "Malcolm Rejects Racist Doctrine," *New York Times*, October 4, 1964, in FBI file on Malcolm X, October 4, 1964.

24. Ibid.

25. "Boston Minister Tells of Malcolm—Muhammad's Biggest Hypocrite," *Muhammad Speaks*, December 4, 1964, pp. 11–15.

26. Ibid.

27. Louis Farrakhan, "I Am an Alarm Clock," *The Black Scholar* (January–February 1979): 12.

28. Perry, *Malcolm*, p. 342.

29. For details of Farrakhan's whereabouts the day of Malcolm X's assassination, see Farrakhan interview by Askia Muhammad, October 15, 1995, syndicated broadcast entitled "Farrakhan '95: A Fresh Look"; Farrakhan's writings quoted from *Muhammad Speaks*, December 1984; Clarence X Gill, "Islam's Gift to Him: Useful Life," *Muhammad Speaks*, August 25, 1964, p. 9.

30. Louis Farrakhan, interview with Barbara Walters, *20/20*, ABC-TV, April 22, 1994; Louis Farrakhan, interview with the author, August 5, 1993.

31. Farrakhan interview, August 5, 1993. It is true that in his posthumously published autobiography Malcolm did not mention his 1959 trip to the Middle East. And while the political scientist Bruce Perry lists in his biography of Malcolm several reasons the NOI leader gave for not going to Mecca that

year—he was ill, he had to cancel the trip to go to Africa, he had to rush home for a rally in Harlem, or Mecca had never been on his itinerary anyway—Perry concludes that the reason he didn't go is "still unclear" (*Malcolm*, p. 206).

32. Malcolm quoted in Perry, *Malcolm*, pp. 203, 254, 255; for details on OAAU events, see FBI report on Malcolm, December 22, 1964.

33. *The Holy Quran*, trans. and ed. Maulana Muhammad Ali (Columbus, Ohio: Ahmadiyyah Anjuman Isha'at Islam, 1995), p. xiv.

34. Perry, *Malcolm*, p. 356; Malcolm X, *The Autobiography of Malcolm X*, p. 428.

35. Malcolm X, *The Autobiography of Malcolm X*, pp. 445–46.

36. Louis Farrakhan, interview with Askia Muhammad, "Black Journalism Review," WEAA-FM, October 15, 1995.

37. From an audiotape of NOI Savior's Day celebration, Chicago, February 26, 1965.

38. Ibid.

39. Ibid.

Chapter 6

1. Farrakhan, *20/20* interview with Barbara Walters, April 22, 1994.

2. "Malcolm X Aide Dead in Boston," *New York Times*, March 14, 1965, p. 57.

3. Aubrey Barnette, "The Black Muslims Are a Fraud," *Saturday Evening Post*, February 27, 1963, p. 28.

4. Ibid., p. 29.

5. Ibid.

6. Ibid.

7. Ibid.

8. Ibid., pp. 23–29. There is a good chance the FBI fed this article to the *Saturday Evening Post*. In a memo of April 22, 1968, agents in the FBI's Chicago bureau advised their superiors in

Washington, "For a number of years, Chicago has had in effect Counterintelligence Programs regarding the Nation of Islam and Elijah Muhammad. Originally, the program was centered around exposing to the public, both black and white, on a nationwide basis the abhorrent aspects of the organization and its racist, hate-type teachings. This was done in such leading magazines as 'Time,' 'U.S. News and World Report,' 'Saturday Evening Post,' etc., as well as through newspapers." Veterans and historians of civil rights groups from the 1960s often point out that internal FBI files may have been written by men currying favor with J. Edgar Hoover. Files especially from this period may also reflect Hoover's racist ideology, which infected most of the FBI.

9. "Wallace D. Muhammad: Reviver of Muslim Faith," *Chicago Tribune*, February 21, 1977, sect. 4, p. 4.

10. Quoted in Adib Rashad, *Elijah Muhammad and the Theological Foundation of the Nation of Islam* (Newport News, Va.: United Brothers and United Sisters Communications Systems, 1994), p. 219.

11. For Elijah Muhammad on the criminal background of many NOI members, see Michael Friedly, *Malcolm X: The Assassination* (New York: One World Books, 1995), p. 216; William Raspberry, *Sepia* (May 1975): 19.

12. Askia Muhammad interview, June 13, 1995.

13. Ibid.

14. On Elijah Muhammad's health, see "Black Muslim Group in Trouble from Financial Problems and Some Crime," *New York Times*, December 6, 1973 , p. 37.

15. Martha F. Lee, *History of the Nation of Islam* (Lewiston, N.Y.: Edwin Mellon Press, 1988), pp. 68–69.

16. "Coxson Murder Suspect Fails to Show up in Court," *New York Times*, August 2, 1973, p. 79.

17. "Farrakhan quoted in Karl Evanzz, *The Judas Factor* (New York: Thunder's Mouth Press, 1992), p. 321.

18. Evanzz, *The Judas Factor*, p. 322.

19. "Black Leader Slain by Boston Gunmen; Muslim Feud Hinted," *New York Times*, May 3, 1973, p. 26.

20. "Three Muslims Seized in Cop Kidnap," *Newark Star-Ledger*, September 6, 1973, pp. 1, 26.

21. Louis Farrakhan, sermon, New York, broadcast on WLIB-FM, September 9, 1973. During his sermon, Farrakhan, as usual, portrayed the black man as having an innate purity that had been tarnished and corrupted by the white man, who "was a murderer from the beginning. He loves to murder. . . . But his spirit is now in the black man. His mind is in the black man. So he makes us now murderers of each other."

22. "On My Own" [editorial cartoon], *Muhammad Speaks*, January 15, 1965, p. 15.

23. *The Holy Quran*, trans. Maulana Muhammad Ali (Columbus, Ohio: Ahmadiyyah Isha'at Islam, 1995), pt. 5, chap. 4, 13:92 and 13:93 (p. 216).

24. Ibid., pt. 6, chap. 5, 6:33, p. 250. Traditional Muslims reject as heretical the edition of the Koran distributed by the Nation of Islam—a 1917 translation by Maulana Muhammad Ali. Ali was a member of the Ahmadiyyah sect, which was founded in Pakistan in the late 19th century to strengthen Islam against the influences of the British raj, Protestant Christianity, and revitalized Hinduism. Ahmadiyyah's founder, Ghulam Ahmad Qadiyani, believed that he was the Mahdi (who would precede the Messiah), the Messiah himself—and a prophet. This last declaration, especially, contradicted traditional Islamic teachings that the Prophet Muhammad was—and always would be—the last divine emissary.

   In Pakistan, the Ahmaddiyas have been declared a non-Muslim minority. And throughout the mainstream Muslim world, the Muhammad Ali translation is repudiated for its theology, anti-colonial politics and implicit anti-Jewishness. Chapter 2, 7: 61 of the Ali translation reads, "And abasement and humiliation were stamped upon them [the Children of Israel], and they incurred Allah's wrath." To which Ali comments in his notes, "the truth of this prophecy regarding the fate of the Jewish nation is amply borne out by Jewish history. The Jews are the wealthiest of nations, but their lot is miserable in almost every country of the world; notwithstanding their great influence in politics, it remains so to this day."

Of this same passage, the translation of the Koran which is accepted by mainstream Muslims comments, "The moral goes wider than the Children of Israel. It applies to all nations and individuals. If they are stiff-necked, if they set a greater value on perishable goods than on freedom and on eternal salvation, if they break the law of Allah and resist His grace, their portion must be humiliation and misery in the spiritual world and probably even on this earth if a long view is taken."

Sources for above material:

"Ahmadiyya," *The Perennial Dictionary of World Religions*, edited by Keith Crim (San Francisco: Harper & Row, 1989), pp. 16-17; John L. Esposito, *Islam: The Straight Path* (New York: Oxford University Press, 1988), p. 193; *The Holy Quran*, translator Maulana Muhammad Ali (Columbus: Ohio: Ahmadiyyah Anhuman Isha'at Islam, 1995), p. 30; *The Holy Quran*, translator Mushaf Al-Madinah An-Nabawiyah (Medina, Saudi Arabia: The Custodian of the Two Holy Mosques King Fahd Complex for the Printing of the Holy Quran, n.d.), note on p. 27.

25. "Decapitated Bodies of Two Found in a Newark Park," *New York Times*, October 19, 1973, p. 47; "Two Found Dead in Weequahic Park," *Newark Star-Ledger*, October, 18, 1993, pp. 1, 6; "Three Muslims Seized in Cop Kidnap," pp. 1, 26.

26. "Eleven Sect Members Arrested in Newark Muslim Slaying," *New York Times*, October 25, 1973, p. 32; "Black Muslim Group in Trouble from Financial Problems and Some Crime," *New York Times*, December 6, 1973, p. 37; confidential telephone interview with former NOI member, January 12, 1995.

27. "Black Muslim Group in Trouble from Financial Problems and Some Crime," p. 37; for NOI businesses, see Clifton E. Marsh,

From Black Muslims to Muslims (Metuchen, N.J.: Scarecrow Press, 1984), p. 90; and Raspberry, *Sepia* (May 1975): 20.

28. "Black Muslim Group in Trouble from Financial Problems and Some Crime," p. 37; for Libyan loan, see "Big Libyan Loan for Muslims Here," *Chicago Sun Times*, May 8, 1972, in FBI memo on Elijah Muhammad, July 18, 1972; on abolition of slavery in Saudi Arabia in 1962, see "The Uses of Malice," *American Spectator* (April 1995): 39. The Libyan ambassador to the United States, sensitive to the risk that the loan would be perceived as interfering in U.S. domestic affairs, stressed that the loan could be used only for the mosque: "We are merely helping to build a church, and this is something American missionaries have done in many countries." But Elijah Muhammad was not pleased with the Libyan demand that the loan be repaid in three years: "We don't mind people giving us the cash, but I don't know if we can pay back $1 million a year." (Source for the quotes from the Libyan ambassador and Elijah Muhammad is the *Chicago Sun Times* article mentioned above.) According to *Muhammad Speaks* (October 20, 1972), negotiations in September 1972 changed the payback deadline from 1975 to 1981: "The reduction makes it possible for the money formerly set aside for payments on the loan to be used to further the cause of Islam among the ex-slaves in America."

29. Pittsburgh FBI office, memo to FBI director, March 28, 1968; ibid.; Buffalo FBI office, memo to FBI director, April 3, 1968, p. 2; Columbia, S.C., FBI office, memo to Washington, April 5, 1968, p. 2; San Diego FBI office, memo to FBI director, April 3, 1968, pp. 2, 3.

30. Quoted in Farrakhan speech, Chicago, November 21, 1982.

31. FBI New York office, memo to FBI director, February 27, 1968, p. 1; on number of NOI businesses in New York, see Sterling X Hobbs, "Miracle Man of the Muslims," *Sepia* (May 1975): 26.

32. FBI New York office, memo to FBI director, February 27, 1968, pp. 4–5. Plans for the booklet were approved by J. Edgar Hoover himself, who thanked the New York bureau for its

"imagination and enthusiasm." FBI director, memo to New
York bureau, April 8, 1968.

33. Memo from Washington to New York bureau, April 8, 1968.
the booklets were apparently prepared at FBI headquarters in
Washington and subsequently shipped to New York.

34. FBI New York office, memo to FBI director, June 26, 1968.

35. Raspberry, *Sepia* (May 1975): 21. Muhammad's mansion and
the three homes across the street he had built for his sons were
valued at two million dollars in the early 1970s.

36. Elijah Muhammad, *The Fall of America* (Chicago: Muhammad
Mosque No. 2, 1973), p. 23.

37. *Los Angeles Herald-Dispatch*, January 9, 1960.

38. Muhammad, *The Fall of America*, p. 23.

39. Ibid. Within days after their "amicable" meeting, Muhammad
criticized King at the Savior's Day celebration for being too
close to whites. Publicly, King glossed over Muhammad's comments and managed to capitalize on the sparse news about his
meeting with Muhammad by using it to signal that he was in
touch with all segments of black opinion in an effort to build
a united front of all blacks. FBI Chicago office, memo to Washington, March 31, 1968.

Muhammad had at least one other meeting with officials of
King's SCLC. In September 1968, five months after King's murder, his successor, the Reverend Ralph Abernathy, met Muhammad at his mansion. As with King's session with Muhammad,
nothing concrete came of the meeting—except for a photo in
Muhammad Speaks of Abernathy joining hands with Muhammad and an NOI minister in Phoenix telling members, "This is
proof that even the great leader of the SCLC is accepting the
Honorable Elijah Muhammad's leadership," and that Abernathy knew he had been teaching the white man's bogus religion for too long to blacks. "Meeting with Muhammad," and
"Dr. King Seizes a Slum Building," *New York Times*, February
24, 1966, p. 75; FBI Phoenix office, memo to Washington, September 27, 1968.

40. Stephen B. Oates, *Let the Trumpet Sound* (New York: Harper Perennial, 1994), p. 390.

41. Quoted in Adam Fairclough, *Martin Luther King Jr.* (Athens: University of Georgia Press, 1995), pp. 109–10.

42. James Baldwin, *The Fire Next Time* (New York: Dell, 1985), pp. 97–98. Elijah Muhammad's assumption that Islam is the natural faith of blacks is reminiscent of traditional Muslims' description of converts: one does not "convert" to Islam, one "reverts" to it, since Islam represents the "original," as well as the final, revelation of the God of Abraham, Moses, Jesus, and Muhammad.

43. Ibid.

44. For the Muhammad family's attitude toward Farrakhan, see Askia Muhammad interview, June 13, 1995; for "Velvet Mouth," see David Jackson, "Ascent and Grandeur," *Chicago Tribune*, March 15, 1995, p. 22; Farrakhan quoted in "Murphy Defends Police Action at Harlem Mosque and Bars Transfer of White Policemen," *New York Times*, April 71, 1972. Of the seventy thousand people who attended the Black Family Day Bazaar, Farrakhan later wrote, not without a touch of sarcasm: "Phenomenal! Stupendous! Think of it. The hated Black Muslims drew 70,000 people in a stadium, not to hear Billy Graham or some faith healer, but to hear the Message of the Honorable Elijah Muhammad." Louis Farrakhan, "The Crucifixion of Elijah Muhammad," *New York Amsterdam News*, March 3, 1979.

45. Askia Muhammad interview, June 13, 1995.

46. The poll describing Muhammad as the "most powerful black man in America" was announced in May 1974 by Black Consumer Research of Freeport, N.Y., according to an article in *Muhammad Speaks*, May 17, 1974, cited in FBI memo on Elijah Muhammad, May 24, 1974; quotes by and about Muhammad are from Raspberry, *Sepia* (May 1975): 22. It was George Schuyler, a black columnist for the *Pittsburgh Courier*, who called Muhammad a "rogue and charlatan."

47. Elijah Muhammad, sermon, Chicago, February 26, 1974.

48. Ibid. In the last sermon, Muhammad's compassion for the oppressed was reserved for blacks. Not even Native Americans, with whom Farrakhan later formed an alliance, got any sympathy. If whites have taken land from Indians, "well, . . . let the Indian fight for his own thing. One thing I can bear witness with the white man—the Indian wasn't doing nothing with it. And if . . . [whites] come here and taken it away from them and build up a great country like this, I say he ought to been here a long time before he did. . . . I love the Indians. But he was not smart enough to keep his home so he let a stranger take it"; speech, February 26, 1974. Two years earlier, Muhammad had assailed Indians as "the enemies of Allah." Apparently, the Messenger's love ended with hues of black and fidelity to Allah, and his attitude toward land was not one of possession, but of pragmatic utilitarianism; *The Fall of America*, p. 22.

49. Jackson, "Ascent and Grandeur," p. 22; "Son Will Succeed Elijah Muhammad," *New York Amsterdam News*, March 1, 1975, p. A–12.

50. From audiotape of FOI meeting, New York, January 18, 1975.

51. From videotape of Savior's Day, Chicago, February 26, 1975.

52. Ibid.

53. Louis Farrakhan, speech, delivered at Your Bakery, Oakland, Calif., April 29, 1979.

54. From videotape of Savior's Day, Chicago, February 26, 1975.

55. Farrakhan speech, April 29, 1979.

56. Ibid.

57. Hobbs, "Miracle Man of the Muslims," pp. 19, 24.

58. Ibid., p. 24.

59. On the fifty thousand dollars, see Jackson, "Ascent and Grandeur," p. 22; for description of Farrakhan's new mosque in Chicago, see Askia Muhammad interview, June 13, 1995.

60. "Farrakhan: New Muslim Direction," *Los Angeles Sentinel*, May 12, 1977, p. A–10.

61. For changes to smoking and drinking rules, see *Chicago Tri-*

bune, September 1, 1975, p. 1; on the change from "black" to "Bilalian," see *Muhammad Speaks*, October 24, 1975, p. 2.

The prophet Muhammad so respected Bilal that he said the slave would enter Paradise before him: "O Bilal, . . . I heard the noise of your shoes in front of me in Paradise, in the night of my ascension." [Edward W. Blyden, *Christianity, Islam, and the Negro Race* (Baltimore: Black Classic Press, 1994), pp. 372–73.]

62. "Muslims to Accept White Followers," *New York Amsterdam News*, June 25, 1975, p. 1; "Black Muslim Movement Is Split in Dispute over Doctrinal Changes," *New York Times*, March 7, 1978; Wallace quoted in *Chicago Tribune*, March 1, 1976, p. 1.

63. "What the Muslims Want" was absent from the first issue of *Bilalian News*, November 14, 1975. The *Bilalian News* replaced *Muhammad Speaks* as the official newspaper of Wallace Muhammd's movement.

64. On demoting Elijah Muhammad, see *Muhammad Speaks*, May 9, 1975, p. 1; for "fully human," see *Time*, June 30, 1975, p. 44; for "I'm not calling," see *Muhammad Speaks*, May 16, 1975, p. 13; on whites being able to join NOI, see "Muslims to Accept White Followers," *New York Amsterdam News*, June 25, 1975, p. 1.

65. *New York Times*, October 19, 1976, p. 33.

66. Farrakhan speech, April 29, 1979.

67. Louis Farrakhan, speech to FOI class, New York, January 18, 1975; Farrakhan speech, April 29, 1979.

68. For Farrakhan on Wallace, see radio broadcast from Chicago, March 9, 1975; *Muhammad Speaks*, July 4, 1975, p. 3.

69. "Farrakhan: New Muslim Direction," p. A–10.

70. Ibid.

71. Ibid., p. A–15.

72. Farrakhan speech, April 29, 1979.

73. For "more important to teach," see Elijah Muhammad, *Message to the Blackman in America* (Newport News, Va.: United Brothers Communications Systems, 1992), p. 204; for "I am a religious man," see Marsh, *From Black Muslims to Muslims*, p. 123.

74. Quoted in "Farrakhan: New Muslim Direction," p. A–10.
75. Louis Farrakhan, speech, Savior's Day, Chicago, February 22, 1981; on Koran classes, see Jackson, "Ascent and Grandeur," p. 22; on Washington meeting, see Askia Muhammad interview, June 13, 1995.
76. For Farrakhan to Wallace, see Farrakhan speech, April 29, 1979; "Farrakhan Leaves Muslim Group," *Los Angeles Sentinel,* December 15, 1977, p. 1; on not being a prostitute, see Jackson, "Ascent and Grandeur," p. 22.
77. Jabril Muhammad, *This Is the One* (Phoenix: Book Company, 1993), pp. 156–57. Muhammad is the former Bernard Cushmeer.
78. "Black Muslim Movement Is Split in Dispute over Doctrinal Changes," *New York Times,* March 7, 1978.
79. "Black Muslim Seeks to Change Movement," *New York Times,* March 19, 1978.
80. "Louis Farrakhan: The Crucifixion of Elijah Muhammad," *New York Amsterdam News,* March 3, 1979, p. 3.
81. Jabril Muhammad, *This Is the One* (Phoenix: Book Company, 1993), p. 253. Of course, the "new teachings" of which Elijah spoke could also be interpreted as those which Wallace eventually espoused.
82. Ibid., pp. 253, 254, 258.
83. For "power of mystery," see Marsh, *From Black Muslims to Muslims,* p. 109. Wallace quoted in "Wallace D. Muhammad: Reviver of Muslim Faith," *Chicago Tribune,* February 21, 1977, Tempo section, p. 4.

Four years after his father's death, when explaining why he had been chosen to replace him, Wallace seemed to be allying himself with those who took Fard's prophecy as a fable:

The other children were already born when Fard Muhammad came. I was the only child born. I was the only child born during his stay with us. I was chosen because . . . they wanted a Christ figure, someone with a mystery about [him]. Here was this newborn baby predicted by Fard

Muhammad and it so happened that the guess was right. I say a "guess" not to laugh at our religion. I say "guess" because that's the language the Honorable Elijah Muhammad used.

Marsh, *From Black Muslims to Muslims*, p. 109.

84. Marsh, *From Black Muslims to Muslims*, pp. 113–14.
85. Ibid., p. 114.
86. Askia Muhammad interview, June 13, 1995.
87. See reference to "grave" in Farrakhan speech, April 29, 1979; see reference to Wallace as "Satan" in Farrakhan speech, February 22, 1981.

Chapter 7

1. From "What the Muslims Want," found on the inside back page of any issue of *The Final Call*.
2. Farrakhan speech, February 22, 1981. Even the Koran alludes to the possibility that it might eventually expire. "For each period," it states, "there is an appointment." *Kitab*, the word for "appointment," is often translated as "a Law decreed," or "a Decree established," with "Law" or "Decree" interpreted to mean the Koran itself. Islamic scripture also states that it will be "revealed by stages." *The Holy Quran*, trans. Mushaf al Madinah an-Nabawiyah (Medina, Saudi Arabia: The Custodian of the Two Holy Mosques King Fahd Complex for the Printing of the Holy Quran), 13:38, 17:106.
3. Farrakhan speech, April 29, 1979.
4. Ibid. Jabril Muhammad quoted in Michael C. Kotzin, "Louis Farrakhan's Anti-Semitism: A Look at the Record," *Christian Century*, March 2, 1994, p. 226.
5. Farrakhan speech, February 22, 1981. Elijah's elevation to Messiah status is inconsistent with traditional NOI theology, since Elijah had declared himself, not immodestly, to only be the last of the Islamic prophets. He had never arrived that he was the Messiah.
6. Ibid.

7. Ibid. Farrakhan's account of Elijah refusing to allow Nation of Islam students to study at orthodox Islamic universities is odd: in the mid-1960s, Akbar, one of Elijah's sons, studied Islamic law at Al Azhar University in Cairo. According to Farrakhan, Elijah told the Arabs who offered him cash to send students abroad "to go to hell . . . [and that he] would not waste the life of . . . [an NOI member] going to Mecca to learn about some spook, mystery God." Then the Arabs "started working on members of . . . [Elijah's] family . . . to teach them prayers in the ways of orthodox Islam, to bring them into the 'true religion.'" "Man," sighed Farrakhan, "how little you [Arabs] understand the book [the Koran] you say you believe in."

   In the same speech in which he spoke about Elijah rejecting the Arabs' bribe, Farrakhan issued the equivalent of a *fatwa* to Arabs about the authenticity of *their* religion:

   > You delight yourself in saying we are not true Muslims. *You* are not true Muslims. . . . You Arabs helped to sell our fathers into slavery. . . . After we came into bondage, God gave us a deliverer and you conspired with the government of oppression to destroy our deliverer. I say to you that your destruction has now entered *your* door. . . . Unless you come and bear witness and bow down, then the whole Arab world is going to be bathed in blood, you devils.

8. Ibid. The plot against Elijah supposedly came to light when, during a conversation between the doctor and other "high-placed Caucasians" at the "orgy," Muhammad's name somehow came up and the physician said, "We got rid of that problem nonviolently."

9. Ibid. This was not the first talk of exhuming Elijah's body. Three weeks after his death, Elijah's body had indeed been exhumed, at the request of the Muhammad family, and rested for almost a year in a back room at the Chicago mosque, protected by an armed guard. He was then reburied after Wallace squashed plans—"This is *not* the Muslim way"—to embalm

the body for viewing, as Stalin's and Lenin's had been in Red Square. (Confidential telephone interview.) Now, five years after reburial, Farrakhan wanted to prove that the tomb was empty, that Elijah had risen, and that his rebirth had given life to what Wallace had slain.

10. Louis Farrakhan, *The Meaning of FOI* (Chicago: The Honorable Elijah Muhammad Educational Foundation, Inc., 1983), pp. 2–20.

11. Louis Farrakhan, "*I Am an Alarm Clock*," *The Black Scholar* (January–February 1979): 10–12.

12. Ibid.

13. Malcolm quoted in "The NAACP's Mistake," *New York Times*, March 7, 1994, p. A16; Farrakhan quoted in "Minister Louis Farrakhan's Stirring Address," *The Black Collegian* (November–December 1983): 36–37.

14. Ibid.

15. For Farrakhan's description of Wallace as "divinely prepared," see Farrakhan, radio broadcast, March 9, 1975; for Farrakhan's later comments, see Farrakhan speech, February 26, 1983; W. D. Muhammad, speech, February 24, 1980.

16. Farrakhan speech, February 26, 1983.

17. Tynnetta Muhammad, *The Comer by Night* (Chicago: The Honorable Elijah Muhammad Educational Foundation, Inc., 1986), p. 108.

18. "A Changed Farrakhan Lights His Peace Pipes," *Chicago Tribune*, October 15, 1986, p. 1; "Rev. Farrakhan Buys South Side Mosque," *Crain's Chicago Business*, September 12, 1988, p. 78. Wallace had sold the NOI's many properties and businesses because he didn't believe a religious body should dabble in commerce (and also because many of the businesses were bankrupt).

19. Farrakhan interview, August 5, 1993.

20. C. Eric Lincoln, *The Black Muslims in America* (Queens, N.Y.: Kayode Publications, 1991), pp. 175–77.

21. *Nostra Aetate* quoted in Eugene J. Fisher, *Seminary Education*

and Christian-Jewish Relations (Washington, D.C.: National Catholic Educational Association, 1988), p. 86.

22. Farrakhan dinner conversation, June 21, 1995.

Chapter 8

1. "Tape Contradicts Disavowal of 'Gutter Religion' Attack," and "Excerpts from Speech," both in *New York Times*, June 29, 1984, p. A12.
2. Farrakhan interview, August 5, 1993.
3. Ibid.
4. Louis Farrakhan, Savior's Day Speech, Chicago, February 26, 1995; for Jews' responsibility for the ozone layer, see Allan S. Galper, "The Foundation for Intercultural Hypocrisy," *Harvard Crimson*, March 6, 1992.
5. James Baldwin, *The Fire Next Time* (New York: Dell, 1985), p. 113.
6. Farrakhan interview, June 27, 1994.
7. Thomas Landess and Richard Quinn, *Jesse Jackson and the Politics of Race* (Ottawa, Ill.: Jameson Books, 1985), p. 203–5.
8. On Farrakhan's Arabic, see George E. Curry, "Farrakhan, Jesse, and Jews," *Emerge* (July–August 1994): 31.
9. Leonard Dinnerstein, *Anti-Semitism in America* (New York: Oxford University Press, 1994), p. 218; for Jackson calling Arafat a "true hero," see "Jews against Jackson" ad, *New York Times*, November 11, 1983.
10. Landess and Quinn, *Jesse Jackson and the Politics of Race*, pp. 196–97.
11. "Candidacy of Jackson Highlights Split among Black Muslims," *New York Times*, February 27, 1984. The size of the contingent Farrakhan led to city hall belied the number who registered along with him: in all of Chicago, only 167 people registered that day, a number far under the one thousand who marched with him to register. The discrepancy further convinced critics that Farrakhan was all flash and little substance.

12. Louis Farrakhan, Savior's Day speech, Chicago, February, 25, 1984.

13. Perlmutter's comments from transcript, "CBS Morning News," February 27, 1984. "Farrakhan on Race, Politics, and the News Media," *New York Times*, April 17, 1984, p. A–16. Although Farrakhan began making his anti-Jewish statements in February, not until four months later did Jesse Jackson fully distance himself from Farrakhan and denounce what he was saying about Jews. On June 28, Jackson said that he found Farrakhan's statements "reprehensible and morally indefensible. I am a Judeo-Christian, and the roots of my faith run deep in the Judeo-Christian tradition." But then he added words that made one wonder if his repudiation of Farrakhan was religiously or politically motivated, or a bit of both: "I will not permit Minister Farrakhan's words, wittingly or unwittingly, to divide the Democratic Party"; he also asserted that Farrakhan "is not a part of our campaign." Yet just a few days before, on *CBS Morning News*, Jackson had taken an ultrastrict civil libertarian approach regarding Farrakhan: He felt "no obligation" to respond to Farrakhan's comments, because "in America, people have freedom of speech to say what they want about whom they want to." ("Jackson Criticizes Remarks Made by Farrakhan as 'Reprehensible,'" *New York Times,* June 29, 1984, pp. A1, A12.)

14. "What Farrakhan Said," *Newsweek*, April 23, 1994, p. 32; and "Meeting Urged with Reporter, Jackson Calls Farrakhan Threat 'Wrong,'" *Washington Post*, April 4, 1984, p. A8.

15. Juan Williams, "Farrakhan's 'Death Threat' Is Disputed," *Washington Post*, May 3, 1984, p. A4.

16. Quoted in Lincoln, *The Black Muslims in America*, p. 205.

17. Farrakhan interview, Chicago, August 5, 1993.

18. Farrakhan press conference, Washington, D.C., April 11, 1984.

19. Farrakhan speech, Chicago, WBEE-FM, June 24, 1984.

20. Farrakhan interview, Chicago, August 5, 1983.

21. On Muslim sheiks, see *Blacks and Jews News* (Fall–Winter

1994): 3; on "dirty" Christian practices, see Louis Farrakhan, speech, Northeastern University, Boston, April 20, 1985; on the NOI as a "dirty religion," see Louis Farrakhan, *The Meaning of FOI* (Chicago: The Honorable Elijah Muhammad Educational Foundation, Inc., 1983), p. 11.

22. Farrakhan interview, August 5, 1993.

23. For back channel negotiations, see confidential interview, New York, April 13, 1995.

24. Farrakhan's virility—and the homophobia he encouraged—was alluded to a week before the Million Man March when the Reverend George A. Stallings Jr. of Washington, D.C.'s African-American Catholic Congregation rebuked those criticizing the march because of Farrakhan's involvement by asking, "What do you want, some milquetoast, sissy faggot to lead you into the promised land?" "Gay Blacks in Quandary over Farrakhan's March," *New York Times*, October 8, 1995, p. 24.

25. Farid Muhammad, interview with the author, Chicago, June 22, 1995.

26. For Malcolm X, Park comments, see quoted from Asociated Press dispatch printed in Newsday, August 19, 1984, and cited in the pamphlet "Louis Farrakhan: In His Own Words" (New York: Anti-Defamation League, October 1985), p. 9; for Farrakhan's comments in Washington, see "Hate Story: Farrakhan's Still at It," *New Republic*, May 30, 1988, p. 19.

27. For Farrakhan's Tacoma comments, see Kenneth S. Stern, "Farrakhan and the Jews in the 1990s," report for the American Jewish Committee, p. 11; for Palm Beach comments, see Louis Farrakhan, speech, Palm Beach, Fla., March 4, 1994.

28. Louis Farrakhan, telephone interview with the author, August 15, 1993.

29. Jonathan Kaufman, "White Racists and Farrakhan's Group," *Chicago Tribune*, October 3, 1985, p. 11; on the talks between Metzger and NOI, see Judith Cummings, "Klan Figure Met with Farrakhan," *New York Times*, October 3, 1985, sect. A, p. 19.

30. Cummings, "Klan Figure Met with Farrakhan," sect. A, p. 19;

for NOI denials, see "Farrakhan Linked to Klan Ex-Leader," *Facts on File,* October 11, 1985, p. 760 C1.

31. "Farrakhan Linked to Klan Ex-Leader," p. 760 C1.
32. Ted Agnes, Jerry Seper, and Glenn Emery, "Race Warriors: Louis Farrakhan and the Nation of Islam," *Insight,* November 11, 1985, p. 14.
33. Wayne King, "White Supremacists Voice Support of Farrakhan," *New York Times,* October 12, 1985, sect. 1, p. 12. Also at the Michigan meeting, according to the *Times,* were Dr. Edward Field, director of the National States Rights Party; Richard Girnt Butler, the head of the Aryan Nations; Don Black, a national Ku Klux Klan leader who had served a prison term for plotting to take over the Caribbean island of Dominica and turn it into a racist state; Roy Frank Houser, a former Klan leader from Pennsylvania; James Burford, a leader of the American Nazi Party; and John Gerhardt, who had been convicted of blowing up a school principal's home in Columbus, Ohio.
34. Agnes, Seper, and Emery, "Race Warriors: Louis Farrakhan and the Nation of Islam," p. 15.
35. Ibid.
36. Malcolm X telegram cited in Thulani Davis, *Malcolm X: The Great Photographs* (New York, N.Y.: Stewart Tabori & Chang, 1993), p. 44.
37. "Special Edition," published by the B'nai B'rith's civil rights division (May 1989), p. 1; for demand that Farrakhan be charged with sedition, see Lyndon LaRouche Organization, "Investigative Leads," April 7–28, 1966, p. 7.
38. LaRouche Organization member, interview with the author, Boston, June 2, 1995.
39. For NOI-LaRouche Howard University program, see Anti-Defamation League, "Partners in Bigotry: The LaRouche Cult and the Nation of Islam" [pamphlet] (1994), p. 2; for LaRouche speaker's comments, see author's notes, Morgan State University forum, Baltimore, April 13, 1994.

40. Lenora B. Fulani, "Open Letter Encourages Black Leaders to Denounce LaRouche," *City Sun,* October 28–November 3, 1992; and " 'We Must Accept the Responsiblity of Freedom': An Interview with Minister Louis Farrakhan," *New Federalist,* June 12, 1995, p. 2.

41. Farrakhan interview, August 5, 1993. The sort of messianic debate that Farrakhan proposed had not been held since thirteenth-century Barcelona, when Jewish and Catholic clergy publicly haggled over the merits of their faiths and over who had a more rightful claim to the messiah. Bishops and monks boasted that Jesus' death had extinguished Judaism's very reason for being; rabbis counterargued that the doctrine of the messiah was not that important to Jews anyway, and that believing in Jesus' divinity had been ruinous for Christians: Rome had ceased to be the master of the world almost as soon as it embraced Christianity, "and now the followers of [the prophet] Muhammad have more territories than they." Paul Johnson, *A History of the Jews* (New York: Harper & Row, 1988), pp. 218–19.

    Farrakhan, of course, could have borrowed the rabbis' argument about the superb conquering abilities of Muslims had he not claimed that Elijah Muhammad had superseded the founder of Islam. NOI members and theology more strictly followed the teachings of the later Muhammad than the early Muhammad.

42. To Shiites, the Mahdi would mark the return of the twelfth imam, or spiritual leader, whose disappearance in the year 874 had broken the chain of hereditary succession among the Shiites. The restoration of the "hidden imam" would usher in a perfect Islamic society in which peace and justice would prevail.

43. From transcript, *Larry King Live,* October 16, 1995. Confessing that he had, in effect, been a closet Jew, that he had traversed the religious landscape from the Episcopalianism of his youth to Islam to Judaism, made one wonder: if Farrakhan was Jewish, who knew which shul Jews' worst enemy might join? Better to head for the exits before he joined the men's fellowship!

    There was nothing new in the formulation of the black as

Jew. At a less conscious, often barely acknowledged level, blacks had always thought of themselves as Jews, not the crucifying kind, but the enslaved kind. America was to blacks as Egypt was to Jews—except that a Moses had led Jews to their Promised Land, and many blacks still awaited their Moses and had *no* Promised Land. Old Testament legends and ancient Jewish songs of deliverance ("Lord, wasn't that hard trials, great tribulations, I'm bound to leave this land!") sometimes resonated deeper with blacks than Jews, whose emancipation was a long-ago feat. But Farrakhan, as was his nature, for he held nothing back, made the sacred openly debatable—and stepped on many a Jewish toe in the process.

44. Farrakhan interview, August 5, 1993.
45. "Nation of Islam Leaders Deliver a Harsh Gospel," *Chicago Tribune*, October 16, 1995.
46. Farrakhan interview, August 5, 1993; Rabbi Robert Marks, telephone interview with the author, July 10, 1993; Rabbi Herman Schaalman, interview with the author, Chicago, June 22, 1995.
47. Skorodin interview, June 21, 1995.
48. Bernard Holland, "Sending a Message, Louis Farrakhan Plays Mendelssohn," *New York Times*, April 19, 1993, p. C11.
49. Ibid. Skorodin also confirmed Farrakhan's statement that he didn't play Mendelssohn because he was Jewish.
50. Holland, "Sending a Message," p. C11; Farrakhan interview, August 5, 1993.
51. Wright quoted in Dinnerstein, *Anti-Semitism in America*, p. 198. For this section on black anti-Semitism, I am indebted to the thinking and research of Dinnerstein.
52. Catechism quoted in Ibid.
53. Quoted in ibid.
54. Quoted in ibid.
55. Bond and Baldwin quoted in ibid., p. 199.
56. Quoted in ibid., p. 199.
57. Ibid., pp. 203–4.
58. On Farrakhan's mother being "slighted," see confidential television interview, July 30, 1995.

59. Quoted in Dinnerstein, *Anti-Semitism in America*, p. 206.

60. Quoted in Murray Friedman, *What Went Wrong?* (New York: Free Press, 1995), p. 78.

61. Quoted in ibid., pp. 78–79.

62. Orlando Patterson, "The Paradox of Integration," *New Republic*, November 6, 1995, pp. 25–26.

63. Farrakhan interview, August 5, 1993.

64. For statistics on Jewish participation in the civil rights movement, see Dinnerstein, *Anti-Semitism in America*, p. 208. Farrakhan's equation of Jews and profiteering was not original: those predisposed to think the worst of Jews invariably ascribe Jews' motives to greed—in this case, they are seen as selling a pound of *black* flesh to line their own pockets.

65. Farrakhan interview, August 5, 1993.

66. Baldwin quoted in Edward S. Shapiro, "Blacks and Jews Entangled," *First Things* (August–September 1994): 34.

67. Ibid., pp. 29–35; Shapiro, "Blacks and Jews," *Sh'ma*, April 29, 1994: 4–5.

68. Farrakhan interview, June 27, 1994.

69. Both columnists quoted in Leon Wielseltier, "Washington Diarist: Naked Lunch," *New Republic*, August 27, 1984, p. 43.

70. Debate between Khallid Abdul Muhammad and Khalid Lateef, WLIB-FM, New York, October 27, 1992; "Anti-Semites at Columbia," *New York Post*, January 26, 19991; "They Call It Diversity," *Wall Steet Journal*, September 29, 1992, p. A16.

71. Farrakhan interview, June 27, 1994.

Chapter 9

1. Khallid, who was also called the NOI's "minister of defense" and the Fruit of Islam's "supreme captain," had a checkered past. Formerly known as Harold Moore Vann and sometimes called "Dr. Khallid Muhammad," he was reputed to have undergraduate and graduate degrees from Dillard University in New Orleans. But according to the Dilliard registrar's office,

Khallid dropped out without earning a degree after being enrolled from 1966 to 1970. And officials at California State University at Long Beach nixed claims that he had been a professor of African studies there: no Khallid Muhammad or Harold Moore Vann had ever been on its payroll. A federal court in Atlanta convicted Khallid in 1987 for using a fake social security number to secure a $175,000 mortgage. He was in prison in Georgia for nine months, then paroled for two years. Jeremy L. Milk, "Inspiration or Hate-Monger," *Chronicle of Higher Education,* January 19, 1994, p. A33.

2. ADL ad, *New York Times,* January 16, 1994, p. 24. The fact that Khallid had taunted such blacks as Jesse Jackson and the film director Spike Lee as well as whites, Jews, Catholics, and gays raised the possibility that the ADL had goofed by being the sole signatory to its *Times* ad. Perhaps if it had asked Catholic, gay, human rights, civil rights, and black groups to co-sign the ad, the fracas might have been perceived not as yet another black-Jewish clash but as a confrontation strictly between decency and hate that affected *all.*

   But if the ADL had pursued that strategy, said Abraham Foxman, its national director, "We'd still be waiting for that ad. And . . . if we had gone hat in hand to other groups, the ad wouldn't have said what it did say. All this is very nice to say, but who are you going to get in the white community to stand up? Jews are a major target [for the NOI], although Farrakhan . . . hates whites in general." Abe Foxman, interview with the author, April 13, 1995.

3. Khallid Abdul Muhammad speech, Kean College, November 1993.

4. For Khallid Muhammad's later remarks, see, see "Khallid Muhammad Resumes Post," *The Final Call,* July 19, 1995, p. 3.

5. Foxman interview, April 13, 1995.

6. "ADL Praises African-American Leaders for Condemning Anti-Semitism," Anti-Defamation League press release, January 21, 1994.

7. Foxman interview, April 13, 1995.
8. "Farrakhan Accuses Jews, U.S. of Plot," *Washington Times*, January 27, 1994, pp. A1, A14; "Farrakhan Sees Jews Plotting vs. Blacks," *New York Daily News*, January 25, 1994, p. 1; "A Bigot Exposed," *New York Daily News*, January 26, 1994, p. 33.
9. "Farrakhan Accuses Jews, U.S. of Plot," *Washington Times*, January 27, 1994, p. A14.
10. Vernon Jarrett, "Meeting's Outcome Reflects Strained Black-Jewish Relations," *Chicago Sun-Times*, February 22, 1994.
11. Mfume, whose home district was 71 percent blacks, defended his efforts to work with Farrakhan: "I was raised all my life to believe that we must find ways to reach out to people in an effort to heal our nation, even if it means that we might fail. . . . Although the effort was fraught with risk, it was pregnant with opportunity."

Mfume did not emerge from the Khallid affair unscathed. Of his circumlocution when asked whether he thought Farrakhan was anti-Semitic—"I believe there have been things that have been said over the years by the Nation of Islam that, without clarity, have been, by many people, including myself, questioned as to whether or not they were anti-Semitic in nature either by happenstance or deliberately"—the *Baltimore Sun* columnist Roger Simon snickered,

> [T]hat fog-bound reply hardly qualifies Mfume for inclusion in the next edition of "Profile in Courage." Compare it to one person who did have the courage to speak out and without equivocation. Rep. Major Owens (D-N.Y.), an African-American whose congressional district in central Brooklyn had the highest percentage of blacks in America, said, "No more time should be wasted on negotiations with hatemongers and rank opportunists. Reject Muhammad and Farrakhan. . . . We must denounce the enemy.
>
> (Roger Simon, "Some People Dared to Tell the Truth About Farrakhan," *Baltimore Sun*, February 4, 1994, p. A2.)

And after meeting with community leaders in Baltimore to explain his posture regarding Farrakhan, one participant wrote Mfume a two-page letter that implicitly chided him for a lack of moral courage: "[I] see political and moral leadership as one and the same. . . . You got snake-bit, but the snake's still around with a seemingly endless source of venom. Perhaps a strong response from you and other black leaders will milk him a bit." (Confidential interview, Maryland, February 10, 1994.)

12. Jennifer L. Hochschild, *Facing up to the American Dream* (Princeton, N.J.: Princeton University Press, 1995), p. 139.

13. Henry Louis Gates Jr., "The Black Leadership Myth," *New Yorker*, October 24, 1994, p. 7. Regarding welfare, Farrakhan said, "The Honorable Elijah Muhammad says 'welfare' . . . backwards means 'farewell' to independent and creative living. So as fast as we can, we move our people away from welfare." (*20/20* interview with Barbara Walters, April 22, 1974.)

14. The National Press Club is a standard venue for press conferences in Washington, but Farrakhan held his press conference about Khallid Abdul Muhammad at the Vista Hotel. He had been barred from renting the Press Club's facilities since reporters attending a 1984 press conference he held there complained about being subjected to "unconscionable searches" by members of the Fruit of Islam.

15. Transcript of Farrakhan's press conference, February 3, 1994. But why hadn't Farrakhan simply dismissed Khallid from the NOI, freeing himself of a defiant insurgent and ridding his organization of a possible insurrectionist? When I asked him that four months later, on June 27, 1994, he responded:

> L.F.: There is no law that we have to turn a person out for speaking out of turn. When Malcolm . . . [made] a mockery of the death of the president of the United States, the Honorable Elijah Muhammad didn't put him out. He silenced him. I didn't choose to silence Khallid. That is his means of livelihood. I chose to rebuke him, hoping that would help him see that he must change the way he represents the mag-

nificent way that . . . Elijah Muhammad has given us to give
to our people. . . .

A.M.: One could argue that he makes his livelihood by mock-
ing Jews.

L.F.: That's ridiculous. No. No. No. No. No. Brother Khallid is
much more than that. Any well-meaning white person
would see that this is a very brilliant man. If he never mentioned Jews at all in his talk, he would still have thousands
come to hear him. That is not the reason he is successful as
a speaker.

A.M.: Some people say the source of your appeal is that *you*
don't hold back. You say exactly what's on your mind. . . .

L.F.: That is true. But let me say this: there are ways to say
things. That's what Paul meant when he said, "When I was a
child, I spake as a child, because I understood as a child. But
when I became a man, I put away childish things." . . . I do
not go before . . . [blacks] to show off that I can say things
that make white people angry or upset. That's not the point.
As one matures with knowledge, one learns how to speak
the truth without being as offensive as one may have been in
one's infancy. . . . God sends prophets, apostles, and messen-
gers as mercies to the people. . . . I must find a way to speak
truth without deviating from it, but in a way that I'm not
speaking it to injure, but to correct that which brings us into
disfavor with God.

16. Farrakhan quote from interview, August 5, 1993; Nation of
    Islam Historical Research Department, *The Secret Relationship
    between Blacks and Jews,* 2nd ed. (Chicago: Nation of Islam,
    1991; 1992).

17. Ira Rosenwaike, "The Jewish Population of the United States as
    Estimated from the Census of 1820," in *Essays in American Jew-
    ish History,* edited by Jacob Rader Marcus (Cincinnati: Ameri-
    can Jewish Archives, 1958), pp. 18–20.

18. Bertram W. Korn, *American Jewry and the Civil War* (New
    York: Atheneum, 1970), pp. xxvii, lv.

19. Ibid., p. lv.

20. David Brion Davis, "The Slave Trade and the Jews," *New York Review of Books*, December 22, 1994, p. 16.

21. Ibid. *The Secret Relationship*'s distortions extend beyond the American South. Economics, not religion, motivated European oppression against Jews: "The pattern and the charges are familiar: monopolization, usury, 'sharp practices,' selling 'cheap' goods, frequent bankruptcies, etc. All such claims seem to preface the expulsion orders against the Jews]." Economics, not religion, spirituality, or ethics, was the very core of Judaism: "Europe's experience with 'Mosaic Law' was that it very closely resembled business law, and that money, not worship, was the main objective." Jews' efforts to convert—and even educate—their slaves were suspect: Diogo Dias Querido converted "several" slaves, then taught them Portuguese and Dutch so they could be "more effective traders." Simply by plying their trade in a complex, interdependent economy, Jews were guilty by association with perpetuating slavery: "Many Jews [in Newport, Rhode Island], if not directly implicated in the slave trade, showed passive acquiescence by engaging in trades directly tied to slavery, such as distilling, financing and insuring, shipbuilding and outfitting." NOI Historical Research Department, *The Secret Relationship between Blacks and Jews*, pp. vii, 34, 101.

22. "Experts Say Few Jews Held Slaves," *Washington Post*, February 15, 1995, p. D4; Henry Louis Gates Jr., "Black Demagogues and Pseudo-Scholars," *New York Times*,, July 20, 1992, p. A13. The only other time the American Historical Association had taken a position on a specific historical topic was in 1991 when it condemned Holocaust deniers.

23. Hochschild, *Facing Up to the American Dream*, p. 106.

24. Farrakhan and Muhammad remarks, dinner conversation, Farrakhan's home, June 21, 1995.

25. Gates, "Black Demagogues and the Pseudo-Scholars," *New York Times,* July 20, 1992, p. A13; Nation of Islam, *The Secret Rela-*

tionship between Blacks and Jews, p. iv; "Farrakhan Speaks on Media, Jews, and Nation's Mission," *Philadelphia Tribune*, February 25, 1994, pp. 5–6.

26. Poll by the Times Mirror Center for The People and The Press, published in the center's "news index poll," April 12, 1990, p. 10. By contrast, the post-Khallid months were a near-disaster for Khallid himself, who, by several accounts, began to suffer financially when he could no longer charge the five to ten thousand dollars per speech that he had levied when he was making headlines. According to Khallid, for at least a year after Farrakhan dismissed him as his national representative, the NOI leader neither met with him nor returned his phone calls. Despite the slight, Khallid denied that there was any symmetry between his break with Farrakhan and Malcolm X's in 1964 with Elijah Muhammad: "Unlike Malcolm X and his spiritual father thirty years ago, I do not find a way to speak out as little as a word or as much as a sentence against . . . [Farrakhan]. . . . I will never speak out against him." On July 1, 1995, Farrakhan reinstated Khallid Muhammad as an NOI minister, and Khallid pledged "to strive to move from that which is profane to that which is more profound." Muhammad's reinstatement was ignored by the media and Jewish organizations that had made such a stink a year and a half before about his Kean State speech. "Khallid Muhammad Speaks Out," *The Daily Challenge*, February 21, 1995, pp. 2, 8; "Khallid Muhammad Resumes Post," *The Final Call*, July 19, 1995, p. 3.

27. *The Arsenio Hall Show*, February 25, 1994.

28. *20/20*, April 22, 1994.

29. Farrakhan interview, June 27, 1994.

30. "The NAACP's Mistake," *New York Times*, March 7, 1994, p. A16.

31. "Black Summit Begins Work in 'Trenches,'" *Washington Post*, June 14, 1994, p. 3.

32. "Chavis Used NAACP Money to Settle a Legal Dispute," *Washington Post*, July 29, 1994, p. A2.

33. "Minister Louis Farrakhan Calls for a Million Man March,"
    The Final Call, December 14, 1994, pp. 21, 29.
34. "Excerpts of Interview with Louis Farrakhan," *Washington
    Post*, March 1, 1990, p. A17; for further details on Farrakhan's
    vision, see "A Final Warning! Minister Farrakhan Tells U.S.
    Gov't: 'Calamities Set for America,'" *The Final Call*, November
    30, 1989, pp. 16, 17, 20, 30.
35. "A Final Warning: Minister Farrakhan Tells US. Government:
    'Calamities Set for America,'" *The Final Call*, November 30,
    1989, p. 17.
36. "Farrakhan Ties March to Jewish Holy Day," *Washington Post*,
    September 20, 1995, p. B3.
37. Ibid.
38. As Jesse Jackson (no stranger himself to being tainted) asked
    from the podium, while tryibg to distance himself from Far-
    rakhan, "Did Minister Farrakhan organize the march? No!
    [The conservative black Supreme Court justice] Clarence
    Thomas and [the GOP House Speaker Newt] Gingrich orga-
    nized the march—just like [the Birmingham, Alabama, police
    commissioner] Bull Connor [who had used police dogs on
    children demonstrating for civil rights] organized the march in
    1963!" "America Will Be Grateful for This Day," *Washington
    Post*, October 17, 1995, p. A23.
39. Kojo Ade-Hassan, interview with the author, at the Million
    Man March, Washington, D.C., October 16, 1995.
40. For the figure 2.2 million households, see Judith Shulevitz,
    "Farrakhan's Secrets," *New York*, November 6, 1995, p. 24. The
    march may have been extraordinarily successful, but Far-
    rakhan did not entirely get his way with it: over dinner with the
    author the previous June at Farrakhan's home, he spoke about
    going to the Capitol the day after the march to meet with
    politicians. That plan was dropped (and never publicly stated),
    possibly because Farrakhan or his advisers were anxious that
    he would be treated as a pariah. (Farrakhan dinner conversa-
    tion, June 21, 1995.) Few politicians, white or black, relished

having their names linked with him—and at least one black
politician who spoke at the march promised his advisers that
he would stay far from Farrakhan so he could not be pho-
tographed with him. (Confidential interview, Oct. 11, 1995.)
41. According to the Koran,

> *Over it are Nineteen*
> *And We have set none*
> *But angels as guardians*
> *of the Fire.* (74: 30–31)

In his translation of the Koran—the preferred version of
traditional Muslims—Mushaf al-Madinah an-Nabawiyah says
of the above passage: "The significance of numbers is a favorite
theme with some writers, but I lay no stress on it. . . . In our
own literature, I think that we ought to avoid too much stress
on speculative conjectures." *The Holy Quran*, trans. Mushaf al-
Madinah an-Nabawiyah (Medina, Saudi Arabia: The Custodian of the Two Holy Mosques King Fahd Complex for the
Printing of the Holy Quran, n.d.), note on p. 1850.
42. Louis Farrakhan, speech at the Million Man March, Washington, D.C., October 16, 1994.
43. Robert Girardi, "Nose Job," *New Republic*, November 13, 1995,
p. 14.
44. Farrakhan speech, October 16, 1995.
45. Ibid.
46. Farrakhan interview, August 5, 1993.
47. Farrakhan speech, October 16, 1995.
48. For a perceptive and sympathetic analysis of King's 1963
speech, see Taylor Branch, *Parting the Waters* (New York:
Simon & Schuster, 1988), pp. 881–82, 887.
49. Price quoted in "March Spirit Draws Leaders to Summit," *The
Final Call*, December 6, 1995, p. 7.
50. Farrakhan interview, August 5, 1993.
51. *The Arsenio Hall Show*, February 25, 1994.

52. Quotes from Mandela and Farrakhan meeting from the *Baltimore Sun,* January 29, 1996, pp. 8–9.
53. Khaddafi quote in Libya and Farrakhan quote in Iraq from the *Washington Post,* February, 1996, p. A19.

    Khaddafi's full quote, one of risible anthropological value, was not reported in most press reports. He justified Libyan intervention in America's internal affairs because "America, which was created by immigrants from the continents of Africa, Asia and Europe, did not belong to anyone but to its ordinary people, the Red Indians, *who are of Libyan origin* [italics added], and nobody has the right to claim that he is a master there, and others merely his slave." (Cited in Clarence Page, "Slavery Today, and Those Who Will Not See," *Baltimore Sun,* February 2, 1996, p. A15.)

    Khaddafi's connections with the Nation of Islam dated back to the early 1970s, when he had loaned the NOI $3 million to purchase a temple in Chicago. In 1985, he gave Farrakhan an interest-free $5 million loan to start a black-oriented line of cosmetics called POWER. When the sales of POWER products did not meet expectations, Farrakhan blamed Jewish bankers and manufacturers. But George Johnson, the CEO of Chicago-based Johnson Products, whose firm was initially slated to supply POWER with products, said he simply could not afford to have a reputation as tolerating anti-Semitism. (Khaddafi's loans to NOI from "Chicago Muslims Gets Qaddafi Loan," *New York Times,* May 4, 1985. Farrakhan blaming Jews from author's August 5, 1993 interview with him. Johnson quote from "Islam's New Entrepreneur," *Newsweek,* July 13, 1987, pp. 38–39.)
54. "Cavorting with dictators" and Justice Dept. letter to Farrakhan from the *Washington Post,* February 16, 1996, p. A26. Farrakhan's dislike of Clarence Page, based on his comments about Page at author's August 5, 1993 interview with him. Page's comments from Page, "Slavery Today, and Those Who Will Not See," *Baltimore Sun,* February 22, 1996, p. A15.

55. Muhammad had been adamantly pro-Japanese since at least 1934. That year, he said that forces of the Rising Sun "can lick this country in 24 hours" and that they were being sent to the United States to protect Negroes. (From CIA files on the Nation of Islam.) And according to the September 22, 1942, *Chicago Tribune* (p. 9), when the FBI arrested Muhammad for violating the draft laws. He was found hiding under his mother's bed wrapped in a carpet. This was neither the properly dignified nor "manly" posture for the Messenger of Allah who would later so effectively portray himself as a brave, unflinching critic of white America.

56. "Farrakhan Vows to Take Libya's Aid," *Washington Post*, February 26, 1996, p. A1.

Index

Abbott, Robert S., 39
Afro-Descendent Society of Upliftment, 81
Ali, John
  fund-raising in Middle East, 102–3
  remarks on Arabs as slaveholders, 102
Ali, Muhammad, 114
Ameer, Leon, 92
American Nazi Party, 155
Anti-Defamation League (ADL)
  portrayal of Jesse Jackson, 146
  published excerpts from Khallid Abdul Muhammad's speech, 174–75, 177
  as target of LaRouche-NOI alliance, 156–57
anti-Semitism
  of American Nazi Party, 155
  among African Americans, 162

Farrakhan's reputation for, xx
  of Lyndon LaRouche Organization, 156
  Protestant, 162–63
Arafat, Yasir, 144

Baldwin, James, xxi–xxii, 109, 141–42, 164, 169
Barnette, Aubrey, 94
Belafonte, Harry, 26–27
Black Muslims in America, The (Lincoln), 65
black nationalism
  expressions of, x–xi
  Malcolm X on, 80
  of Nation of Islam, 73
black people
  differences in skin color, 11–12
  force of religion for many, 55
  Northern migration (1910–20), 37–39
  perception of NOI, 133
B'nai B'rith, 156–57. See also

Anti-Defamation League (ADL)
Bond, Horace Mann, 163–64
Boston
  Louis X as Fruit of Islam captain, 60
  Louis X as minister for Nation of Islam, 58–62, 65–66
  Malcolm X in, 32–35, 59
  NOI assignment of Louis X to, 58–60
  Roxbury's black community, 5–8
  Roxbury's West Indian community, 1–4, 13
  Universal Negro Improvement Association in, 15–16. See also Roxbury, Massachusetts
Boston Boy (Hentoff), 13–14
Boston Latin School, 18–19
Brown v. Board of Education (1954), 59
Butler, Norman 3X, 89
Bynoe, John, 3, 8, 21

259